Capitalism and Human Values

Tony Wilkinson

SOCIETAS
essays in political
& cultural criticism

imprint-academic.com

Published in the UK by
Imprint Academic, PO Box 200, Exeter EX5 5YX, UK

Distributed in the USA by
Ingram Book Company,
One Ingram Blvd., La Vergne, TN 37086, USA

ISBN 9781845407889

A CIP catalogue record for this book is available from the
British Library and US Library of Congress

For Emma

Contents

Introduction

Capitalism is not enough

Whether we like it or not, material and economic concerns suffuse and dominate modern culture. Not only is public policy largely dictated by economics but overwhelmingly our individual economic role and status define our place in society and our relationships to other people. Getting and spending have come to define who we are.

Then, in the grip of this materialist obsession, the world in general has narrowed its gaze to capitalism as the one dominant form of economic organization. Today, private enterprise is embraced or at least allowed in almost every part of the world, even where political organization is overtly undemocratic. But let us be clear: in itself this is not something to lament, for capitalism has brought us such prosperity as we enjoy. It and its engine, free enterprise, provide innovation, efficiency and abundance like no other form of economic organization yet devised.

Yet we know that capitalism also has a dark side of excesses and abuses — excessive inequality, for example, exploitation, instability and even violence in the pursuit of profit — which governments have often sought to mitigate or control but with limited success. There have been and remain many who believe that such problems reveal something fundamentally wrong with the world's dominant form of economic organization and that therefore we need a radically different system.

But with what could we replace capitalism when other systems have been tried and have failed even more spectacularly? Revolution, the wholesale destruction of institutions in the hope that something better will emerge, may appeal to those who think they have nothing to lose or may even sound romantic. The reality usually involves violence and misery on a massive scale followed by a return to something remarkably like the way things were.

On the other hand, proposed solutions to reform or tame capitalism rather than replace it obviously need repeated legislative or institutional adjustments. But this political process is often a losing battle in which the balance of power is against politics. Without doubt some such political innovations have a part to play but, crucially, no such solution has worked so far. We continue to gain considerable benefits from capitalism, yes, but also still suffer the excesses, abuses and failures.

The key contention of this book is that what is wrong with capitalist society is not primarily the way economic activity is organized. It is that capitalism and free enterprise do their limited job so well that we have mistaken what they do for the purpose of our lives and society. Reining in the excesses and abuses of capitalism may well involve economic or institutional reform of some sort but the root of the problem lies deeper. This is a problem about our values.

The fragmentation and in many cases decline of other — particularly religious — beliefs has left a vacuum where shared values might once have been. Of course history is full of examples where economic advantage crushed human or religious decency anyway, but values only stood a chance when they were strongly held and widely shared. We have now come by default to believe that our collective and private lives should be so defined by our economic lives that we scarcely have values any longer, just economic aims. It is as if we created a machine so glittering and powerful that we came to worship it, forgetting that economic output and consumption are only part of what we are or could be. Capitalism, like many of its products, is a good servant but a bad master.

If, however, we had strong, shared values they could provide a counterweight to capitalism and its implied materialism, pointing up the tendencies which otherwise result in abuses and leading us to insist, collectively, on something better. A society in which values were strong enough to hold an equilibrium with the power of capital could work wonders. Our contention is that capitalism fails when we forget that it does not make sense for it to stand alone. We need values of some kind to stand beside it, shared values which give us direction and provide boundaries to the power enterprise can unleash.

But as things stand we simply do not have such values — not, at least, on a basis we can agree upon and share. Any form of "ethical capitalism" must remain a fantasy as long as we cannot agree what our values are and why. The way we live and the fate of our society are both tied up with our ability to rediscover or reconstruct our values.

Values

So we must look hard at values. Most of us have a sense that there must be some sort of standards to help us shape our lives and actions. There are, for example, important lines we just won't cross in our personal lives. However, when we try to pin down this sense or the detail of whatever picture such lines make, we begin to struggle. To change the image, values can seem like mirages that retreat as we approach.

It can also seem that other people see quite a different picture. We live in a world of many cultures and beliefs, in which there are many different ideas of what values are and which values should guide us. But such variety seems to make any particular values optional, or perhaps only valid relative to certain circumstances, cultures or traditions. If we are not careful values dissolve altogether and we are left living without guidance or direction, amid others who play by different rules or none.

Getting clear about our values is surely then something of great importance even without considering how to tame capitalism. Values help us make major choices, of course, but they also influence the day-to-day fabric of our lives, the small choices which make us who we are. They define our characters and are critical in how we relate to others. Political or collective values, we might hope, help us make (or contribute to) the kind of collective choices which determine what kind of society and indeed world we live in. In so doing they bind people together into communities, nations, or congregations. In fact, communities really only work if there are shared values and if we don't have them it is difficult to live together without conflict.

But what kind of things are these values? Where do they come from? What gives them their authority? How do we decide or find out what ours are or should be, or why we have the values we may have? Immediately we find ourselves in difficulty. There are too many conflicting answers from which to choose.

The foundation of values

It is tempting to conclude from such confusion that values are somehow an outmoded idea or belong to some realm of wishful thinking. But the source of the confusion is easily identifiable. There is little point in arguing about whether this or that action is right or wrong (for example) when we don't agree about what criteria should be applied to decide the question, or even about what the question basically means. We don't agree what makes a value a value and hence there is no bedrock on which we can build the structures that make up our lives. We no longer agree what the foundation of values might be.[1]

A common stance we have already met, for example, is that life and society are all about economics, possessions and consumption so that values, political as well as personal, are primarily about our attitudes to such things. But this does not take us very far, for some believe that those who can should maximize their share, others believe in material equality, others in finding some balance between reward and need, for example. Or perhaps values are after all just a sham, part of a story people are told to keep them obediently in their allotted economic place. But which of these versions should we believe? And why?

Another common stance is that values are just a matter of personal taste or private conviction. On this view, I have my values and you have yours and, while we may try to explain them to each other, if we don't agree there is nothing much more to be said.

At another extreme there are many, including some of those for whom religion is an important aspect of their lives, who think of values as something eternally fixed and applicable to everyone, perhaps even regarding values as supernatural laws.

None of these stories can convince adherents of the others and none of them commands general agreement. Overall we have no shared or common idea about what values are or even what we are talking about when we try to discuss them. Instead we rely on various, mostly confused, strands of history, religion, tradition, culture, feeling and whatever else. As a result, values cannot even be rationally discussed because we are quickly at cross purposes. They are especially difficult to apply in agreed ways to new situations, which severely restricts their usefulness. Whether one person can accept another's values depends on both accepting the same starting point, which in our radically pluralist, multicultural, multi-religious world is increasingly unlikely. Often, we just end up shouting.

So we will look, in what follows, for the missing foundation on which values could rest by common agreement. This foundation, we will suggest, must be secular — not because we want to disparage religion but because there is no other way to find common ground in a world of so many diverse views. Hence our focus is on "human values" and the foundation on which they might rest.

It is high time in any case that secular society grasped this nettle. It is astonishing that we have no stronger commonly accepted basis for secular ethics than the vague strands we have mentioned or well-meaning but hazy lists of do's and dont's. We will suggest that (almost!) whatever your views on religion it makes sense to be interested in secular values which are common to us all, believers and non-believers alike.

Because values shape our lives and society the foundation of values is no less than the foundation of both. It is not hard to see from this point of view how confusion about values could ruin lives or threaten the cohesion of society. If we cannot locate shareable values at all, we are likely to have something else imposed by whoever is strong enough to do so. If we are lucky we will be left as economic units, consumers and workers with economic aims leading more or less prosperous but empty lives. But beyond that is always the threat of worse — the possibility of a world ruled by violence or barbarism.

As was once memorably said about football, this is not a matter of life and death.[2] It's far more important.

What do we tell the children?

Discussing "the foundation of values" may seem a bit abstract but we can bring it down to earth with one key question.

"What do we tell the children?"

This question offers an excellent test of whether we really understand any subject at all. To explain, for example, some theorem of geometry, or the basics of natural selection, or string theory to a ten-year-old you need not be an expert but you need to have a decent grasp of the basic ideas. (Good luck with string theory!)

But the question bites even harder where values are concerned. The ability to explain them to children is an absolute and essential requirement if any system of values is to work at all. If we can't convince our children that our values should be their values, what kind of lives are we leading, or are they likely to lead? How will our culture and society continue if we cannot successfully transmit our values to our children? But if we are not sure what our values are or why, where do we even start?

Children for example tend to be particularly good at asking "Why?". In this case perhaps, why is it right to do X or wrong to do Y? Why should we be "good", sanctions apart? Why do you have the values you profess? But these are precisely the questions to which we lack commonly agreed answers. Sure, we can produce lists of "do's and don'ts", or we can extol kindness over violence, for example. But in each case, what reasons can we give? Of course kindness is better than violence, but why?

It is often said that we must teach values by example. It is surely true that we are unlikely to succeed in persuading anyone, particularly an observant and skeptical child, that a certain way of living or acting is right if our actions do not support our words. That doesn't mean, however, that actions are all that matter in the transmission of values. We need to explain as well. We need to give sound reasons for our choices and that means that our values must be rational or reasonable. They may not be like mathematical theorems, logically necessary or deducible from some kind of incontrovertible first principles, but they must make sense. There should be sound and satisfying reasons why this way of living is better than others. That, in fact, is just what we mean by having a foundation for values.

If we don't have answers to such fundamental questions about values how can we satisfy the need of the next generation to find direction and meaning in their lives? When they ask what it's all about, in whatever form they ask, can we offer them no help at all?

So, what <u>do</u> we tell the children?

Satisfied mind

The answer we are going to develop lies in what we will call "satisfied mind". Satisfied mind, we will discover, is the essential, necessary condition for living well and happily.[3]

Satisfied mind is about our subjective experience, our inner life. We will suggest that the way we experience and react inwardly to whatever happens to us is the crucial component in whether we live happily or not. Of course, the inner life is not disconnected from our external life, including what happens around us, what happens in our bodies and how we relate to others. The two aspects are continuous. But our inner life is how we experience the world and that consciousness is to a significant extent what makes us human. We will explore how our experience, or our inner life, can be moulded or improved by developing "inner skills". Satisfied mind is not a simple matter of positive thinking or intellectual effort, but involves an approach to life in which we take systematic responsibility for our own happiness.

At this stage of course the expression we have chosen is little more than an empty box, perhaps like one of those frames into which cement is poured to form building structures. Part of the book is an attempt at showing and clarifying what satisfied mind really means and what is needed to achieve and maintain it. If satisfied mind really is the key to living happily, that in itself would surely be worth a bit of anyone's time.

As you would expect, however, there is much more to the story. We will explore how and why satisfied mind is capable of providing the rational, shareable foundation for our values, both private and political, that we need. We will also explore at least in outline what private and public values, ethics and politics, would look like with satisfied mind as that foundation. And we will see how secular human values built on this foundation can give us a rational basis to insist on a more human capitalism.

Reconstruction

Questions about values are far from new. They have been rattling around for centuries, puzzling some very clever people. The sensible thing might be to tiptoe away and find something easier to do. On the other hand as we have seen the answers really matter, which is why people keep trying.

We could incidentally equate values with ideals, or we could talk in terms of right and wrong, or good and bad, or just and unjust. We are in the realms of ethics or morality or political philosophy, although for me at least talking about values seems easier to relate to everyday life and less likely to lead us off into abstractions. These "ethical concepts" are not completely identical but they are so closely connected that if we understood one we could hope to understand all the others with a bit of effort. But that is the problem: at present we don't really understand any of them.

What sort of exercise is this? Are we for example analysing how values actually work today, or how the language of values works, or perhaps examining the history of how we got to wherever we are? We suggest that the main work is none of these, but one of reconstruction.

It is as if the language of values has become detached from the context it once had,[4] maybe indeed from every one of a string of different contexts it has been through historically. As a result we still have all the words but have lost or abandoned the sense that lay behind them. The words no longer mean what they used to mean. But the job these words did was such an important one, tied up with the way people understood their own lives and their institutions, and the way both people and institutions made important choices, that we cannot live well without that job being done somehow or other.

We must therefore reconstruct a meaning which makes sense for us today, something which allows rational discussion and sharing of values in a world which shares few basic assumptions. This is not really philosophy as it is now understood academically, although perhaps it is related to what philosophy started out trying to do. It is a matter of creating a meaning which makes sense of our history and intuitions about values, but also restores our ability to use values to make sense of our lives and create the world we really want. That is a tall order, of course, but ultimately the only other choice is to live in a world which does not recognize any values at all.

Part 1.

Things Fall Apart[5]

Chapter 1
Crumbling Values

A hollow centre

Values guide our choices and decisions about how to live our lives. Even when we don't think about them that doesn't mean they are not with us or we are not using them. It's usually just that they are not being challenged. A person's values define that person's character and the same is broadly true of societies. A life without any values at all would be incoherent, aimless. If we cared about nothing in particular and just followed the whim of the moment, we and our lives would be without direction.

We live in a profoundly pluralist society in which the determinants of what we care about are hardly the same for any two of us. We have many religions, many cultures, classes, traditions, levels of education and knowledge, even languages existing side-by-side. These differences can cause values to conflict even within a single individual, leading to dislocation and bewilderment. Perhaps their cultural background inclines them one way, their religious beliefs another and their role in society a third. It is the stuff of personal crises: which priorities are uppermost, which should prevail when there is a conflict?

Not everyone is confused, of course. Some people have very strong and clear views about what their values are, or what matters most to them. Such clarity is usually based on some particular distinguishing element of their lives like their faith, some ideology they have adopted or their culture or class. (Faith, Ideology, Class, Culture: we will abbreviate this variety of causes and say that such values depend on an FIC.) Well, that is fine for them, but not everyone will share that FIC and there will generally be no way to convince others that it is so superior it should dominate the choices of everyone else. Hence, it is difficult to share such values outside the group which shares the particular FIC. Clarity of this kind is therefore not transferable.

Most benefits have a cost and it seems this variety is a cost of the tolerance and openness of pluralism. If all values are equal then no values are any more acceptable than any others. In the end such radical tolerance means that anything goes. But even if we don't go this far, some conflict of values is "built-in" because there will be many competing sets of values.

Such competition can give rise to a particularly awkward kind of problem. If values rest on a particular FIC, to question or even entertain evidence about that FIC can mean calling the values into question. But that involves questioning not just facts but a person's whole way of living, a much more serious and painful matter. What typically happens therefore is that people will consciously or unconsciously protect their FIC, holding it immune to reason or evidence—for if ever the FIC weakens values are destroyed. So the defences go up, listening stops and it is only a short step to various kinds of fundamentalism.

The more common case, in our own society anyway, is that our lives are not driven by strong convictions about religion or ideology. In this case, the lack of rational roots for our values is desperate. Without such roots, our values float on nothing more than a vague feeling of what is right without even the support of some ideological theory or supernatural "facts". If we cannot justify our values to others we cannot really justify them to ourselves, for if I can't give you convincing reasons, what reasons can I give myself? Thus the most important choices of our lives can be left without rational support or foundation.

Rationality of course has its limitations, but without some rational justification or foundation the personal values we cling to can begin to seem arbitrary at any time. Relativism sweeps them all away. If we ever do think about <u>why</u> this or that is so important to us we find that we don't really have an answer. We can't discuss values rationally with others, we can only shout and hope we are loudest. But in the silence of our own minds, there is nothing to help us. The centre cannot hold. We either retreat back to dogma or our values and therefore to an extent our lives can seem hollow.

The symptoms of dislocated personal values are all around us. Depression, stress, anxiety, feelings of alienation, rage, violence, alcohol and substance abuse, addictive consumption—the list could go on. Of course many other factors are involved in each case. But while we can argue about detailed causes it is surely clear that there is a value dimension to these widespread malaises.

People often do not know which way to turn or how to live. Their feelings and aspirations are at odds with their surroundings and circumstances. They live in a world in which getting and spending, in particular, are the essence of normality and success. Yet getting and spending, even when they are possible, do not seem to solve their problems and even cause many of them.

A hollow society

If values give direction to our individual lives they are also instrumental in creating the society in which we live. They may not be the only thing that binds societies together, but they are a very important part of what turns a crowd of people occupying the same geographical space into a society. If people have no values in common with their neighbours then the condition of society is likely to be fragile or fragmented at best.

But now, if the values of each person come from different sources and if no source is considered authoritative by everyone then any sharing of values across society is a lucky coincidence and nothing more. That, you may retort, is what democracy is for, to tot up the various views and produce if not a consensus at least a workable view. But this is expecting far too much of democracy.

If values matter to us we cannot expect anyone to change their values just because others disagree and they are outvoted. Democracy may produce a practical decision but can never produce agreement about values. It can at best paper over, not resolve, fundamental differences about values and is itself likely to be an early casualty if it constantly leads to people feeling that their values have been violated.

Democracy works best therefore when at least some important values are already widely shared and where there is agreement on major objectives. It can break down into unrest and even civil strife when values are sharply divided. Besides, to the extent that we cannot give a reasonable justification for our values it is hard to see how we can have reasonable political discussions about them. If we have no rational way of explaining or perhaps even deciding on our individual values how can we bring them into any process of forming the values of society? Which way do you vote if you don't know what matters most to you? How do you begin to persuade others if you cannot explain why you believe what you believe? But democracy without some basis of reasonable discussion is a very strange beast, little better than a lottery.

Broadly the same arguments apply if markets are your solution to resolving fundamental issues within society. Both are simply ways for individuals to express their choices, but the irony is that both therefore require that there is first some way for individuals to make those choices. That is fine if the choice is between, say, cheaper cheese or more expensive, better tasting cheese. Matters of taste and budget don't need deeper reasons and anyway there is no one right answer in such a case but a spectrum of answers. But not every collective decision can be left like this as a crude sum of disparate individual choices. Besides, to accept that <u>every</u> individual choice is a just "a matter of taste" is already to have given up on the possibility of values. In some of the most difficult cases we fetishize individual choice as the alternative to collective decision-making without having a sound method for individuals to make rational individual choices.

The processes and practices of the marketplace, though, have a way of filling the vacuum left by the absence of well-founded values. It's not a conspiracy, it's just what happens. If we are closely focused on getting and spending and nothing more then the things that help us get and the things on which we want to spend become the most important aims we have. They fill our horizons and we cannot see beyond them, indeed we may feel there is nothing to see. Thus consumer capitalism comes to provide our social values by default. To the many who are the victims rather than beneficiaries of capitalism (or as those who regard capitalism as part of the natural order of things might say, losers rather than winners) this will seem a harsh result. But surely to everyone it must seem just a little strange. We may agree that capitalism provides innovation and efficiency (for example), but why is making and consuming the most important function of our species? If capitalism claims to provide our values as well as our goods, we should at least expect an explanation of how and why.

It would be an exaggeration to suggest that everything that is wrong with our world is the result of our confusion and lack of agreement about values. But we suggested at the individual level that many major problems have a value dimension to them, and at the collective level this is also true. We could cite terrorism, wars, economic crises, debt problems, global and indeed local poverty, our unwillingness to curb greenhouse gas emissions, drug trafficking, people trafficking, social deprivation, disputes over health care provision, intolerance and discrimination of whatever kind and so on and so on. Each, again, is the product of many complex factors but in each case we can point to a value dimension, an aspect where a basic disagreement exists between groups about what is the right thing to do or the right outcome. More clarity about values would not make the world perfect or abolish all these problems overnight, but even a little more clarity might help.

But where can we turn for clarity? Religion seems separate from politics except for fanatics, politics mainly a game for the personally ambitious. Economic life seems to be played on a global stage by global forces few of us understand, let alone control. What role can values play and how do we establish what those values should be? Are there even such things as political or collective values anymore, anything real we can grasp and use to steer our lives and our society, or are there just the cultural preferences of each group pitted against all the others?

Chapter 2

A Failure of Secularism

The value-shaped hole

The fragmentation of our values is surely related in particular to the fragmentation of religious belief, whether because we no longer believe at all or because so many varieties of religious belief are now familiar and available. People often talk about the "god-shaped hole" left when religious belief is lost, but to a large extent the real damage is a "value-shaped hole", a hollow centre in our lives where values should be.

Religion has in many countries retreated from the public arena except where the specific interests of religious groups are threatened. Since this was often an important step in creating tolerance in society it is hard to argue that it is completely a bad thing. There is no accepted way to settle disputes between religions so it is (rightly) deemed safer not to argue, because history shows that the arguments can get ugly. On the other hand, in areas of the world where religious agreement is both widely shared and central to everyday life there is no lack of certainty about values—which is not always a good thing or even a source of sensible decisions, but it confronts our own confusion as well as making dialogue with those countries difficult.

For many people in our own society, though, religion and values are still if not synonymous at least tightly linked. Yet there are strong motives for trying to find a foundation for values which does not depend on religion.

The first is simply that many people do not have a religious faith at all. It is deeply unsatisfactory, then, to depend on values and moral guidelines whose roots and justifications lie so deep in religious history. A second motive comes from the sheer variety of cultures and beliefs which tend to make up modern society and the modern world. A third motive is that without strong values the world is organized by power and power alone. We consider each of these motives in turn.

The lack of a secular foundation

The shocking fact is that there is no sound and generally accepted basis for secular values, despite centuries of recognition that ethics and religion should in principle be separable. We can pick out many causes of this sorry state of secular affairs.

One is the prevalence of forms of "emotivism" (which we will examine more closely later) which suggest that values rest solely on our feelings, desires or tastes. This may leave values as something we care about, but not something we can discuss or share except to the extent we can describe and canvass for our tastes.

Another cause is the deep influence of Marx particularly on progressive or left-leaning politics, which leads to suspicion of any kind of values as cultural artefacts which either reflect or mask (or both) economic realities and relationships. On this view values are no more than a propaganda tool to further the interests of the economically powerful. A consequence is that trying to justify or find a foundation for values is itself regarded as a politically dubious activity which is really just propping up the economic status quo.

Yet another cause is the fetishization of science as the only form of understanding, a metaphysical view which is itself not science but "scientism". On this view we might search for the basis of values in biology or neuroscience,[6] but what we will find, what we can only find, are the causes of how we come to have the values we do. The vital human question of how we should live is not even allowed because it is not "scientific".

There are indeed good scientific theories about how we might have come to behave as we do, for example what evolutionary advantage there might have been in altruism. The problem is that these explanations even if true do not offer any reason why any individual should behave in similar ways today. We would need to have some reason, for example, why one evolutionary outcome might be ethically preferable to another and it is not even clear what that might mean. In any case we generally do not know where evolutionary advantage lies at any given time.

But whatever the causes of why we have no generally accepted secular basis for values, the fact remains that secular society and secular people really need one—otherwise our secular values are, as now, incoherent. They are little more than a jumble of prejudices, inarticulate feelings and religious left-overs, even leaving aside propaganda. That might not matter if we lived in a static, unchanging world where no new questions were ever asked of us and no new situations arose to challenge our values. In such a world we might get along by relying on the traditions of the tribe, so to speak. But the pace of change in our world could hardly be faster and we need a foundation for our values that helps us adapt and direct our decisions and our changing lives.

Binding cultures into society

A second motive driving the search for a secular basis for ethics comes from the fissiparous nature of the pluralist, multicultural society we live in, both within national boundaries and globally. Because religions are often looked to as taking the lead in ethical matters, the argument below will be framed in terms of different religions. Bear in mind, however, that we could say similar things about many kinds of FIC. We are not picking on religion.

It is obvious that there are very many religions in the world with different cosmologies, supernatural beliefs and authorities, and different values which hinge to various degrees on those specifically religious foundations. Thus when different religions have a disagreement about values it is likely to rest on an underlying disagreement about (for example) supernatural beliefs which there is no way to adjudicate −not, at least, without simply adopting the religious beliefs of one religion or the other (or a third!). Hence it is unlikely that religions will be able to find agreement on values. If their conclusions agree it will be good news but pure coincidence.

So unless we can find some neutral ground, the prospect of gaining agreement among religions on value matters will always be problematic. But that neutral ground cannot itself depend on supernatural beliefs, since we know we cannot arbitrate or find agreement on those. Even leaving aside the many people who accept no supernatural belief at all, if we are to have any chance of supporting values in a way which allows us to share them across religious communities it must be done on a basis which itself makes no appeal to supernatural or religious beliefs.

That basis must therefore be secular. Even if we set ourselves a less ambitious goal, that of being able to discuss values reasonably in a language we all understand and can relate to, rather than resorting as we often do to shouting slogans at each other, we have to find some neutral and thus secular substrate on which the discussion can rely.

So the second powerful motivation for finding or constructing a secular foundation for values is that it offers the only chance for broad agreement on values within, across and between groups in society and even between whole societies. Without it, multicultural or multifaith societies are inherently unstable. Peace on earth needs human values.

Power and the price of everything

A third reason why we need secular values is that without strong values the world is organized by power and power alone. That may mean, for example, it is organized by violence and overt force, or perhaps by structures of power which generally do not need to use force but can call on it as a last resort. Values can stand against power, by saying for example that there is a way in which things <u>should</u> be organized whatever the preferences of the powerful. This has no chance of working unless, crucially, we can give convincing reasons for opposition based on values, which is again why values need a rational foundation. History is of course full of examples where values have been swept aside by force, but to accept that human life <u>has</u> to be organized like this is to accept barbarism, however politely clothed.

But common as violence and force are as ways of determining human lives, the more insidious danger comes from economic power. It is not just that economic power may occasionally turn to force when all else fails, or even harness or capture the structures of power which, for example, make up the state. It is that economic power constantly sets up goals and norms which we are invited or obliged to pursue. Economic power seduces us into accepting it as the basis of values.

Without clear, strongly based and widely accepted values economic goals come to be seen as the life goals of both individuals and states. In this way our economic lives, public and private, come to dictate what we consider right or wrong. What is good comes to be equated with what is profitable, or what promotes economic growth, or just what we yearn to spend our money on. And thus we come to have no real values, just the shifting goals and targets of consumer capitalism.

A society in thrall to consumer capitalism perfectly fits Oscar Wilde's definition of cynicism: it knows the price of everything and the value of nothing. We will not argue that there is a better way to organize our economies — there probably isn't. But we will argue that there is a better way to organize our values and thus our lives.

Capitalism may be fine as a way of getting things done, but the question is, what things and why? Without values to set its goals and boundaries, capitalism is a headless chicken. More seriously, capitalism on its own is amoral — which is not even a criticism, for the mistake is to think that capitalism could ever generate values or meaning in our lives. The same is true, would be true, of any other economic system. Economics does not generate creeds or values, just more or less effective ways of getting things done. So we need some other way to set directions and boundaries for ourselves and our societies.

We need strong, rational, shared values which can stand alongside and against the dictates of economic power and hold their own against economic arguments. For that our values need a strong, rational foundation. But since economic power is exercised globally, that foundation has at least in principle to be acceptable globally, which means it must be as culturally neutral as possible. At the very least it must be secular.

False trails and dead ends

When we start to think about a foundation for secular values, however, we immediately run into a thicket of different views, all with long histories but all still very much part of the prevailing confusion. In the next few chapters we will look (very briefly indeed!) at several such commonly met views about the foundation of values, only to suggest that they will not do the job.

In some ways it is a pity to start by considering what <u>doesn't</u> work. But this is not a matter of knocking over straw men for sport. These mistaken views are widely held and strongly influential and it is best to deal with them head on, otherwise they will confuse the picture as we go forward. We certainly do not claim to do justice to all the subtleties of every such view but there some important fundamental points to be made. Moreover, in the course of considering such views we will gain some insight into the nature of the task we have to accomplish.

To summarize, we will suggest that values cannot be based on laws or rights and particularly not on any kind of laws or rights independent of human beings, whether natural or supernatural. Neither can they be based on our feelings and preferences, nor on science, nor on calculation. We are heading towards "teleology", also known as virtue ethics, the idea that values are based on aims or purposes. Later, of course, we have to show how satisfied mind (remember that?!) fits into this scheme of things. But, first things first.

Chapter 3

Laws and Rights

The myth of law

Values are not laws. We will call the view that they are, "the myth of law" or "the legal paradigm". The myth of law has persisted for centuries[7] and still today when people realize it is untrue they are often inclined to think that values are therefore worthless or inapplicable. If we are to fill the hollow centre where values should be, we need to understand why values cannot be laws, but also that they are no less important for that.

The model here is that values ("moral laws") are like the law of the land, only (so to speak) more so. They have the character of regulations we should obey, perhaps but not necessarily on pain of punishment. But they stand above and beyond the laws of the land, indeed they might be thought of as the laws of the universe.

The origins of this view are probably religious, founded in the idea that values or moral laws represent the will of the gods or God. But there is a powerful argument against at least the most obvious version of this view. I will call it "Plato's fork".[8]

Plato's fork is an innocent seeming question: "Do the gods[9] will what is good, or are things good because the gods will them?"

Devout people might prefer the first option. It seems attractive not least because it is essential if they want to say that the gods are themselves good, but unfortunately it destroys the idea that the will of the gods is the foundation of values, or of what is good or right. If the gods are drawn to what is good, whatever they choose must already be good before they choose it, otherwise what is the basis of their choice? There must be some other basis, some other foundation for what is good and the gods are just recognizing it. Their will might be a reliable guide, but it does not make things good as such because things are already good or bad independently of the gods and their will.

But the second option (prong) is much worse. If the gods have a free hand in what they favour they might choose, for example, cannibalism or incest, which would thus have to be regarded as good. The mythical Greek gods did occasionally stray along such paths, but the point is that even the possibility of such will-driven choices takes us way outside any acceptable understanding of what is good or right. The unconstrained will of the gods becomes the whim of the gods, so that absolutely anything could be good or evil and even change moral status from one day to the next.

It is of course no use objecting that the deity you believe in wouldn't behave like that because your god is inherently good. If "good" means nothing but what your god wills that statement means no more than that your god wills what your god wills, which doesn't help at all. If you want to say that your god is inherently good and have it mean something you have to take the first prong of the fork, but then goodness isn't dependent on divine will.

Plato's fork, simple as it is, is utterly fatal to the idea that values are divine laws. All that is left of it is the possibility that the gods might choose to back up pre-existing values with rewards and punishments of their own. If that were true it would certainly add to the advantages of being good or living a devout life but would not alter the foundations of values which would lie elsewhere. Frankly, once the idea of values being themselves divine laws has gone, such rewards and punishments do not belong in the realm of the ethical but in the realm of the prudential. Besides, such prudential calculation makes sense only in the context of particular religious beliefs and need concern only those who hold such beliefs.

This does not of course mean that religion has nothing to say about values – there are many other ways in which particular values might be supported by religious belief. But divine law is not one of them.

The myth of law, secular version

This paradigm of values as "divine laws" is probably the main source of the idea that values are laws at all. Once it goes the myth of law is left very exposed. If values are laws, but not divine, the questions quickly mount up. Who does make them, how are they legislated, how altered if at all? What are their detailed provisions, or indeed any provisions, and how do we find them out?

A law like "Do not kill", for example, may sound straightforward, but most people allow at least some exceptions, for example self-defence. Presumably it means "Do not kill humans" anyway, or is even the killing of bacteria not allowed? This example is of a rule we all more or less subscribe to, but how do I know or find out what the detailed exceptions are? Perhaps, for example, it is permitted to kill people I disagree with on certain matters, or worse, for them to kill me! The point is that this "law" is severely under-drafted in its simple form and indeed we can observe that much of what passes as practical ethical discussion is about the fine print of such supposed laws.

The problems go on, however. Why should I obey this law, what is the source of its authority? If the law or its application to a particular situation is not clear, who decides? What if there is a conflict between two different laws? Are there "ethical judges" or must we all judge for ourselves? If there are judges or even experts, who appointed them or how do you get to be one? But if we all judge for ourselves what kind of law is that? Imagine even deciding for yourself whether or not you should be given a parking ticket—what do you think you would decide?!

There have been many attempts to answer such questions over the centuries. In one of the strongest and best known[10] each individual indeed legislates for herself but subject to a constraint. In choosing how to act we must choose as if we create a law which applies everywhere and to everyone.

This has many merits. For example, our own actions must themselves have some measure of consistency (if, that is, we act rationally); our laws can be developed to cover genuinely new situations; and the same laws are in principle applicable to everyone. But there are still many problems.

It is not clear for example how we can have enough information at any given time to make these important, indeed universal, legislative choices. If I have promised to meet you for coffee, for example, do I really have to take a view on all promises made in all circumstances by everyone before cancelling? That seems a heavy responsibility to take on for missing a cup of coffee! But on the other hand the fine print of my personal law-making could always make the whole question of universal laws pointless—if I declare that everyone should act as I do now in these circumstances I might specify the circumstances so narrowly that they never apply again.

Even if all the problems about making, interpreting and changing laws were solved, though, there is a more general problem. Why should I decide to be law-abiding? It might be rational to obey, it might be prudent to obey, but many people act irrationally at least some of the time or decide not to be law-abiding even where the ordinary criminal law is in point. The fact is that even with the ordinary law there is a choice about whether to obey, with consequences depending largely on how well the law is policed and enforced. That in itself suggests that laws are the wrong sort of model for values, because people with a certain kind of values will obey and those with a different kind will not. Where morals or values are concerned laws cannot be the foundation, because the foundation would really lie in whatever determined the individual choice to obey the law, or not.

Many people are reluctant to give up the idea that values are laws because they fear the consequences, particularly perhaps what other people will do if freed from the fear of law. Just as we rely on the deterrent effect of the criminal law to protect our lives, loved ones and property, it may seem that we rely on moral laws or values to make dealing with others tolerable and safe. This fear of moral anarchy is perfectly understandable, but fear cannot justify a belief in something which can be shown to be nonsense. We cannot just pretend that values are laws if they are not. We have to be brave, abandon this mistaken legal paradigm and find a better one.

Moral Rights

Closely related to the myth of law is an idea we could call "the myth of rights". According to this, we are each endowed with certain rights simply by reason of being human or perhaps just being alive.[11] We might call these fundamental rights.

Separately, we may also acquire rights through our actions or our transactions with others. However, if we can acquire such rights it is likely that we can also lose, trade or give them up so that these acquired rights may be secondary and not fundamental. Rights (of both kinds) are essentially rights against others, a demand on others that they do something or allow us to do something.

Strictly speaking, rights are not of course identical with values. It is more exact to say that respect for <u>my</u> rights is part of <u>other people's</u> values, while my values are concerned with my respect for other people's rights. But many people feel that "standing up for their rights" is in itself an important value, without which perhaps rights would be so violated that they would count for nothing. In any case we seem to have a network of rights, yours and mine and theirs, and the values which bind society together are the result.

Rights of the fundamental sort are not inherently legal rights or such as the law of the land will enforce: the law of the land may recognize them or not. Just as adherents of the myth of law would see a distinction between the law of the land and the moral law, theorists of rights can uphold a distinction between legal and moral rights, with the moral being in some sense prior and superior to, even if less enforceable than, the legal.

For our present purpose it doesn't really matter whether rights are enshrined in or enforced by law. In politics for example it is a common move to assert a moral right as a way of expressing a belief that such a right <u>should</u> be publicly enforced, or that the law should be changed to make sure this claimed right is recognized. I may have a legal right, for example, to a certain piece of land, meaning that the law will uphold and if necessary enforce my right to go onto and remain there. Suppose, however, that I or my ancestors obtained that right by force or deception so that others consider themselves to have been dispossessed unjustly. They may feel they have rights which are not recognized by the law — moral rights which they might campaign about and which over time the law might indeed be changed to recognize. At any rate, it is clear that the law is not the source of fundamental rights, for the law can be changed at the stroke of a legislative pen.

The trouble is that moral rights are subject to many of the same issues and problems as moral laws. How do we know precisely what the details are of their scope and reach? Without such detail we can do little with them, because they are most relevant when they are disputed or when one person asserts rights which conflict with those of another. Indeed, conflict may often concern exactly who has or can have rights, as when we consider the rights of animals, or the unborn, or even the deceased. Again, who or what gives rights authority and how does this work? Can I acquire a moral right to land, for example, just by occupying it when no one else seems to want it? Who says, one way or the other?

Conflicts pose particular problems for the myth of rights. Moral laws might conflict but need not, while moral rights are inherently set up to conflict. The whole point of my having a right is that it is a right against or in opposition to someone else and their possible claim — or as they see it, their right. How do we decide then whose right should prevail? The likelihood is surely that I assert my right and you assert yours and in the absence of a neutral arbiter we are headed for battle. So if values are primarily based on rights we are little better off than if we had no values at all because we must dispute and defend our rights endlessly. We may not be much better off than if nobody had any rights!

This is not of course to say that there is no place for the language of rights in society, nor that the language of rights may not often be the best way to put across a difficult or novel idea which changes society. The assertion of rights for slaves in the nineteenth century or for their descendants in the southern USA in the twentieth are shining examples. But the language of rights can be and often is used simply as a rhetorical device to express the idea that a particular group wants to make a demand on the rest of society and we have to turn elsewhere to decide which demands are justified.

The trouble with the myth of rights is that, like its cousin the myth of law, it borrows from legal and legislative institutions we are familiar with to suggest an underlying realm or sphere where rights are already, indeed perhaps eternally, clearly set out. The task then seems to be to discover them by some means of clearly perceiving this transcendent realm, some metaphysical enquiry. So if a right is not yet recognized it is as if there has been a mistake about interpreting the hidden realm of rights. But how can this be true? We can talk about the rights we have in a given legal framework and indeed about the rights we think we should have, but these are matters of law and politics, respectively, not of metaphysics.

The stark fact is that moral or natural rights cannot form the basis of shared values, because what they are and how they come into being does not really make sense, even leaving aside the difficulty of resolving conflict between different people's rights. This is a dramatic departure from prevailing fashion, for many moral dilemmas are commonly presented in terms of conflicting rights and the assertion of presumed rights often has a strong emotional charge. Nevertheless, when we look closely there is little we can do with such claims. We must keep looking.

Human Rights

We should not be confused at this point by the idea of "Human Rights", which are an important political and legal idea but, we suggest, not something which can be made immediately useful in the sphere of morality and values. We will look at this question in more detail later but Human Rights are essentially an expression of the rights which citizens might aspire to have against the state.

They are embodied in (various[12]) documents which represent diplomatic compromises reached at particular points in time, for indisputably worthy and highly laudable ends. But despite the sheer rhetorical brilliance of calling them "Human Rights" they are not expressions of any rights which human beings inherently enjoy. On the contrary, it is necessary to write them down because they express standards which states systematically and regularly violate.

Human rights could be regarded as elements of a model constitution, a model for how nations should treat their citizens and others. As such, they have their own drawbacks. When embodied directly in law as legal rights they can produce the usual difficulties of written constitutions when a very brief (but inviolable) expression must be stretched to cover cases not remotely considered by the drafters. When used in international political polemic they may have great power – but only against those states who care about the opinion of subscribing states.

They are thus limited in scope to aspects of the relationship between state and citizen and they express what the originators think that relationship should be like, not what it actually is. Like the predecessor idea of the "Rights of Man" they are, if taken out of their proper context, nonsense, and the idea that they are inviolable, while a wonderful dream, is yet "nonsense upon stilts".[13]

Chapter 4

Emotivism

Preferences and feelings

At an opposite extreme from the theory that values are laws or rights is the theory that they are based simply on preferences of different kinds. Depending on which particular member of this family of theories you choose, the proposed basis might be individual tastes, desires, feelings, will or something else.[14] On all such views, I make choices about what to do and how to behave simply as an expression of my preferences. If I use the language of values or terms like good and bad it is just to back up my choice and persuade you or others that I am right, perhaps because I don't want you to get in my way or because I want you to join or agree with me.

So in its simplest form "Kindness is good" works in much the same way as "Bananas are tasty". Both express how I feel about the subject and make you aware of my preference, for whatever reason I want you to know about it. Both perhaps invite you to share my enthusiasm. But on this view the language of values has no substance beyond those limited tasks.

Forms of this kind of theory are very widespread and the general term for them is "emotivism". They seem to be the most common place of flight when the idea that values are based on some form of law is abandoned. In some forms, the underlying theory is expressly nihilist. It says there are really no values and people's use of language about them is either cynical, mistaken or in some versions even craven, an attempt to persuade the powerful to moderate their use of power.

Such views may be presented as being mainly about how the language of values is used and what it does, hence the stress on justifying myself to others and persuading them. The emotivist may contend that this is the only way to make sense of what people are doing because what they think they are doing is not coherent. People may think, for example, they are referring to some sort of laws but (as we have seen) they could not explain the origin, nature and detail of those laws if challenged, so the theory is that they must in fact be doing something else.

The entirely individual quality of values for emotivism is quickly clear. A theory of this kind leaves values without any objective substance at all. If there are shared values based on shared preferences it is a coincidence or a fact about people which has no moral significance in itself. The most we have are individual preferences and feelings, tastes if you like. If I say that it is wrong to kill people I am saying little more that I don't like that kind of thing, although perhaps by telling you this I am testing your opinion or trying to bring you round to mine.

Oddly, if you and I express different views on what is the right thing to do in some particular circumstance we are not really disagreeing, we are just expressing our different tastes. Unless I am accusing you of lying about your preference there is no more disagreement than if you said you liked chocolate cake and I said I didn't. If only one of our preferences can be accommodated we may have a different kind of problem, but it is a problem about power or politics not values.

The destructive power of emotivism

If some version of emotivism is true then in talking about values we are in the first instance reporting on our own tastes, as when we say we like cheese but don't like Brussels sprouts. Beyond that there is just spin, persuasion and rhetoric, or at best perhaps an attempt to identify where and how our preferences converge into some sort of consensus. The language of values may have a function to announce, warn or persuade others about preferences, but the underlying idea of values itself becomes redundant — or worse, a trick.

While I may care about group "values" for many reasons, including my desire to fit in with the group, I may simply decline to play the game. This riff is understandably a contributor to social fragmentation. We can easily conclude, for example, that talk of ethics or values is simply an expression of the preferences of some clique or ruling elite. Worse, it may be a fairy story told to keep people in their places.

So the rich and powerful tell the poor and dispossessed it is wrong to steal because they don't want to be robbed, while the same rich help themselves quietly and cynically to anything they can. Or the more gifted (privileged) tell the less gifted (less privileged) it is wrong to depend on the state and everyone should find work because the gifted don't like paying taxes but can create work opportunities for themselves.

From the opposite perspective, those without jobs and money can persuade themselves that they really have a right to anything they want, their lack being somehow the fault of "the system". Violence and theft can even be painted as noble, unfettered expressions of will.

Something strange often happens here though, as if the idea of objective values will not let go. Even if we incline to the view that values are based on feelings or will, <u>our</u> position always seems true or based on "good" feelings or desires, while <u>their</u> position seems false or in bad faith. No one likes to admit openly that there are no true values because that would mean no position was any better or worse than any other, so they confine themselves to rubbishing the values of the other side. Such indignation always has to claim that somehow there really <u>is</u> a moral high ground, which by the way it happens to occupy. But of course the other side makes the same claim. The rhetorical idea of morality is used, because of the persuasive force it still possesses, to clothe a prejudice or preference. More shouting.

In any case, your preferences, tastes and feelings are unlikely to be identical to mine in all respects, whether we are talking about food or values. So, if values are to be based on our personal feelings or preferences, our values are likely to differ. Perhaps one of us can persuade or cajole the other into agreement, but it is unlikely this trick can be repeated right across the community, let alone across whole countries and continents. So everyone, more or less, has their own unique system of values which may have features in common with the values of others but may not.

But—this just doesn't work. Too many systems of values amounts to no values at all. What it comes down to is that we just have preferences, indeed there is nothing to be had but preferences. It would be great if we all had some built-in aversion to certain things, like cruelty or killing, but human history does not support such naturalism as the basis of universally shared preferences. Even the persuasive aspect of values disappears, or at least is reduced to wheedling or perhaps trying to get others to agree because they don't like to be different. We can't appeal to values to persuade anyone because no one else shares our values! There is never a "right thing to do", only what you or I would prefer to do which may or may not be different things. You like sweet, I like sour—there can be no reasoned argument.

Something like this has already happened in modern society, perhaps not right down to the level of each individual supporting their own preferences but pretty close. We influence each other sufficiently perhaps that there are "clumps" of preferences, based around inter-sections of religion, place, culture, social class, education and so on. But each clump may view the others in at least certain respects with sus-picion and distaste: "Their values are not our values and who are they to try to impose their values on us?" Or more simply, especially since values even in these circumstances still often carry a high emotional charge: "What makes them think they are better than us?"

Consensualism

There is indeed a variant of emotivism in which preferences are replaced by shared preferences. Killing people, for example, is held to be wrong not just because I think it is or because I don't like it, but because by and large we all agree on the matter. Agreement may even be regarded as the price of entry to our group or society. This variant, which we might call "consensualism", may even suggest that the foundation of our preferences hardly matters because we all (or enough of us) happen to share them anyway. There is sometimes a supplementary suggestion that widely shared preferences might have a biological or evolutionary basis so that the consensus itself points to a natural phenomenon or (better still) a scientific fact, a suggestion which gives an air of scientific respectability to the underlying position.

This view may be a brave attempt to avoid the atomism towards which emotivism based on individual preferences seems to lead but its drawbacks are still considerable, probably insurmountable.

First, this theory leaves us all in a very odd position. I may know what my <u>preferences</u> are, but I don't know what my <u>values</u> are until I find out who shares which particular preferences. If my liking for Scandinavian detective dramas (or dislike of theft, to take a different sort of example) is not widely shared, that may make it just my personal taste. But if this preference is actually disapproved of by many, does that make it actually wrong? On the other hand, if it should turn out that everyone likes ice-cream (or shooting people) does that make this taste into a value? It is very odd to have to find out what everyone else thinks before I know something actually counts as one of my values. How many people do I have to canvass?

Second, we will probably find we agree on broad outlines but start to disagree as soon as we get to details, which is typically where morality matters. We may agree that gratuitous killing is wrong, for example, but disagree about whether particular cases are gratuitous, for example to what extent war or punishment or self-defence may excuse killing.

Third and perhaps most important, are there any limits to what we can agree upon? What if we were all persuaded or cajoled to agree with something terrible, to support a genocide for example or impose slavery? Would that make it morally neutral or even right? On this view it must. It is no help to say that such a thing would not or could not happen in practice. Even in principle, if we agreed that something was right that would make it right. (That pesky fork again.)

Consider finally what might happen when there was a shift in public opinion, as surely there often is. There might be a point where the majority (Simple? Qualified? What are the rules in these cases and who decides them?) tipped over from one view to the other on a particular subject. This would mean that what yesterday was right was now wrong, or vice versa. Not just, "We were mistaken and what seemed to be right is now accepted as wrong" — which has indeed happened many times in history — but flat out, "What was right is now wrong". Surely this is nonsense.

Consensualism thus cannot be the truth of the matter. What we all agree to be right may be so, but our agreement or our shared preference is not the reason why.

Nihilism

Any form of emotivism as a theory of values either amounts to or inevitably leads to value nihilism. It may dress things up with talk about how moral language is used but implies ultimately that there are no values, only different sorts of preferences.

At most there are maybe practices and behaviours that people treat with care because they prefer them, find them useful or observe them as traditions or cultural practices. Cultural practices may even be maintained and imposed, in good faith or bad, by one group in society to keep another group in its place, and this increases the suspicion that values are just somehow a trick, a piece of spin. There is thus moral rhetoric, but no rational moral arguments worth anything. There is nothing behind preferences to say that one such practice is better or worse than another.

Such "nihilism dressed up" is a very common view although it produces astonishing conclusions. Slavery, cruelty to children or genocide are not really wrong, on this view, just disapproved of by many. So we live in a valueless world in which anything goes, if you can get away with it, and if we oppose certain things that is just an expression of our own tastes. This is maybe not a bad description of some aspects of Western society today, but should we accept it as the last word about values?

If we do, there is only a paper-thin wall between us and outright barbarism. But unless we can come up with an alternative it is the destination towards which emotivism and indeed any form of relativism about values inexorably takes us. Surely we should not give up the search unless it is certain that there is no alternative.

Capitalism and preferences

Many people as we have noted consider economic materialism itself as a source of values. This is indeed the position towards which consumer capitalism encourages us, if quietly and implicitly. The market dictates what is valuable and what is not, based on the preferences which are there expressed. Whatever (and by implication whoever) is successful in the marketplace has right on its side. This is clearly an attractive theory for the wealthy, because it suggests that wealth is the reward of virtue. Less attractively, it suggests that poverty is a punishment for some kind of turpitude.

But if this view is explicitly treated as a theory of values it is clear that it is no more than another form of emotivism or consensualism. Values are here being built on the back of preferences and nothing more. The market is just a way of adding up the score. If we ask what should inform or constrain the buying choices individuals make, there is no answer. Individuals are supposed to act as "rational agents", but even if true that only means that they will express their preferences in non-contradictory ways, for example they will not pay a higher price for goods available at a lower one. The nature and quality of their preferences are otherwise left to them.

This leads us straight back into all the problems we have already seen with values based on preferences alone. On this view, if there is a demand or desire for something, the market is right to supply it, whether it be nuclear bombs for private use or slaves. But as soon as we accept that some preferences are illegitimate, we have moved away from the marketplace and asserted the existence of a separate regime of values.

Perhaps not many people regard capitalism as explicitly providing a theory of moral values in itself, however, except perhaps more aggressive but less reflective financial traders. Capitalism is able to set the values of society in more subtle ways. By setting out to meet demands and taking no stand on values itself, it declines to look behind the preferences expressed in the marketplace and encourages us to do the same. But in a society which is confused about values or in which relativism has taken such a hold that there are few shared values, that very neutrality of the marketplace endorses emotivism and ultimately nihilism.

Capitalism is at best amoral, a mechanism with nothing to say about values. It may meet material needs as long as people can freely enter the market process (which may be a problematic condition in itself) but like any mechanism does no more than what it was designed to do. It tells us something about what preferences people have, but makes no judgements about how those preferences are formed, still less about what preferences people ought to have or whether what they want is in their best interests. Indeed such questions hardly make sense in a nihilist world.

This, however, is actually a relatively benign view of capitalism, a best case, because as we know capitalism does try to persuade. It explicitly offers people a vision of how they should live their lives, promising fulfilment based on consumption and possessions. Usually of course this is done with no evil intent, it is just a way to sell stuff. But cumulatively, it helps to create a climate in which people come to believe that consumption and possessions are all that matter.

Marxism[15]

The other major branch of materialism offers values based not on consumption but on the surprisingly abstract idea of service to historical destiny. Marxism promises peace and plenty in the distant future when true communism prevails, but in the meantime demands struggle and obedience. Individual values are condemned as indulgent, collective values are all that matter and there is no difficulty such as democracies might face about how collective values can be decided upon because the party leaders will let you know. All other purported values are explicitly held to be either self delusions, attempts to delude the workers of their rights, or fabrications built on the economic status quo.

On the other hand there is a sense of determinism in Marxism which makes even collective values largely irrelevant, because the eventual destination of society is held to be historically inevitable. To the extent that this is an empirical prediction it shows no sign so far of being anything like true, but since the eventual destination of society is always in the future the prediction has an irrefutable quality more like a religious goal. In effect, though, it makes Marxism inherently nihilist about values, since they make no difference to the outcome.

It is sometimes said by Marxists nevertheless that the true source of values is to align oneself with history, to act so as to further or hasten the historically inevitable destination. To the extent that values are about what matters most to people this does suggest a goal which might fill someone's life and become the driving reason for their actions and choices. The problem comes in knowing what history demands. Again, the usual answer is that the party will let you know, but that merely pushes the question back to how the party knows. Marxism tends to take the second prong of Plato's fork, which as we saw earlier permits any excess on the grounds that (in this case) what the party wills is automatically good. Any refusal to obey is disloyal or merely squeamish. We know where this has historically led.

Marxism thus requires blind faith either in the underlying theory of historical inevitability or in the wisdom of its leaders, or both — faiths to which history has not been kind. To the extent that it allows for values at all and is not a form of nihilism it offers a secular theory of values, certainly, but one in which anything goes if the party says so and which, moreover, has all the drawbacks of a system of values based on faith. Add in the suspicion which Marxism has of any dissident or independent forms of thought and it seems impossible to extract from it the rational foundation of values we hope to find.

Chapter 5

Science and Calculation

Science

In an age dominated by science and technology it would leave a large gap if we did not at least consider science as a possible source of ethical truth.

What do we mean by science for this purpose? Science deals in facts and theories about the world. We could thus reasonably define the activity of science as a collection of methods for finding out or testing facts about the world. It is continuous with other sorts of fact finding, the sorts we use to find out what we need to know about our everyday world, as also the kind of fact finding which goes on in law courts. We may be able to make distinctions between science and other kinds of fact finding based on subject matter, but what really distinguishes science is that the methods used are (supposed to be and generally are) more systematic and rigourous, with extra care taken to rule out false interpretations.

Science is often thought to be about generalization but it is rigour rather than generalization which distinguishes science from ordinary fact finding. If, for example, we establish something unique about our planet or about a particular animal we may be doing good science even though the facts are singular and not general. So science is a fact finding activity distinguished by its care and rigour. The facts so found are often referred to as scientific facts, scientific knowledge or, with only a small risk of confusion, just as science.

Hence for science to give us a foundation for ethics would suggest that the foundation is itself a fact about the world or rests solely on such facts. There is a long tradition in ethics[16] which disputes how this could possibly be true or at any rate be the whole truth—and with good reason. Ethics is about what we <u>should</u> do, how we <u>ought</u> to live, what choices we <u>should</u> make—all "should's" or "ought's", not "is's". Whatever the facts are we can always respond, "OK, but why should I do that?".

The point is not that no factual argument has any force or bearing at all on our actions, but that no argument based on fact <u>alone</u> can compel us to act or even prove that we are being unreasonable not to act in the face of the facts. We need another step in the argument, something which adds an imperative, something which says in effect: "In these circumstances you <u>must</u> act like this." Science, however, does not deal in imperatives. In the classic formulation, you can never get a conclusion which says "You ought..." from premises which say "There is...". The Ought has to arrive from somewhere else, there can be no OUGHT just from an IS. Or as an adolescent of any age might put it, "Why should I?".

It is unlikely then that science will give us a foundation for values, simply because values are not facts about the world, or they are different from the facts in which science deals. That does not make science irrelevant as far as values are concerned and it will certainly inform ethical discussions and choices, not least because we need facts as well as values to fill out the picture and take any kind of decision. Science may tell us, for example, that certain people cannot help themselves when they do certain things which might be considered evil in others, or it may fill in the detail about the circumstances in which we act so that we better understand the implications and consequences of the choice we are making. But science will not give us values, because values are not themselves facts about the world.[17]

Reductionism

There is another way in which science is sometimes claimed to colonize ethics. Strictly speaking, we begin to pass here from science to scientism, neither the application of rigorous methods of fact finding nor their products but the often passionate and nearly always unscientific belief that science has all the answers.

This claim involves the argument known as reductionism. Human beings, whatever else they might be, are biological systems, made of various biological structures which are made in turn of molecules, atoms, fundamental particles, quantum fields, etc. — as far down the chain of the nanoscopic or even the abstract as we care to go. It is often true that what happens at one level of this progression can best be explained by what happens at the next level smaller, or certainly that another level of abstraction is needed to shed light on what is observed at the more aggregated level.

For example, something we see happening in biological structures, let's say in the division of chromosomes, can partly be explained or certainly illuminated by the biochemistry of what is going on, in this case the replication of DNA. This can lead to the claim that the larger or more easily observed phenomenon is equivalent to the underlying mechanism which helps explain it. The explained is "just" — the fateful word—the explanation. Phenomena are not only explained, they are explained away.[18]

Where human behaviour and experience are concerned for example we may be told that consciousness itself, for example, is "just" a by-product of the neurological or biochemical activity of the brain. Because our feelings, our thoughts, our desires are correlated with certain brain states or neurological events we are invited to conclude that there is nothing more to them than these states or events, or the biochemistry underlying those states, or the physics underlying the biochemistry, or wherever you want to stop. Hence, one version of the argument goes, ethics could be regarded as simply a set of quaint recipes for producing certain sought-after brain states, which in more enlightened times in the future we may be able to produce more directly with drugs or electrodes.[19] Since the universe is presumably indifferent about this or that state of our tiny brains, ethics is irrelevant or illusory except as a folk remedy among humans for reaching certain neurological states. In any case, producing these states is just something we like and thus in one sense we are back to emotivism.

What this reductionist argument misses out is that explanations of what causes or comprises any phenomenon do not exhaust the useful descriptions of the phenomenon. Very little is "just" the sum of its parts. "Everything is what it is and not another thing."[20] Your furniture, for example, is certainly made of atoms but you have to deal with it as furniture, not at an atomic level. Rearrange the atoms and you can make a table into a set of chairs—care to try? Of course you can't, it doesn't work like that, but it is still true that your furniture is made of atoms—and this is one of the simpler aggregations.

Living things, including human beings, are a great deal more than the sum of their parts, however minutely the parts are described, in fact especially when the parts are described minutely. It's not even a matter of there being something extra, like structure or organizing informa-tion, although that extra is usually present as well (think of furniture again). It's more that one description is fit for one purpose but simply misses out everything that's useful and even necessary for another, like different maps of the same territory made for different purposes.[21] One map might show, say, height above sea level, another annual rainfall or cultivation patterns, but it is wrong to say that only one map is the "real" map.

Consciousness, for example, is notoriously hard to capture with a physical description. Even if we had a full description of all the neuro-logical and other states underlying every mental phenomenon, which we are nowhere near yet, the problem would remain. It's more a question of different types of language doing different jobs, like different maps or the language about atoms and furniture. But it's not possible or sensible to say that one of them describes "reality" and the others describe some type of illusion or secondary phenomenon.

The necessity to have different descriptions for different tasks is, perhaps paradoxically, well recognized within science itself. We don't say that biology, say, or genetics are irrelevant or not real sciences even though we know that in principle most of what happens in an organism could and might one day be described in terms of biochemistry, which in turn might be described in terms of physics. (Well, maybe they do say such things in physics departments, but quietly…)

We don't say that psychology is irrelevant because it describes behaviour which must have underlying physical contributors. Each layer of description has its place and contributes to the whole, one does not replace all the others. Descriptions at different levels do not collapse into each other—some may, but it's not the usual case. Phenomena are not "reduced" by being described differently or more minutely, we just have a more complex description on different levels.

The humanistic level

So now at the level of human beings and our awareness of ourselves and dealings with each other we have a particularly important level of language and description, which we will call the humanistic. (It's probably not one level but many, but that doesn't matter here.) This level is vitally important to us, because it's where we live our lives.

This level is the language which describes our experience of being human, what it's like to be us. It includes not just the bald physical facts but the interpretations and meanings we as humans ascribe to things and events, the feelings, thoughts and beliefs which attach to and interpret the world as seen through human eyes. It's a different point of view from the objective, scientific point of view but it has its own function and does a different job.

We each have a huge amount of knowledge at this level, and we have a huge amount of shared or available information including both fiction and non-fictional disciplines like history, for example. In fact, it's the level of description we absolutely need to function as human beings and although it is constantly illuminated by discoveries at other levels, they do not and cannot replace it.

We need not deny that there are biological, chemical and physical mechanisms which underlie our lives. But still, we have to try to make sense of what we do and choose in terms that are human, that interpret our actions as human actions and our choices in the context of human lives. In fact, we have no choice but to operate like this. Just as we cannot use quantum mechanics to rearrange the furniture we cannot use our knowledge of biology or physics alone to make decisions or answer questions about what to buy in the supermarket, let alone how to live and how we should relate to others. And even for those who are fascinated by the scientific questions, these humanistic life questions are among the most important we face.

Of course, knowledge or facts at a humanistic level still face an IS/OUGHT gap if we are to arrive at values: humanistic facts are still facts. But we should not allow the reductionist fallacy, for a fallacy is what it is, to persuade us to give up looking for a foundation for values and assume that they will be "explained away" by science. Since values are what we use to take real life decisions and steer our lives it is likely that the ideal we are seeking is essentially humanistic and relates our ideas of right and wrong to something about human lives. At any rate, it is likely to be expressed in the language of the humanistic level and not to be reducible to another.

Determinism and free will

The idea of scientific reductionism leads to the idea of determinism. This is the idea that we have no choice in what we do because every-thing can be assigned a biological or neurological cause and the chain of causation leaves no room for us to intervene.

We might think, this story goes, that we make choices, but that is some sort of illusion and all that "really" happens is that brain mechanisms (or molecules, or energy fields or quantum froths) work themselves out in their own way. We are, in effect, deluded robots made of meat (or something still more basic) and there are no such things as free will or choice. Values, therefore, are at best part of our illusion, for we will do what we are destined by biology or physics to do anyway. The only real events governing how we live happen quite unconsciously and inevitably in the depths of the machines we call brains.

Such determinism, though, is a curious story. Nobody can or does live as if it were true: it's not even clear how that would work. It matters to us because it suggests that the search for the basis of values is ultimately pointless since there are no choices, just the illusion of choices. To the extent that it rests on the reductionist fallacy we have already seen that it cannot be the whole truth. But it has a fascination of its own which we need to escape.

We can be transfixed, for example, by the idea that if all our actions are the result of natural processes our wills do not matter. But if our wills are themselves natural processes or parts of such, surely they matter as much as any other part of the process. We could say that free will describes the natural process by which the complex organisms called human beings determine what they will do when they are not coerced in certain ways.

Somehow, however, this seems unsatisfactory: we want our wills to have acted outside the course of nature or the prior chain of causation in order to be assured that we are free. But what would be the point of that? Surely our wills have to be fully engaged with the "chain of causation" or they will have no effect on what comes next? Free will must be part of a natural process, not something which conflicts with the working of the material world.

Of course it may be true that everything that happened since the Big Bang "led up" to a particular person making a particular choice at this moment in this particular universe—as well as several trillion trillion other things. We can leave to one side the possibility that the outcome could ever have been predicted: if a single toss of a coin is difficult to predict, this is mind-bogglingly so. More important, if human beings form part of the (very recent) evolution of the universe as they strive and struggle to make choices, all that striving and struggling is part of the process of arriving at any particular point and that part of the process cannot be left out of a full description. We all know in any case that even at a humanistic level there are all kinds of influences, habits and dispositions which make one choice more likely than another in any given set of circumstances. We do not assume that we lose free will merely by having a history. Why then is it any different that our atoms have a history?

By way of analogy, suppose I offer you a choice of tea or coffee, either being equally providable. It's not as if you might think: "I really want tea but I feel an inner compulsion to ask for coffee." It's not even clear what that would mean: if you feel compelled to ask for coffee you do not really want tea. Of course you have preferences and those preferences influence your decision on this particular occasion so that the choice of drink is not a "blue sky" choice. Then again, there are many factors you might take into account: the time of day, the amount of caffeine you have already had today, your knowledge of the quality of the drinks I am likely to offer, etc. etc. In a few seconds at most these factors are balanced against your natural preferences and you give an answer.

We can be sure that all this mental activity is underpinned by processes in your brain and body, which in turn are underpinned by biochemical processes and all the rest of it—but we can also be sure that you chose a drink. It's not right to say that you had no choice but it is equally not right to say that your choice somehow took place outside the natural order of things. If this sounds like a contradiction, it's no worse than the opposition which exists between my saying that my desk is solid and static while at the same time composed of fast moving particles and (to a much greater degree) the space between them. The tension we feel between free will and causation or determinism is at least in part a tension between different types of language which have different jobs to do. We may want to ask, "Yes, but which describes reality?" — but in different ways, both do.

Another analogy: suppose an engineer has to design a bridge. She has to perform all the right calculations carefully to make sure the design is sound. In one sense whether she gets the right answers and whether the bridge stays up may be predetermined from the Big Bang. But that does not mean she does not have to do the calculation properly, following the appropriate mathematical rules. It would be no defence in the event of a disaster to say: "Well, that was obviously what the universe had in store all along — who knew?"

In this example the rules that must be followed are in no sense ethical rules (though the engineer no doubt has an ethical responsibility to do things right). It is simply a matter of careful measurement and putting the right variables into well understood formulae. But the process has to be done properly and the engineer cannot rely on determinism to provide the right answer. So here we have a human process in which there is no shortcut for a human being doing the hard work in the right way as if they were entirely free. If this is true of building a bridge it is surely true of the greatly more complicated process of living a human life.

Utilitarianism and calculation

We have already announced that we are heading towards the idea that satisfied mind can serve as the foundation of values, although how and why we still need to show. But the idea that happiness in any form is the basis of values almost inevitably raises the spectre of utilitarianism, the theory that what is good or right can be calculated by working out what will lead to the greatest happiness of the greatest number.[22]

If happiness or living happily is to be the basis of ethics, all we have to do in any given situation is tot up what produces most happiness and we have a winner. Or if this is not possible in individual situations perhaps we can tot up which rules will tend to produce the most happiness overall and adopt them as our moral laws, leading us back to the comfort of the legal paradigm. Simple?

Unfortunately not. Utilitarianism is still a powerful influence on many people's thinking, perhaps not least because something very like it applies in theories of choice in economics (for example) and even influences political and business decision-making in the form of "cost-benefit analysis". Admittedly, in these cases a neutral-sounding "utility" or a measurable quantity like money stands in for happiness, but there is often a suggestion that such quantities are just more easily measurable proxies and happiness is what we are really calculating.

Yet it is well known that there is something very strange about the idea that we can derive values or decide what is good or right by any kind of calculation which uses happiness as the raw material.

A "felicific calculus", a way of adding and subtracting happiness, has never been produced and there are good reasons why such an idea could not work. How would the basic quantities even be measured for any given individual, for example?

We may be able to produce a happiness ranking ("I am happier now than then", for example). We may even ask people to grade their own subjective experience, although we have no check on honesty or how one person's assessment compares with another. But even if it were all theoretically possible, we cannot do a survey every time we make a choice! That would assume that everyone affected by an action was available to be canvassed. How do we even decide who is to be brought into the calculation, who is affected? How far into the future must we look for consequences and do we reduce future happiness and pain by some discount factor in some way? How do we factor in the uncertainties involved in these predictions?

Subtraction is a fundamental problem: how do we treat unhappiness or pain? Are they the same and are they really just negative forms of the quantity we call happiness, happiness with the sign changed so to speak?

The assumption that they are leads to all sorts of absurdities, as we can see especially when we try to do the sums for populations rather than individuals. For once we have measured the happiness of individuals with sufficient precision (if we can) we have to add and subtract across and between different people. Does each person's happiness (or otherwise) count equally or should we apply weights, for example to help the more worthy (however we define that) or the more miserable? Does an increase in happiness for someone already very happy count the same as the alleviation of someone else's extreme suffering, assuming we decide that the quantities are the same? How does my happiness offset your unhappiness anyway?

So we quickly reach absurd conclusions. It might be right, for example, to inflict horrific torture on an innocent person if we could show that such an action led to even a small benefit for sufficient numbers of people, so that the benefits in total outweighed the harm. Or, if it makes A sufficiently happy to kill B whom C loves, causing C immense grief (not to mention poor B!) that would be fine as long as A's happiness equalled or outweighed B and C's suffering. Killing in fact offers many difficult problems anyway, for if we do not consider the possibility of life after death (although who says we can ignore that possibility?) then presumably happiness and suffering end with death. Thus to kill someone painlessly is only wrong if it adversely affects others left alive, unless we have to predict and deduct what happiness the victim might have enjoyed in the future. It is surely clear that we have strayed very far away from any recognizable idea of morality or values. Even common sense is struggling!

It might be thought that this lack of numerical precision is merely a technological problem, something which could be overcome if only we could advance our knowledge further. For example, it has been suggested that if we could scan or measure brain activity with sufficient speed and precision – at a technological level far in excess of what is possible today – we would know precisely whether a given action made a person happy and to what extent. If good and right are in some way numerical functions of happiness we might thus gain the raw data from which we could calculate the ethical value of actions.[23]

But even if we imagine that every conceivable technological problem with this plan could be overcome, we still have the same issues about how to combine data from different people, from different times (what about the future consequences of today's actions?) and with different signs (how do we calibrate happiness against pain?). The problem with utilitarianism is not technological, it is a much more fundamental conceptual issue. Happiness is just not something to which we can easily attach numbers that make any objective sense. In other words, it is not a quantity.

There are no doubt more sophisticated versions of utilitarianism which fix some of these basic problems but there are so many problems that the whole enterprise of calculating our way to ethical decisions seems to be doomed. This is a pity in many ways and awkwardly at odds with the spirit of our scientific age in which calculation forms such an important part of our understanding of the world and how it works. Nevertheless, our broad if rather speedy conclusion is that utilitarianism just does not work as a way to tell right from wrong.

So when it comes to deciding how we should live we cannot calculate, we must make judgements and comparisons which do not depend on numbers. We may, indeed we must to some extent, be able to compare, for example to say that one action is preferable to or better than another (ordinal ranking). But we will struggle to assign precise numerical values to these judgements (cardinal ranking). The difficulties of calculation are present even where our own happiness is concerned, and the attempt to calculate collapses altogether when we try to compute values using the happiness of different people, or of populations. Yet another theory falls.

Part 2.

A Foundation for Values

Chapter 6

A Central Goal

Purposes, teleology and virtues

We now know quite a lot about what <u>doesn't</u> work as the foundation of values. The question is, what is left?

The major traditional answer we have not yet considered is "teleology", which goes back at least to Aristotle.[24] It has been adapted over the centuries to form the basis of other influential ethical systems, notably that of Aquinas and through him the Roman Catholic church.

The idea here is that values are built on purposes. If you know what anything is for, what its purpose is, you can describe what distinguishes a good specimen of that kind of thing from a bad one. So for example a good knife is one that cuts well, a good musical instrument plays and sounds well and so on. If a class of things has several different uses there may be many different ways of being a good one, depending on the particular use you have in mind — think, for example, of cars.

In the crudest terms, then, identifying the purpose of human beings should enable us to say what makes a person good or bad. There is thus a continuity between "ethical" or "moral" goodness, the sense in which we might say of someone that they are a good person, and functional goodness, the sense in which we might say of someone that they are a good butcher or baker, or indeed that a pen is a good pen, a chair a good chair. What makes particular choices or actions good, in turn, is whether they are the choices or actions a good person would undertake or which would be conducive to a person being or becoming good.

If we can get this far we might hope to be able to identify <u>qualities</u> which describe the good person, qualities which a good person will possess and display and which someone who aspires to be good might try to develop or strengthen. Those qualities would traditionally be called virtues, hence an alternative name for this tradition, virtue ethics.[25]

But a massive problem with this kind of approach is immediately obvious. We can say what the purpose of a car or a musical instrument or any artefact may be, because it has been deliberately made with a purpose in mind. But what could possibly be meant by "the purpose" of a human being?

Many religions offer answers to this question based on the idea that a deity has designed human beings for a specific divine purpose, which is one reason why virtue ethics often play an important role in religious values. But this obviously does not help in a secular context.

If there is no external, non-human "purpose setter" we have to find some other source of purpose. Purposes and goals, however, are something human beings themselves—and if we set aside the supernatural, pretty much <u>only</u> human beings—form and follow. (Of course other animals may have limited purposes but human beings are unique in the complexity, longevity and range of theirs.) So we are quickly pointed to the idea that values are tied in some way to human purposes and goals.

In passing, we should note that attempts to shoehorn evolutionary or biological purposes in here will not work. The great merit, in some ways the whole point, of the theory of natural selection is that it does away with any need for a purpose in biology. Whatever works given the prevailing circumstances, survives. If circumstances change what once flourished may perish, like the dinosaurs. There is no sense that nature or its organisms are moving forward towards some goal and if we ever get that feeling it is only because we look at the past with knowledge of where the process has led. There is no such thing as an evolutionary goal or purpose, either for human beings or more generally. Hence it is impossible to base values on such a purpose.

But even if human beings are the only relevant originators of purposes, the idea that there is a single purpose common to everyone on which we could base human values seems tricky, to say the least. We all have thousands of different purposes, some stable and long term and some which shift every minute. Moreover, purposes differ widely from person to person, across time periods and across cultures.

Nevertheless, we will see that this is definitely the right track. What takes us forward is the simple idea of ranking.

The centre of our lives

Clearly, some things matter to us more than others. It usually matters a great deal for example whom we live with, where we live, how our children fare, what we do for a living and how we like to enjoy our leisure, though even these major concerns are by no means equal. It matters much less whether we get tea rather than coffee on a given morning or whether we get to watch our favourite TV programme on a given day—but it still matters a bit. From such examples we can get the idea of a rough ranking of "things that matter" to us.

We needn't expect precision, or to be able to rank everything exactly in relation to everything else, but the idea of such a ranking is implicit in the way we live. For example, we might be prepared to sacrifice something that doesn't matter very much to secure something that matters a lot. But it doesn't make sense to sacrifice something more important to get something we rank low in our priorities. Straws do sometimes break camels' backs but nobody ends an otherwise healthy and happy relationship, say, because someone buys the wrong brand of coffee!

Ranking what matters to us gives us a hierarchy. A hierarchy is often thought of as a pyramid, with, typically, many things on the lower levels and fewer things on each level as we go up, until we reach the top where (in this case) there would be relatively few very important or absolutely vital things in our lives. But alternatively we can think of a hierarchy as made up of concentric rings or spheres, successively smaller but more important layers being found as we move inwards. Think perhaps of an archery target. The numerous, "Yes, I mildly prefer it that way" items would be right on the outside and the vital things in the centre.

I prefer this second model because it leads us easily to the metaphor that there may be certain things (people, ideas, activities, states) which are absolutely central in our lives.

This simple idea offers a key to re-imagining values, to under-standing what they are and the part they play in our lives and society. All our tastes and preferences, for example, matter to us to some degree, but our values are based on what matters most, or what, using our simple model, we put at the centre of our lives.[26] This point of view allows that we may have many "lesser" tastes and preferences and others progressively deeper and therefore more important to us, per-haps based on culture and tradition for example. But eventually we come down to the core, to what really matters most. (Interestingly, we even talk sometimes about "core values".) The prompts and constraints on our actions which are generated by this core or central level of our purposes override all else.

Notice that having such a central goal does not exclude other con-cerns and other interests, indeed the whole variety of ordinary human concerns still operates. I can and will still have many lesser aims and ambitions, lesser preferences and desires. Even the ardently pious or the deeply politically committed still share everyday concerns and have their personal likes and dislikes. (Anarchists prefer herbal tea...)[27] But the central goal would take priority over anything else. If ever there were conflict between another aim and the central goal, the lesser aim would have to be abandoned. In another idiom, we could say that the central goal makes sense of the narrative of a person's life and actions but that narrative would be coloured by all the lesser goals. A central aim doesn't mean that nothing else matters, it means that nothing else matters <u>as much</u>.[28]

A decision to adopt something as my central aim in life could not be a decision taken lightly—arguably it is <u>the</u> most important decision I make if this aim overrides all others. A central aim becomes the touchstone of our life and actions, the way to settle inner conflicts, the way to consider direction when the path seems unclear.

A deeply religious person might, for example, have a central goal which was based on religious faith, on living so as to achieve some religious target. Such an example makes clear that our approach is not new or iconoclastic but closely related to mainstream ways of thinking about values and ethics, including in particular some religious ways. We will obviously differ from religious approaches by suggesting that values can be founded on a secular central aim or purpose, a goal common to all humanity but not a supernatural goal. But the basic idea that our most central or most important purpose is what drives our values and makes sense of the narratives of our lives is the same whether the central purpose is natural or supernatural.

The purpose at the centre of our lives, or what matters most to us, needs to be as fully imagined and articulated as possible. If it isn't, then the implications and requirements of that central aim will be obscure and we are likely to end up with as much confusion about values as if we had no central aim at all. A slogan or a buzzword, for example, won't do. Once we have done the work of fully imagining a central goal we might of course abbreviate it for easy reference, but just to seek a goal represented by a slogan—wealth, consumption, happiness, world domination (that old favourite!), respect, salvation, enlightenment, whatever—is to chase a shadow.

The same of course applies to political goals. It is common for people to advocate, say, justice or liberty or equality in the abstract without fully working out what they mean in detail. Often this causes much misery at the social as well as the individual level. As we frame our central aim we have to do the work of filling in the detail as far as possible. We could say, as was memorably said of language: "To imagine a central aim is to imagine a way of life."[29] That is no simple matter but without the broadest picture of what our central goal involves we might be building our lives on nothing at all.

Imperatives: "Why should I?"

We noted earlier that no amount of factual information is sufficient to generate an imperative—we cannot deduce an OUGHT solely from an

IS. Fortunately this gap is easy to bridge with an aim or purpose, especially one we ourselves have decided upon, for that is the nature of a purpose. Adopting a purpose is not at all the same as recognizing a fact.

Consider how this works. Having thought carefully about my central aim I am likely to recognize that to reach it I must do certain things and refrain from others. I may not have mapped out every step, in fact I probably can't because I don't know what conditions I will meet along the way, but I know that certain things must be done if I am to get to my aim and certain things will take me in the wrong direction. Such insights were once called "hypothetical imperatives" — they have imperative force for me, they command my actions and choices, simply because of the importance to me of that chosen central aim. It's a matter of "Do X and avoid Y or you won't achieve Z", where X and not-Y represent my values, the things I must do and the things I must avoid, all based on the premise that Z is my aim.

When nothing is more important to me than Z, which is true by definition of a central aim, this imperative is very compelling. Some people believe it is not strong enough, that values or morality must somehow be based on a "categorical imperative", something that is binding on me whatever my aims and goals.[30] But that is just the myth of law in another guise. The incentive or imperative to follow my values because of my overriding commitment to my own central goal is as strong as it gets.

It is thus <u>commitment</u> to our central aim which underpins and gives imperative force to our values and the <u>centrality</u> of this aim which gives our values greater imperative force than anything else in our lives. Our relationship with the central aim is thus not simply one of recognizing what it is, but of choosing it, committing ourselves to it. This is how we bridge (or maybe go around!) the IS/OUGHT gap. A commitment to a goal, as we said, is quite different from an observation of a fact.

We are of course fallible and we might not always do what takes us in the right direction towards our central aim, but that is not the issue. We must hope we can recognize when we have made a mistake and change course. Nevertheless, the test of whether an action accords with our values is whether it has brought the realization of our central aim nearer or pushed it further away.

What might a central aim look like?

Obviously the choice of a central aim in life is a big deal for anyone. There are typically many things that are important to us and to single out one as potentially overriding all the others is not a trivial task.

What could possibly justify our choice of a central aim, something so important to us that it defines our life? What will convince us that we have made the right choice?

We must at a minimum be able to give sound and satisfying reasons for our choice, otherwise we cannot justify it to ourselves and we cannot take others with us, in particular those who matter most to us like our children. So we will need to explore this further.

But reason or rationality won't take us all the way, for commitment is rarely a matter of reason alone. We might even expect reason or reasonableness to be more useful to rule things out than to push us to the level of commitment needed to choose a central aim. Something else is needed. We will suggest in fact there is a second formal require-ment which helps to identify an important goal as a possible central goal, to distinguish the "merely" important from the absolutely central. We will call this "unconditionality". It has to do with being able to assure ourselves that our central goal will be stable and lasting throughout our lives, and so can safely be placed at the centre of our concerns.

There still needs to be a third factor, however, maybe rather difficult to pin down, which prompts us to add the assent of the whole person to that of the intellect, or as we might say, the assent of the heart to that of the head. We will call this "resonance". The chosen goal must reso-nate with us in a way which makes the choice something to which we can willingly commit our lives. So we have three conditions which will help us to test any proposed central goal:

1. Reasonableness or rationality, necessary to qualify a goal as worth consideration;

2. Unconditionality, which we will suggest is necessary to achieve centrality;

3. Resonance, necessary to complete our commitment.

In the next chapter we examine each in turn and we will hope to show that satisfying these conditions is both necessary and sufficient to qualify an aim as a central aim. It is hard to prove this formally but together these are very demanding conditions which very few aims can meet. If an aim meets all three conditions it would certainly be difficult to argue against it. Perhaps again that means that there may be more than one central aim left in the arena of choice, even when only secular aims are considered. We shall see.

Chapter 7

Conditions for a Central Goal

Reasonableness and consistency

A minimum requirement of being reasonable is consistency. At the very least my central aim should be self-consistent or I enshrine a contradiction at the heart of my life, which cannot end well. But it should also be consistent with my other beliefs. If for example I do not believe in an afterlife it would be absurd to frame my central aim as if I did – and of course it would be equally absurd to ignore the afterlife if I do believe in one. Either way I must decide the question of whether there might be an afterlife by some other means, of course, and certainly not by considering whether it makes sense of my central aim!

This suggests, however, that the beliefs on which anyone's choice of central aim is based can only be their own current beliefs, whether right or wrong. This is obviously inconvenient to a degree, because it implies that everyone may very well be driven to a different central aim from others because they have a different understanding about the way the world really is – and that is indeed what we observe as we look around us. Religious beliefs, for example, to the extent they are regarded as a species of fact about the world, may give rise to central aims based on whatever the particular beliefs entail, which essentially means different views of how the world works and what it is to be human.

Thus we do not automatically get to a unified central aim for everyone by applying the test of consistency alone. We may of course be able to demonstrate by some other means that, for example, some beliefs are inherently unreasonable or inconsistent with commonly accepted facts, but that is another debate entirely.

The requirement of consistency, however, underlines the ethical importance of getting our facts right and hence the importance for ethics of education and open enquiry, of science for example. We need to acquire and use the skills, for example, of obtaining and assessing evidence or identifying and examining assumptions. Without such skills we are liable to make mistakes about how to live and what our central goal should be because we will make mistakes about what the world is like, or about the context in which life is lived.

But exactly these sorts of skills are what we mean when we talk about using reason, so we can look at this as the principal influence which rationality has on values. Most cruder forms of supernatural belief, superstitions for example, would fall at this fence. If a faith suggests that reason should be set aside altogether or that we should embrace the inherently unreasonable as a justification for our actions, we should at least be suspicious.

Reasonableness and making sense

What else, though, does reasonableness require? It must "make sense" that a person should adopt a given aim and organize their life around it. We have to be able to understand why someone would live like that, even if we think they are wrong. If someone professes to have a central aim for which they can't give intelligible reasons at all, or (because they themselves might not be very good at giving them) for which no one can give reasons, we would have to say that such a central aim was unreasonable.

If someone told you, for example, that the central aim of his life was to collect nineteenth-century matchboxes you would probably assume that he was very keen but simply exaggerating. If his actions showed that nothing, really nothing, was more important to him—that he would commit any crime, make any sacrifice, take any risk to further his aim—you would rightly conclude that he was deranged. Not all commitments are reasonable—this collector's values may be sincere but they are not reasonable.

Suppose again someone said: "I am going to live my life without any plan, I'll just act randomly, I'll do whatever comes into my head at any given moment." We could perhaps understand this as some sort of radical, randomizing approach to the uncertainty of life, but in reality a person could posture in this way but hardly behave like it. We can only understand actions at all in the context of an inner life, a life of human aims and motivations, desires and so on. It might be possible to live without a central aim, to live with just a jumble of aims some of which conflict with each other and give us headaches from time to time, but it's not possible to live without aims at all because aims are what make a life human.

So this person would be trying to live a deliberately unintelligible life. But why on earth would anyone live like that? It might be an experiment or an artistic statement but that's sort of the point—it needs a context, a story to make it even marginally intelligible. To have randomness as an aim is to have no aim at all. More broadly, reasonableness demands intelligibility.

We may insist, then, that a central aim is reasonable in at least the sense that intelligible reasons can be given for a person having that aim, reasons which allow us to understand the aim in the context of a human life. But even such intelligibility may not give us something we find "reasonable" in all respects. It may not rule out every aim we might prefer (and which most people's intuitions about ethics and values would strongly tend) to have excluded. Many examples could be ruled out by the test of consistency with established evidence. For example, if the "values" of a committed Nazi were based on a belief that he represents a race superior to others, we could easily find evidence to refute such a belief. But perhaps the belief is not sensitive to evidence, as in the case of some religious beliefs. Thus as we expected at the outset reasonableness (rationality) alone may not give us a unique and satisfying solution to the question of what should be our central aim.

Reasonableness does, however, eliminate a lot of candidates as central aims and the demand that we use our reason to the utmost to check what we believe are facts and make our aims consistent with them is strong. Some will be convinced that it eliminates most religious aims, for example, but we will not follow that route because such discussions are generally fruitless. We have in any case already suggested that there are good reasons to look for a secular ethical basis if we are to find values which can be common to all. If reasonableness need operate only in the secular sphere – so that for example we do not have to entangle ourselves in questions of whether this or that religious belief is reasonable – the condition is even stronger.

Reasonableness and change

One particular aspect of reasonableness involved in assessing facts is that we need an honest assessment of what can and what cannot change in the world and our circumstances. Reason and experience suggest that our circumstances are seldom unchangeable. They will likely change whatever we do although we all hope that if we direct our efforts suitably they may change in ways that suit us and which further some of our aims.

This has particular relevance for our choice of central aim, for if we base our central aim on an assumption that everything will remain as it is, we are more likely to be bewildered by rapid and continuous change. Even traditional, pre-modern societies can experience great changes in a single lifetime through, for example, weather patterns, incursions by other societies or ecological changes. So a failure to face and acknowledge the likelihood of change is already a serious mistake about the facts.

A closely related issue is our degree of control over our circumstances, in other words over change. Sometimes we can manage the way the world goes or shape the changes to our liking, sometimes we can't. If we can, why wouldn't we? But we know perfectly well that however powerful we are we do not control everything about our circumstances. Shit happens, bad things happen to good people, the best laid plans, etc. etc. This is fundamental to the way the world is and our central aim must surely take it into account. An aim which assumes a smooth progression to some end which, once achieved, will last for ever may be a highly motivational delusion but it is a delusion nonetheless. And the danger with delusions is that circumstances have a nasty habit of exposing them and thus leaving us aimless and lost.

Prominent among the uncontrollable circumstances we all face, for example, are ageing and death, which force us to think about all our aims but in particular our central aim in the context of our own finiteness. Nobody gets out alive. We are astonishingly good at ignoring or denying this fundamental and simple point about ourselves. Vast and complex systems of belief have been constructed to keep the thought at bay with the reassurance that death is not the end. But even from a religious point of view death is not something to be taken lightly for at the very least it marks an important transition with crucial consequences, whether the transition is one among many or the last chance before eternity. From a secular point of view this is it: one life, one brief enough blazing of matter into consciousness — and the question is, what to do with such an amazing gift?

A central aim which does not recognize the finiteness of this existence is self-evidently built on a false foundation. So, far from assuming or anticipating that everything will go well and the story will have a happy ending, we already know the end of the story. We don't live happily ever after. Our idea of what matters most in life has to be framed in the full recognition that there isn't as much of life as we might like. Values are about how to live this life, but the question can only be framed in the full knowledge that this is a finite issue, regardless of whether anything of us survives death.

There is of course a strain or mood of thought which suggests that finiteness and mortality imply that life can have no meaning, so it doesn't matter what we do. That of course would only be adequate if our actions had no consequences within our own lives, which is not often true. But it is a very strange belief anyway, if it is even right to call it a belief.

Most commodities become more precious the less of them is available, so why should life itself be any different? Surely each moment of a finite life is more precious than any moment of an infinite one? This nihilist mood in fact has it completely backwards, for it really would not matter what we did or chose if life were infinite, since we would have infinitely many chances to try things again in different ways. Death and finiteness do not destroy meaning, quite the opposite. They make each moment pulse with it.

As it is, each choice we make, even minor ones, may be the only chance we get to jump that particular fence. That can be scary, of course, and part of the point of thinking carefully about our central aim is to allow lesser choices to be made in a purposeful context. Driving our choices with values and our values with a central aim enables us to become comfortable with finiteness and with the significance it brings to every moment.

Unconditionality and the constant aim

The previous sections confirm that the constraints imposed by reason (or the requirement of reasonableness) on what we might choose as a central aim are impressive but far from conclusive. They would certainly be disappointing, for example, if we were expecting "Reason" to take the place of "Authority" and give us definitive proofs about how to live and what is right and wrong. We clearly need something more.

A central aim is something anyone might be expected to change only with great reluctance, for a central aim which changes with every fashion is surely not central at all. It is the mark of a person who is bewildered or confused, or who has just not made their mind up about where they stand and what their life is about. We have already suggested that a central aim has to acknowledge that we live in a world of change. We now suggest that anything we could genuinely install as the guiding aim of a whole life should rely as little as possible on circumstances which might change, because a central aim which depends on changeable contingencies is likely to need to change whenever they do. A central aim should be as constant as possible.

We don't normally think like this, it has to be admitted, because we don't normally think of our lives in terms of a central aim. In practice we scramble to adapt our aims to circumstances throughout our lives. We might make initial assumptions about what our lives are about without thinking very much about the consequences of change. So, for example, we adopt values when we are young which we abandon as we get older. If we are born in fortunate circumstances we might form views about how meritorious it is to be wealthy which are likely to be shattered if our wealth disappears. Or someone might believe that getting rich or famous is their essential goal only to feel empty or depressed when they get there. If we are looking for a central aim which runs through a whole life we have to abstract from all such possible changes, which means the aim must somehow be independent of the contingencies both of our present condition and our possible but unknown futures.

This is clearly a difficult demand. Where does the process of abstraction stop, what is contingent and what can we count as fixed? Even when we consider seemingly unchangeable conditions or qualities about our lives they are seldom absolute. Take for example ethnicity. We are born into an ethnicity, of course, but what ethnicity means is something cultural which we learn. Young children, for example, are often quite blind to it. The significance of ethnicity is very largely a matter of prevailing beliefs and ideas, of how it is viewed by ourselves and others or even, in some unpleasant cases, of legal definition. This significance can change vastly within and between societies in a single lifetime. Without all these contingent accretions ethnicity is no more than an incidental physical characteristic, like having big ears. So the bare fact may be fixed, but almost every important consequence of that fact at a given time is not fixed.

Again, take gender. Even leaving aside the small number of people who actually change gender in their lifetimes, the social construct that is gender, the social significance, status, power, expectations — everything other than the bare biological fact — may and does change. Feminism, for example, is not a demand that women become like men, it is a demand that the social and cultural limitations placed on women should be no different from those which apply to men. Thus gender differences are also to a large extent social constructs, not biological facts. So even what appear to be "fixed" conditions or qualities are not necessarily fixed in their significance and the way they affect our lives.

Unconditionality and human values

We thus arrive at the demand that a central aim should be unconditional. To be truly acceptable as central it should not depend on any contingency, any attribute I may possess which I may lose, or which may so change in its significance as to make the chosen central aim irrelevant.

But there is a progression here which does not stop with attributes I might possess but recognize as being at risk, like youth or health. A central aim should not depend on any attribute I might not have had in the first place. You might be beautiful or not, clever or not, rich or not, of high social standing or not — and it might be difficult to see how such a thing might change. But it is still contingent, even accidental. Such things usually could change, even if in circumstances which seem very unlikely. But if it is possible to imagine them otherwise they need not have been so in the first place.

Where do we stop with this progression? It is difficult to see a defensible stopping point until we get down to the most basic fact about us: we are human beings.

And there we have it. Unconditionality requires that our central aim depends on none of our characteristics beyond that of being human.

This requirement corresponds to Aristotle's idea[31] that what we are looking for is our purpose <u>as</u> human beings, which we have here adapted and translated into the discovery of a central aim. If we stop the stripping away of contingencies at any point before this, we are choosing a central aim which life may render pointless, thus taking away the point of our lives as we understand them.

You may argue that even our humanity is a contingency in a sense, for we might not have existed at all. But then we would not be in search of a purpose! On the whimsical side, it might be argued that we might have been cabbages or butterflies, for example. But such an imagining is not really intelligible. What would it be like? Are we not just imagining a human being with the shape of a cabbage or a butterfly, as in a children's story? In any such case, <u>human</u> goals or values would not be in point anyway, even if such an existence and its goals or values could be made intelligible to us at all.

Given that we exist at all, then, our humanity is the only unconditional fact about us. We are not required in this exercise to consider a goal for the universe, for all things, all beings or even all rational beings, if such there be outside humanity. We are simply considering what goal a particular human being might adopt for themselves as central in their human life — though that is quite enough! If we pare back contingent circumstances to find a central aim for a human being there is simply no point in going <u>beyond</u> the bare fact of being human. The question is only whether there is a justifiable place to stop before we get to that point. We suggest that there is not.

However, just as we discussed for gender or ethnicity, there are different notions about what it "really means" to be human so that being human is itself in a sense a social or cultural construct. One of the ways great evils (including slavery and genocide) are often advanced is to claim that the victims are less than human, for example. This is not too worrying, for we can reasonably argue that such claims are always false. The people thus excluded from humanity for whatever purpose are arbitrarily and falsely excluded, usually according to some theory or classification which can always be shown to have no factual basis.

Still, there remain some very different notions of what it means to be human. Ideas of humans as embodied spirits or fallen angels, for example, have some very different consequences from the idea of humans as a certain kind of evolved apes. We may rely here to some extent on the requirement of reasonableness: which of these views can be justified on the facts as we know them? It may still simply be, however, that there is more than one central goal which satisfies the requirement of unconditionality, because there is more than one concept of what it is to be human. But if we accept that values must be secular to be shareable, as we argued before, then we can at least narrow the field of acceptable central aims for this purpose to include only secular views of what it is to be human. In any case, if unconditionality brings us to the point where we can agree that a central aim must depend on nothing more than the requirements of living a human life, it will have taken us a long way.

Reasonable commitment

We have suggested there are some important constraints on what we can reasonably choose as our central aim, but we have also seen that reason does not settle the question. Neither does unconditionality. No amount of constraint on our choice can actually force us to commit ourselves to any given aim. Something else is still needed.

Commitment, in other words, needs more than reason or logic or formal conditions, which is why even the cleverest thinkers have been unable to sustain the idea that values or morality can be deduced from some first principles or in some way made a function of reason alone. If it were so simple there would be no disagreement, just as we do not disagree about whether twice two is four.[32] The blunt fact is that logic alone does not provide a basis for a choice. Neither does anything else, if what we are looking for is something which <u>compels</u> us to choose good over bad, kind over cruel, compassion over selfishness.

This stark conclusion is perhaps inevitable in any case, however much we may crave a certain outcome, but it is clearly inevitable if values are founded on a choice about our central aim in life. That crucial choice cannot itself be governed by values, because the choice is made prior to values having any basis. Thus any attempt to find a cast iron reason why we <u>have</u> to choose a particular aim is bound to fail. If the basis of the imperative force of our values is our commitment to a central aim we cannot expect some "super imperative" to tell us what we should choose or force us to go one way rather than another. We cannot look to logic, reason, science or even religion to provide a complete justification of why one central aim should command our allegiance above all others without us having to make a choice.

But this is not as terrible as it sounds. The situation is no different from what occurs with many decisions we have to make in life, including – perhaps especially – the most important ones like, for example, whom we choose as a partner. We will have lots of information but the picture is never complete and in the end we just have to take the leap. We choose, we commit ourselves – for better or worse. There's <u>always</u> a gap in the argument and we bridge the gap with a choice or, in the case of choices with long term consequences, a commitment.

It's not a question of commitment <u>instead</u> of reason, however, but commitment supported by reason – reasonable commitment. Head and heart working together. Reason takes you so far but in the end you have to take the plunge, leap the gap. There are no guarantees that you will get the perfect answer. Some of the lesser choices we make are silly or unreasonable and sometimes we even see that but make them anyway: it usually doesn't work out well but it makes a good story, which is why such "heart over head" choices are one of the great drivers of fiction. Some choices look eminently reasonable but, as we say, "our heart isn't in it". They seldom work out well either. With a commitment to something as important as the central aim of our lives, head and heart absolutely have to work together because the choice, the commitment, is too important to regret.

The central aim is a constant, a commitment around which life can be organized and actions tested. Perhaps the fact that we can and must choose such an aim is reminiscent of emotivism because there is nothing in the end beyond the choice. But if this is emotivism, it is changed out of recognition. First, the aim must be central, any passing preference, will or desire does not count. Second, there are strict conditions of reasonableness to qualify an aim for choice as central. Third, the condition of universality narrows the field to just those aims which are common across humanity because they depend on nothing beyond being human. Perhaps, then, we should acknowledge the spark of truth we have in common with emotivism – that choice lies at the heart of values – but we can insist that values based on a central aim rest on a much more solid foundation which, in particular, does not lead to relativism, value atomism or value nihilism.

It is important with our central aim also that we do not just have the opportunity to choose if we want, we absolutely <u>must</u> choose if we are to live with values at all. We cannot back away. If we do not make the choice thoughtfully and explicitly then we will make it carelessly and implicitly by the way we live. If we do not think about the central aim of our lives we are likely to have an unsatisfactory aim foisted on us, perhaps consumerism for example, or to live without being clear what matters most to us. Furthermore, we commit ourselves to a particular central aim taking into account of course everything we know about it, but also knowing that we don't know everything about it. Making this commitment, taking this responsibility, is what being truly human is about.

Resonance, meaning and fulfilment

What, then, could push us off the fence to make such a vital decision? Since it cannot be reason or fact alone it has to be something else — intuition, feeling, enthusiasm? Something has to make this life seem better than any other, inspire us to achieve this aim to such a degree that the consequent commitment follows. The process is at once mysterious and familiar, we can't specify exactly what is involved but we know it happens because it's how we take all major decisions and make all major choices. What is different in this case is the sheer magnitude of the choice and the reach of its consequences.

This is what religions and ideologies have been so good at through the centuries, painting a picture — of an afterlife in the case of religions, of the future with ideologies — so vivid and compelling that people will accept any price to achieve it. It is an ideal, the promise of fulfilment, the prospect that this is the best thing that could happen, a goal that outshines anything else that could come within our reach. It is vitally important that our choice of ideal is constrained in the ways we have discussed if we are truly to take responsibility for our lives, but the choice still requires accepting a vision of what those lives could be. That vision must resonate with us as the way we want to live.

An ideal or vision of what we want our lives to be like is not of course something we can go out and observe, because by definition it does not yet exist for us although we may observe it in others.[33] It involves imagination but not, we should note, in the same way as religious faith. There is some relationship with faith, certainly, but the choice of a central aim requires belief only in verifiable facts about ourselves and the natural world and trust that a good life is achievable. We are not imagining, for example, a future discontinuous with what we can observe, and we are not required to invoke the supernatural (for example) to explain how it might come about.

Whether we can convince ourselves that a particular ideal can fill this role remains to be seen, but that is where we need to go. We have to find an ideal which is not merely desirable but can inspire our lives and rise above all other goals. For the reasons we looked at earlier we must do it independently of supernatural beliefs, but we do not need to pretend that we can do it by logic alone. We need to be inspired, the goal must have a compelling resonance. That, of course, is what we hope the ideal of satisfied mind can provide.

Chapter 8

Satisfied Mind[34]

Closing in on a central goal

If we are right so far, values can be given a sound and satisfactory secular basis if, but only if, we can identify something which could be accepted as a central goal in life by any human being. It would not be their only goal but the most important, the one which would override all other considerations. This chimes incidentally with earlier notions of morality, for example the idea that conscience or a "moral compass" might override immediate temptations and selfish motives. The imperative aspect of values (the "shoulds" and "oughts") would flow naturally from the central importance of this goal.

With such a goal a person's life would have a shape, a narrative and meaning. The guidance provided by the pursuit of the goal might not banish indecision in every difficult case but as we will see later there is no requirement that it should—that's why difficult cases are difficult! But it would give us a way of thinking about moral issues. Even better, if the same goal is the obvious choice for everyone we could hope for some kind of rational agreement about values, or at least open the way to a rational discussion of moral issues, rather than leaving us dependent on dogma or the assertion of tastes.

One answer to the question of what this all-important goal might be crops up again and again throughout the history of thought but has never been fully accepted. It is the answer Aristotle described in his own way, although we will not follow his particular description. The most rational central aim of human existence might simply be to live happily.

Everyone, surely, wants to live happily. Those who believe that this life is only a preparation for another life (or one in a series of such lives) may not care too much about happiness in this life but that is only because they are focused on maximizing happiness further down the line, in their expected future life or lives in comparison with which this life is fleeting. Living happily is still their goal and they may well take this long-run happiness more seriously than more obvious pleasure seekers take their pursuit of immediate gratification. The universality of our desire to live happily is surely not something that has to be argued for very long.

At first glance, however, living happily doesn't seem to have quite the right stuff to qualify as a central aim. It is insufficiently serious; or it refers to a transient and at times even inappropriate state of mind; or it is too various and vague to be pinned down – what could it even mean when everyone has their own idea of what living happily might entail? We can try to narrow the field by talking about flourishing or even "eudaimonia" if you like Ancient Greek. But still, how can living happily be the root of values?

This is where the idea of satisfied mind comes in.

The inner life

A key aspect, indeed a necessary condition, of living happily is that it depends on our inner lives.[35] By "the inner life" we mean here all the various contents of our consciousness – our thoughts, perceptions, beliefs, desires, emotions, feelings and so on – everything of which we are aware. The inner life consists of how we think, what we believe, how we interpret what happens to us and around us, how we react inwardly to people, what emotions we feel in what circumstances, what wishes and desires affect us, what loves and hates we experience and so on.

In one way, this inner life is all very complicated and perhaps even mysterious, because nobody knows everything about how it all works. But we do know a lot, both because we all live with it every day and because people have been observing and writing about this life of the mind, emotions and desires in both literature and science for millennia. Earlier we talked about layers of language used for different purposes and how descriptions at one layer are not necessarily reducible to another. Description of the inner life has its own "humanistic" layers which may one day be mapped onto layers which describe, say, brain states. But even if that happens – and it is not obvious that it will – the inner life will not lose its importance. It is where we live.

In another way indeed our inner lives are almost too commonplace and familiar. We tend to pay little conscious attention to them because they are just there all the time. We don't usually observe ourselves thinking or feeling, for example, we just think or feel. So, paradoxically, when we do think about the inner life we may perhaps conclude there is something strange or even supernatural about it. But there isn't: we just have to observe.

The inner life is at least as important as a factor in whether we live happily as any external circumstances and conditions, even if we count our bodily health as external. Other than in the most extreme circumstances, the inner life is in fact the dominant influence on our happiness. Any external circumstance is usually less important than our consequent or simultaneous thoughts, beliefs and feelings. Thus it is that two people can experience identical external conditions, whether nice or nasty, but one is happy and the other not.

A rich woman can be discontented because she wants to be richer or used to be richer or envies her friend who is richer: a poor woman can be happy with the little she has. To cite two often used but powerful and well-documented examples, people who suffer major spinal injuries are often understandably depressed initially, but after a period of adjustment return typically to being as happy (or unhappy) as they were before the injury. Conversely lottery winners return remarkably quickly to the same level of contentment as before their good fortune – when people say their win will not change them they are speaking more truly than they perhaps realize.

Your happiness is certainly affected by what happens to you, that we do not and cannot deny. Whether you have enough to eat, whether you have good health, whether you have material security and your loved ones have it too, whether you live in a safe environment or, further up the chain of external well-being for example, whether you are successful in what you set out to do—all these things matter greatly, of course. But their importance depends, as far as happiness goes, on the effect they have on your inner life, at least until we reach a point where there is a physical or physiological threat to your survival. For example, a lack of basic food is ordinarily one of the great miseries any person can endure, but sometimes fasting, for example for religious or spiritual reasons, may be a source of satisfaction, even joy. How we "take" what happens to us is more important to our happiness than what actually happens. Happiness is famously not "out there", it is "in here".

Of course someone's inner life might be in a state of bliss in the midst of terrible external conditions because of some kind of delusion and we would hesitate to call that person truly happy in this state. (Think for example of the human "batteries" in the film "The Matrix".) So genuine happiness is certainly not wholly a matter of thoughts and feelings, for example, it has to be based at the very least on an approximate awareness of external circumstances. That condition of external accuracy seems to take us back outside the inner life itself for an empirical check on our beliefs. But it is wrong in any case to think of the inner life as existing in some separate, self-contained realm cut off from the rest of the world. The inner life is itself an aspect of the world, our human consciousness or subjectivity is part of the world. Living happily clearly requires some kind of balance between external and subjective conditions. We do not need to describe every detail of this balance, for the important point is that the appropriate conditions of the inner life are a <u>necessary</u> condition of living happily in any circumstances. We do not have to insist that they are always <u>sufficient</u>.

This idea may be easily accepted as soon as we stop and think about it, almost to the extent that we retort "So what? We know that!". Yet it is of profound and subtle importance. It is also contrary to everything we are generally encouraged to believe. It is the very opposite of how our consumption-driven capitalist society works, for example. If the inner life is a necessary condition of living happily and living happily in some form is our central aim, there is an immediate implication that economic concerns cannot be the centre of our lives, however important they may be, because they concern only external goals. No amount of material acquisition or success will guarantee that we live happily unless we attend also to the inner life and its requirements. So if living happily is the rational, shareable central goal we seek, and depends critically on the inner life, economic goals in general and capitalism in particular cannot be the foundation of our values or the centre of our lives, at least not on their own. We are worth more than that.

External circumstances

Another immediate reaction might be that of course we can get used to, say, bad housing or hunger or disappointment and stay cheerful, but if happiness is our goal it would be better to fix these external problems rather than cultivating some kind of inner acceptance.

This reaction is partly correct, but it conceals a misunderstanding. Of course our external conditions can often be improved and we will be happier as well as materially better off as a result. If we can make external changes, we should: there is nothing in this approach which requires passivity. The simple but vital point is, however, that no amount of rearranging the world will guarantee that we can live happily in it if our inner life stands in the way. If we cannot learn to be content in a wide variety of circumstances — especially when things do not go our way — we are doomed to live discontented lives because, first, things have a habit of not going to plan and, second, even when things do go our way we may still not be happy.

If for example we make the external changes we think are needed but neglect, or worse damage, our inner lives (for example by becoming angry and bitter, or hard and unforgiving) we may be no happier. But we may be unable to change external circumstances anyway. Poverty, for example, is not something a person can always easily or quickly change by their own efforts or even by contributing to social change. That is no reason not to make the effort, but must such a person be condemned to unhappiness until the work is done, which may take several lifetimes? Would it not be better <u>as well as</u> working on external change to cultivate an attitude (if we can figure out how!) which allows that person to live as happily as possible in their difficult external conditions?

What we are talking about here is a way of living, or an attitude to living. It involves many factors such as inner resilience to difficulties, appreciation of available positives, a realistic but hopeful attitude to negatives, the ability to rest with a quiet mind and a peaceful heart whether the day brings disappointment or plenty. This is a deep kind of happiness, for which indeed we do not have a single accepted word. We have announced from the beginning that we will call it "satisfied mind". But new concepts cannot start with a definition and we must still put flesh on the bones of this idea, which will be the task of the next chapters.

So it is a necessary condition of lasting happiness whatever our external circumstances that the inner life is in tune — that, as we will now say, we cultivate satisfied mind. If you had achieved satisfied mind and, crucially, knew how to maintain it you might live happily in any but the most extreme circumstances. If not the task could be bewildering.

Satisfied mind and inner skills

One of the things we can quickly observe about our inner lives is that our thoughts, emotions, etc. are not completely or even usually under our own conscious control. We don't usually, for example, decide to daydream about what happened last Saturday, the thoughts just appear unbidden. We don't decide to get angry and then do it, we just find anger welling up in us. We don't decide to like or dislike chocolate cake, we just try it and we like it or we don't.

We seem thus to be predisposed, primed, to react in certain situations with a thought or a desire or an emotion, so that something happens either outside us or within our own inner life and the reaction follows. There are no doubt complex biological mechanisms which create and govern such dispositions, involving the usual suspects like genetics, nurture, experience and training. Some reactions are instincts, some are acquired habits, some are reflexes, some are the result of a desperate inner scramble to cope with a new situation. We cannot always stop ourselves reacting even if we don't like the reaction, many reactions happen as if they were automatic. So does this mean that we are hopeless slaves of our habits and instincts?

It does not, and this is the key. We can change the way we are primed. We do it all the time, in fact. Every time we learn something, think or feel something, resist a temptation or indulge a whim we initiate, strengthen or weaken a tendency to experience the same reaction in similar situations. If the same external circumstances recur or persist and we react each time in the same way we might expect that the inner reaction will become more of a habit. But in many cases we can choose different reactions which we find helpful rather than react instinctively. In this way we can form, change or replace habits so that our inner reactions are more useful and suit our purposes.

Just as an athlete or a musician practises by repeating certain quite specific movements or techniques over and again until they "become instinctive" or "become second nature" (the phrases we use are telling in themselves) we have the opportunity to rehearse the reactions of our inner lives all the time. So, if we know what effect we would prefer, we can try to shape our habits bit by bit in that direction. It may be difficult or take time, there is no guarantee of quick fixes. But we can deliberately change our inner habits over time so that our inner reactions change.

For example, if you are conscious that the way a certain person talks to you always makes you feel angry, there are many things you can do about it. You can perhaps talk through the situation with them because they may not realize what effect they are having — this is an external fix, altering the world to suit you. It is a good solution if it works, but it will not always work: perhaps the person enjoys upsetting you, or can't help themselves! The alternative, inner fix is to find ways of not reacting, or reacting differently. Sometimes just observing the effect as if from a distance will rob it of power. Or you may ask yourself why the person needs to do it (are they insecure or jealous?) and perhaps start to feel a little sorry for them rather than angry. You might imagine the person in a ridiculous situation which makes it impossible for you to be angry. These are all just techniques but by finding one that works for you, you can change the way you react. You can weaken your tendency to be annoyed.

If we work out what inner reactions will help us to develop and maintain satisfied mind we can set about cultivating those reactions. We can thus shape our inner dispositions and habits so that whatever happens we can live happier lives. It's not that we will never encounter trouble, or even that we will never react badly. But we can shift the odds in our favour, so to speak. With time and determination we can dramatically change the way our inner lives operate so that we can deal far better with whatever happens.

Habits we deliberately mould and cultivate are what we call skills and we acquire and develop them all the time — for work, in social situations, for sports. They crop up everywhere in life. Satisfied mind requires a certain range of skills, inner skills, to do with our thoughts, beliefs, desires and emotions, the whole range of what makes up the inner life.

Some people will naturally be more skilful than others through no merit of their own—it just happens in much the same way as some people are naturally more athletic or better at arithmetic, for example. Skill is not in itself meritorious, just useful. But everyone can acquire or strengthen a skill through practice, maybe not to the point of perfection but often surprisingly far if they are persistent. It is only to be expected that inner skills, like any skills, will need practice and development over time. As they are strengthened our ability to live happily is strengthened in turn.

So if we can find ways to manage the habits and patterns of our inner lives and steer them in the direction of satisfied mind, we will live more happily whatever our circumstances. If of course we could combine this enterprise with some suitable level of external comfort we would be as happy as it possible for human beings to be. If we could spread these blessings throughout society so that everyone lived with satisfied mind and suitable external comfort we would have achieved something extraordinary. But external comfort at whatever level will never be enough on its own to make us happy if we have restless and unskilful minds.

Survival

Before we go on, we should perhaps mention and dispose of one particular "red herring" as a central goal, namely survival. It is tragically true that for much of humanity and for much of our history survival has been a constant struggle and perhaps the most a person could hope for day to day. That remains true today for far too many. But although survival may be a preoccupation in difficult times it cannot be the central goal of our existence, for several reasons.

First, we know that in the end we don't survive. To adopt survival as our central goal is to fly in the face of the most basic fact about our humanity, namely that we are mortal and our time is limited. Our central goal must surely be about how we spend that time, about how to live not how long to live.

Second and closely related, the quality of our lives (including our inner lives) must surely be relevant. If you were offered, for example, the chance of immortality but in a permanent dreamless coma, would that seem an attractive option? Surely it would be pointless and yet it would fulfil a central goal of survival.

Third, if survival is not an immediate issue because, for example, the external conditions we face are not threatening, what becomes of our goal? It is hard to see that it offers any guidance in everyday life. A goal which is only in point in extreme times — times we may never encounter or only encounter once and then find ourselves helpless — is a strange sort of centre for our lives.

Finally, we can all think of examples of heroism of many types in which people risk and on occasion sacrifice their own survival for the sake of others.[36] Yet if survival were our rational central goal this behaviour would at best be incomprehensible, at worst immoral. Thus it seems there are times when behaving well demands that we risk or ignore our own survival.

We can make the same point with a contrary case. A person who puts their own survival selfishly above that of others, for example a man who pushes others aside to get a place in the lifeboats of a sinking ship, is certainly not someone we admire or who seems motivated by high values. But if survival were a reasonable central goal this criticism would make no sense, for such a person would be a paragon of virtue.

Of course survival is important and our natural instincts will fight for it. It is even sometimes all that we can hope for in desperate situations But for all the reasons above it cannot fill the role of a central goal for our lives.

Part 3.
The Structure of Satisfied Mind

Chapter 9

The Skills of Satisfied Mind

How to play tennis

We have suggested that satisfied mind depends on developing skills. In this Part we will explore that idea further to fill out the concept of satisfied mind. Then we can return to the crux of the matter, the idea that living happily through cultivating satisfied mind can serve as a central aim and thus as the foundation of our values.

If you want to play tennis you can just pick up a racquet and do it, but you will probably not play very well. (I speak from personal experience!) You need to learn certain skills. The essential strokes, for example, require a certain technique. The racquet has to make a certain shape in its swing, the ball has to be struck at a certain point in the swing, the follow through has to be right, the position of your feet and the movement of your body have to be right, timing has to be spot on and so forth. You could read a book or visit a website which told you the details, but reading wouldn't do you much good. You have to practise, even though that may mean getting it wrong hundreds of times.

There are so many variables that if you think about it too hard you will probably fall over! But deep thought in this instance would obviously be silly, it would be like trying to solve mathematical equations of motion while the ball was in the air to decide where it might land, instead of just watching it. It's not the way. So instead you pick an aspect of the game and work on that until it has improved a bit, then another, then another, then go back to the first. You practise, you repeat, if you are lucky you get a coach to point out what is wrong because you often can't tell for yourself, you just know it isn't going as it should. You loop or spiral round cycles of improvement and disappointment. Gradually you get better, gradually you find that more and more of what you have practised is there, as if by magic, when you need it.

What you are doing is not primarily to increase your knowledge as such, which is why the book/website didn't help except as a guide to what you should practise. What you are doing is to train yourself so that the appropriate habits — meaning in this case the ones that help you hit tennis balls — become part of you. Where habits are concerned what matters is practice: intelligent, guided repetition until the effect you want happens — well, habitually.

This process continues even with the world's best players who still practise and learn and improve however good they are. Skilled help is still invaluable, but interestingly the coach does not need to be a better player than the champion. Coaching at that level is a different skill, involving the ability to spot tiny weaknesses, to invent ways of changing them and to communicate all this with precision, clarity and sensitivity. But practice is still the way even the best get better.

There is little point after all in telling yourself what you should be doing when the pressure of the game is high. The game is too fast for conscious calculation so it is a matter of practising until the right reactions are there when you need them. "Right" of course does not here mean right in an ethical sense, simply the reactions that work and give the effect you want, so it means useful or helpful. The right habits are what we call skills.

If there is a problem with a certain habit we have to find a way to change it, to weaken one habit and replace it with another. Sometimes, for example, you can pick up a weakness, perhaps a technique which may get you by at a certain level but isn't good enough for the next. If you want to progress to the next level you have to break that habit back down again and build up a better one.

Our suggestion is that satisfied mind, like tennis, depends on the development of habits or skills, giving us helpful reactions to all kinds of situations which are there when we need them. But in the case of satisfied mind the relevant skills are inner skills or skills of the inner life rather than the physical skills of tennis. (Tennis needs inner skills too as is well recognized,[37] but that is not for us to pursue here.)

Of course, skills need not only to be practised but used, indeed to be able to use them is the point of practice. There may be aspects of practice which are separate from use, as when a sportsperson employs drills outside the context of the game to sharpen skills which will be used in competition. But actually playing the game is also practice. Practice is use and use is practice.

The practice of inner skills is not just a means to an end. It is part of what it is to live well. Using these skills is the key to living well, living with satisfied mind, but to use the skills is also to practise them so that we have a beneficial "loop". When we discuss the practice of skills therefore it would be misleading to give the impression that this is simply a process which leads to or results in satisfied mind at some point in the future. Practice is a way of life, a way of living with satisfied mind.

Practice and belief

This emphasis on practice is important because we are accustomed, certainly in the West, to think that the way we live and the conditions of our being happy are matters of truth or belief. Two thousand years of Abrahamic faiths have made belief central: we think if we believe in the right doctrines or seize "The Truth" all will be well. This was never the whole story of faith, of course, but it was a sufficiently important part for people to be excluded or even killed for unorthodox beliefs — and still is.

As and when religious belief began to weaken its grip, science became the dominant model of rationality. Again the emphasis was on truth or belief, just this time empirically tested belief rather than doctrine. This was a beneficial change in our approach to belief as such. But there was no change in the dominant position given to belief in our culture.

In the all-important realm of the inner life belief is just one species of habit among many and by no means the strongest or most powerful. We all know, for example, that desires and emotions can sweep away calculation — reason is said to be the slave of the passions.[38] So if satisfied mind matters to us then practice, the process of moulding or shaping the habits of the inner life to make satisfied mind possible, is as important as getting our beliefs right.

This is a major cultural shift. It could mean for example that the truth of beliefs may in some contexts be less important than their usefulness. People may embrace what they know are myths or metaphors because these myths are useful in motivating the practice of useful inner skills. This tolerant approach to belief characterizes some of the Eastern religions which recognize that the important issue is the development of the inner life, however the process may be described or transmitted. But the idea that there can be 'truth" which is not literal truth is also familiar from the arts in our own culture.

Just to be clear though, truth is still important if not vital in many contexts and even in the context of inner skills. If you hold beliefs that are not true you might, for example, be in danger of favouring habits which you think are useful but in fact are harmful. Imagine a tennis player who was (somehow) convinced that gravity did not affect a tennis ball in flight: do you think she would be successful or could become skilful? Truth still matters because belief sets the context in which we practise. Nor do we have here any licence for deception, for example the use of myths to trick people into practice "for their own good". But as far as our inner lives are concerned practice is the key, not correctness or certainty. Practice matters even, perhaps especially, if truth is uncertain because it is our inner skill that determines whether or not we can create and maintain satisfied mind. We should practise whether we understand the world or not.

The importance of practice for the inner life is reminiscent of religious practice, especially spiritual practice of the more advanced and dedicated kind. The two contexts are quite separate of course but the association is a good reason not to attack every religious belief we may find untenable or even bizarre. Religious practitioners are not the fools or monsters the New Atheists sometimes suggest and some have extraordinary inner skills, so that we may learn much that is valuable from them about inner practice and skill even if we cannot follow their beliefs. Distinguishing between beliefs which we might question or reject and practices which we may adapt because of their proven value is a useful skill in itself.

Another way in which belief is subordinate to practice in this context is that the manipulation of our own beliefs can itself become a valuable technique to loosen the grip of unhelpful habits. Going back to the earlier example of someone who makes us angry, it may be that by imagining scenarios which, though plausible, are untested and perhaps untrue we can bring ourselves to see the person in a different light. If such thoughts allow us to interrupt the habit of getting angry they are useful at least in that limited context. It does not matter whether they are true or untrue and we need not even bother to find out which. They are tools which do the job. Things would be very different if we were to set out to redeem or transform the other person: before doing that we had better make very sure of our facts. But in the shaping of our own inner skills whatever works, works. Practice, not truth or belief, is the issue.

The importance of structure

If, however, we need practice, what exactly are we to practise? What are the inner equivalents of the tennis strokes, the subroutines we need to assemble to form a game or, in the case of the inner life, our experience of living?

The analogy of sporting skills suggests that we will not get very far by trying to achieve the final outcome without breaking the problem down into smaller parts, sub-skills each of which can be practised and developed in relative isolation. Only by a continuous process of doing this rigorously, advancing each skill little by little, can we hope to advance towards our overall goal.

There are many different approaches to the important question of what to practise. Each religious tradition, for example, has its own "recipe". Buddhism, possibly the least doctrine-fixated of the religions, has the Noble Eightfold Path, eight categories in which the right attitude and skill has to be cultivated.[39] But even within Buddhism, there are different sub-traditions with different suggestions as to what to cultivate, how and in what order.

But we need to answer the question of what inner skills are essential for satisfied mind in a secular context, without doctrinal props. This problem can be addressed by taking a broad look at the major elements of the inner life and asking what obstacles they produce which might prevent us from attaining or maintaining satisfied mind and how these obstacles can be overcome. In that sense some might prefer to say that we do not so much build satisfied mind, we merely remove internal obstacles to it.

For example, we all know that our emotions or feelings can sometimes get the better of us. But emotions are not all bad in themselves, in fact it would be surprising if we could be happy in life without strong positive emotions like love or joy, for example, or without a sense of fun and humour. Sure, we can sometimes be led into making mistakes of judgement if we are carried away by some of these positive emotions, but on the whole they are enhancements to our lives and they are certainly not problems in themselves.

Other emotions are, however, almost wholly negative—anger, hatred, jealousy, envy, the thirst for revenge for example. Not only do they lead us to actions which often have further seriously unhelpful consequences in the external world, but they play havoc with our inner lives. It is, for example, difficult if not impossible to be very angry and be calm and content, let alone happy, at the same time; in fact it may not even be possible to imagine such a state. If you are very angry you can sometimes think of nothing else but the wrong done to you, you "burn" inwardly, your judgement may very well be compromised, you want nothing except retribution or restitution.

So there are certain emotions which, while they may be perfectly "natural", both in the sense that we understand them as part of normal human motivation and behaviour and even in the sense that they served some useful biological or evolutionary function in the lives of our ancestors, are nevertheless obstacles to satisfied mind. If the tendency to get angry, say, is stopping us from enjoying a peaceful and happy inner life, we are stuck with an unhelpful inner habit.

Creating a structure for practice

Using this reasoning we can recognize that obvious obstacles to satisfied mind arise from different sources, different categories of habit or
pattern which occur in the inner life. We will focus on four broadly
drawn categories: thought, emotion, belief and desire. For each we will
suggest that there is a family of skills which can be practised to weaken
unhelpful habits and replace them with habits which give us more contentment and peace. There is a fifth family of skills which completes the
set, about which more below.

For example, obstacles can arise as we have suggested from certain
negative emotions like anger and hatred. There is a family of skills we
will designate as the benevolence skills which focus on shifting our
perspective so that we are less at the mercy of these emotions.

Again, obstacles can arise from our fixation with our desires or
aversions, with what we want or crave and what we detest. The solution here is broadly to disassociate, to separate ourselves from the
craving and let it go, so this family of skills is called the "letting-go"
skills.

Then obstacles can arise from our beliefs, which can warp our inner
life by, among other ways, distorting the lens with which we view the
world, filling us with prejudices and misconceptions. The counteracting skill family is called "story" and involves among other things
cultivating the ability to look at the world from different angles so that
we avoid fixation.

In the category of thought we may encounter problems from the
thoughts which flit across our minds and distract or disturb us even if
we do not really believe what they tell us.

There may of course be other problems which cannot be fitted into
these "boxes", or the boxes might be constructed differently, condensed
into fewer or expanded into more. That's fine — there is no point trying
to get away from doctrine and then creating a new doctrine about what
categories to use. Different schemes may suit some people just as well
or better. But it matters a great deal less than you might at first think
whether these are exactly the right categories to use, because we need
really to do only two things at this point.

First, we need to round out the concept of satisfied mind so that we
can see more of what it entails especially as a central goal. Second, from
a practical point of view we need a plan, a training plan that will help
us start developing the skills we need. If we come to understand at a
later stage that there are additional skills we need, we can address that
problem when it happens. Most of us will have our work cut out to
address potential problems in the categories we have identified

already, but if we are right that practice and inner skill are the keys to satisfied mind it would be absurd to refuse to start until we can see the whole territory mapped out.

Two more things, however, are needed. First, we need to be able to observe our own habits and patterns of thought, belief, emotion and desire, and such observation is just not what we usually do. Just as an athlete needs to be aware in training of what they are doing wrong (or get a good coach to point it out) so that they can correct it, we need to be able to spot the unhelpful habits which govern our inner life. We need therefore to cultivate the ability to observe what happens in our own inner life—how stimulus leads to response, how we jump to certain kinds of conclusions, for example, more readily than others, or find certain emotions surging through us even when we know they are not helpful.

This observational ability, fortunately, has been studied extensively in both religious contexts and in therapeutic practice, so there is plenty of help available.[40] The ability is called mindfulness and it will be the first of the families of skills we will discuss. It is, moreover, so closely related to the skill we need to deal with obstacles in the thought category that we can let one skill family do both jobs, so we still have only four families.

Finally, however, we have to "accentuate the positive". By removing internal obstacles to satisfied mind we can make ourselves immeasurably happier but, rather like physical training or dieting, if the process is tedious or depressing we just won't stick with it and it won't take us very far. So we need to cultivate habits which let us enjoy the moment and enjoy the process of being on the road to an even more satisfied mind.

This journey after all is literally the journey of a lifetime, but as we know the goal is not reached at the end of the journey, the goal is to enjoy the journey. How sad it is to meet deeply committed and spiritually eager people who have squeezed enjoyment from their lives in the pursuit of perfection! Skills like gratitude, patience and humour —for they are skills—help to counteract such dangers and draw our attention back to the wonders of even the hardest life.

This fifth family of skills, then, we will call the enjoyment skills. It is not of course radically different from the other four because it does also counteract an unhelpful tendency, broadly speaking the tendency to overlook the good things which enrich the inner life without harm. But this family might also be seen as cultivating the positive while the others eliminate the negative.

So we have five families of skills, the practice of which adds up to the cultivation of satisfied mind:

- Mindfulness
- Benevolence
- Story
- Letting go
- Enjoyment

In the next chapter we will explore each in more detail.

Chapter 10

The Five Families[41]

Mindfulness

Mindfulness has undergone a welcome rediscovery in the last few years, but for a long time it seemed to have been largely omitted from Western culture. To be fair, it is not a skill whose importance is really appreciated anywhere in the world in everyday culture as opposed to specific contexts like religion. It has tended indeed to be regarded as a religious skill, most notably in Buddhism but also in the contemplative traditions of other religions. But there is nothing inherently religious or supernatural about mindfulness in itself and this is increasingly being recognized. Versions of it have more recently become "respectable" in medical and scientific circles as therapeutic techniques for those suffering from depression or other psychological disorders.[42]

Mindfulness is the skill of being aware of the way in which our own inner life is operating, what habits are at work and how they are affecting what we think and feel. With this ability, we can begin to observe what it is that stands in the way of satisfied mind, what stops us being happy. Instead of inner habits and patterns simply pulling us this way and that, we can become more aware of what is going on.

Where external skills are concerned another person can help with the equivalent process. If an athlete or an artist is not getting the result they want from their performance they might ask a coach or teacher to observe and help them identify where they are going wrong, as an essential first step towards putting it right. Sometimes just to have a "bad habit" brought to their attention will be enough for them to start to fix it, but sometimes they will need much more because the habit has become engrained through the repetition of tiny errors — think tennis again, or golf or indeed any physical activity.

Mindfulness acts in a similar way in the inner life, where no external coach can watch the performance. It allows us to observe what we do and how: how anger arises in us, why we crave to eat or drink too much, what are the patterns of thought which deflate our confidence. By increasing our awareness we can sometimes change our inner lives instantly ("I never realized I was doing that!") but at any rate give ourselves the opportunity to create change where habit is an obstacle to satisfied mind.

Like most skills, mindfulness is not an "all or nothing" matter—it's not a question of being fully mindful or not mindful at all, lights on or lights off. As mindfulness is practised it grows and becomes stronger. In the beginning it might take great effort to "catch yourself" in the act of subverting your own happiness, but with a little patience you may notice (for example) "Oh look, I seem to be getting angry about being stuck in traffic even though I'm not actually in a hurry"—and because of that awareness the anger no longer has you completely in its grip. A little (or a lot!) later the anger in similar circumstances may only be a mild irritation, or may not arise at all.

Thus mindfulness has many beneficial effects in itself but even without them it is the essential diagnostic skill for the inner life, helping us to discover what it is going wrong and what unhelpful habits are at work. Only with such a skill can we begin to shape our inner habits in the direction we have chosen, that is to say in the direction of satisfied mind. Some have described this process as taming or mastering the unruly mind, some traditions using the metaphor of taming a wild horse or an ox[43] to picture the process of overcoming unhelpful habits. This metaphor rightly emphasizes the difficulty of perfecting the skill, but perhaps represents it as too much of an internal battle, which is less helpful because the state required is one of alert but relaxed attention. Others talk of becoming focused on the present moment, realizing that we can get lost in thought or emotion or carried or swept away. The remedy is to be calmly but acutely aware of whatever is happening inwardly right now, because it is only with such focus that inner habits can be observed or disrupted.

Mindfulness practice

Since mindfulness consists of paying close attention to what is happening in the inner life it is practised by any technique that can remind us to observe and only observe. There are many ways of doing this.

The best known practices are forms of meditation, for example those which try to focus attention on the breath. Just watching your own breath is surprisingly difficult at first, because your mind jumps and flits and gets bored very quickly. That, however, is exactly the point. We are not used to holding attention steady, even regarding it as a virtue to be able to do many things at once. There is nothing wrong in itself with doing many things at once, of course, it is just difficult to remain fully focused on any one of them!

One of the great modern masters of mindfulness, the Vietnamese Zen master Thich Nhat Hanh, encourages the use of a "mindfulness bell" in his communities. At random intervals a bell is struck and people stop what they are doing to recall themselves back from wherever their wandering minds or imaginations may have taken them. It is a way of increasing mindfulness by at least devoting certain moments to it, because in busy lives we can sometimes run through the whole day without ever being aware of what effects are governing our inner lives.

Meditation practices are often thought to involve sitting still, but physical stillness is not necessary. If sitting still does not suit you, there are many ways in which mindfulness can be practised which involve movement, like walking, or even intense activity like dance, martial arts, running, yoga and so on. Like sitting watching the breath such activities can be done mindfully or not, but all of them are done better if done mindfully, with full attention to detail and without allowing the mind to wander. That does not mean that we strive to keep them under conscious control, any more than we try to control the breath. It is a matter of minute observation. If extraneous thoughts or feelings do arise, they are just to be observed and allowed to pass as one returns to the job in hand.

Like any other skill, then, mindfulness is practised by attempting the thing aimed at, in this case being mindful, getting it wrong and trying again. As with any other skill the more you practise the better you get but you never reach a point beyond practice. "Practice makes perfect" is a silly saying in most contexts: "Practice makes better" is both more accurate and describes a worthwhile outcome, even if it lacks alliterative punch!

One of the first benefits of trying to practise mindfulness is to make us aware of how unruly our thoughts can be: they tumble in and out of our consciousness from whatever recesses of our brain generate them and we ordinarily have very little control over what thoughts appear in our minds. Sustained practice tends to calm this process and leads to a less frenetic inner life. But from an early stage when we become aware of what happens we might question why we so often allow ourselves to be dominated by what seems like a chaos of thoughts. Allowing ourselves not to identify with this torrent is useful in itself: thoughts mostly just happen, rather than being the product of purposeful thinking.

Mindfulness can also take us into mental states of great clarity and peace, for example the states known as samadhi in Eastern traditions, where the chatter of the mind has stilled to the extent that what can be observed is peace and stillness. But while very pleasant and no doubt beneficial, these states are not the primary aim of practising mindfulness and indeed can become distractions if we strive or worry about achieving them. The states described by Western psychology as "flow"[44] are closely related, I suspect, although usually with an external focus: perhaps "inward flow" or "flow focused on stillness" would be helpful ways to describe samadhi.

Socrates, the father of analytical thought in the West, reportedly said at the trial which condemned him that the unexamined life is not worth living.[45] Certainly a total absence of reflection may diminish a life but if examination means analysis there are many activities in life in which it is a hindrance. Perhaps, though, we can adapt Socrates' remark so that examination is understood as a matter of being mindful. Truly, the unmindful life is not worth living.

Benevolence

For the second family of skills we use the umbrella term benevolence, to include in particular compassion, kindness and that ubiquitous but confusing prescription for well-being and the life well lived, love. At first glance it may come as a shock or even seem absurd that such qualities or feelings are described as skills. They are more usually regarded either as emotions (love, empathy) or as virtues (kindness, compassion). But, looking closer, they can all be or become habitual patterns of feeling, even if we see them in different contexts as emotions or virtues. There is nothing strange in the notion that we can learn to love, or learn to be kinder by making the effort to be so.

Thus compassion, kindness, love and their cousins can certainly be skills whatever else they may be, especially once we have deliberately set out to strengthen their influence on our inner lives. We can have habits of feeling just as much as habits of thought. Feeling is anyway almost always mixed with belief, thought or desire: our categories are analytical and not meant to imply that each is found only in a pure form.

The reason why these benevolence skills are so important is that they weaken and counteract negative emotions which put us at odds with other people but also—and for our purposes crucially—cause turmoil in our own inner lives. Anger is the prime example, but hatred, jealousy, envy, spite and so on are members of the same family of negative emotions. It may be possible while angry, for example, to be exultant, to rejoice in the defeat or discomfort of your enemies, or in revenge gained, which might be a sort of happiness. But such limited happiness, first, can only be momentary because it is occasioned by a particular event; and second, it is dependent on external circumstances which might be reversed. It is at most a respite from a life lived grimly and in struggle, nothing to do with satisfied mind.

The negative emotions are not of course unnatural. They may have — or perhaps <u>had</u> at some time in our evolution — their biological uses or presumably we would not have them. But they are not useful in the context of a life committed to satisfied mind. They destroy satisfied mind and they also tend to perpetuate external conflict, with unpredictable results. There is much to be said anyway from a practical point of view that aggression is better met dispassionately, with a calm that can defuse, deflect or deal with attack without the distraction of wild emotion. Few successful armies are made up entirely of berserkers. But we are here concerned with the inner-life aspects of the negative emotions and it is surely beyond doubt that anger, hatred and their cousins are not compatible with satisfied mind.

The more our inner lives are prey to these negative emotions, therefore, the further we are from gaining and sustaining satisfied mind. If we can reduce the occasions on which they arise or even reduce their force when they do arise we will inevitably become calmer, more peaceful, happier.

Counteracting negative emotions with positive inner skills is very different, however, from controlling or suppressing them. Opinions differ about whether such control or suppression is useful or even possible anyway. But in any case it doesn't help our inner life at all if we learn to disguise our feelings externally or restrain our actions. Our peace is gone anyway. We are thus not interested for this purpose in the external management of anger (for example) or in learning how to live with anger, however useful such skills might be in other contexts. We are interested in weakening the habit of becoming angry, ideally until anger no longer arises at all but more realistically until when it does arise we can catch it quickly and dissolve it so that inner peace returns.

Cultivating benevolence skills

We might start by cultivating different ways of looking at the actions and motivations of others as a way of displacing anger, hatred and so on. Instead, for example, of regarding someone's rudeness as a personal insult, we might look at it as an expression of their anxiety or insecurity, or as stemming from a confusion that they cannot help. It does not matter, as we saw earlier, that we get the story right because we are not trying to change the behaviour of the rude one, we are trying only to change the inner effect it has on us. We don't even need to fix on one particular explanation, we might even be content to reflect, for example: "I do not know why they are being so rude, there are many possible explanations of which at least one and possibly more may be true, so I will try not to react anyway."

On a different scale, when we hear of great atrocities in the world committed, for example, in the name of politics or religion, it is easy to jump quickly (a sure sign that a habit is at work) to the view that the perpetrators are fanatical, or evil, or inhuman. We react with anger and hatred in our turn. The perpetrators may indeed be vicious, but in these contexts historical enquiry is a useful tool. There is no conflict, no fanaticism in the world which springs up without roots, which does not have a history going at least part way to explain why intransigence and hatred have taken hold. Historical understanding may not dissolve our hatred (or theirs) or solve the problem, but it may allow us to react with a sense of what has shaped the attitudes on display. We cannot condone atrocity, but if we can avoid knee-jerk hatred on our own part we can preserve our own inner balance and may have a better chance to find an external solution.

We might reflect more generally that most people passionately want to live happily but not everyone knows how. Hence for example someone whose actions seem to be driven by anger or hatred, which might otherwise provoke us to anger in our turn, is quite likely to be in a state of confusion about the importance of inner skills. (This is closely related to the Buddhist formula that ignorance is the root of suffering.)[46] Alternatively, this angry person may have realized the importance of satisfied mind but be struggling in their attempts to achieve it, which may be even more deserving of sympathy. This is not to recommend smugness about our own wisdom or progress, which apart from anything else is seldom a good way to meet anger unless we are really looking for trouble! It is again a matter of inner attitude, of cultivating the inner space not to respond to anger with anger.

Another approach is to reflect that we allow ourselves far more indulgence and latitude when we judge our own behaviour than we afford to other people. It is not unknown of course for people to be genuinely angry with themselves. But generally if we are angry with ourselves we are angry that we did not perform better, that we made the wrong decision or lacked sufficient skill for the occasion. Mostly, perhaps because we tend to believe or feel that our own motives are transparent and our actions for the good (whether they really are is another matter), we judge our own actions less harshly than those of others, giving ourselves the benefit of most doubts. So we could say compassion for others is no more than regarding their actions as we regard our own, which means we look for the best interpretation. (This is closely related to the Christian formula that we should love others as ourselves.)[47]

Thus the benevolence skills are a matter of regarding others as kindly, compassionately or benevolently as we can, looking if necessary for reasons to excuse or explain their behaviour towards us if that is what it takes. The practice of these skills consists of constantly attempting to make the inner shift to see others in that light. This is likely to result in a kinder and more benevolent approach to others in our external actions, but it is the inner and not the external effect for which we are looking.

So this is not a suggestion that we should be nice to people because that's what nice people do. It is a programme of building inner habits which allow us to react inwardly without anger, hatred, desire for revenge or any other negative emotion, because only thus can we avoid the inner turmoil which comes with those negative emotions. We may still need to take action against someone, for example to defend ourselves or others or prevent harmful behaviour. The point, however, is to do so as far as possible without our actions being coloured by our own anger or hatred, just as, for example, we might seek to deal with a dangerous natural phenomenon.

There is of course a significant reversal here of our usual ways of thinking about benevolence, in fact there are two. In the first place, we cultivate these skills because they help us deal with the negative emotions which can prevent us living happily, in other words because we cannot be happy without such skills. In this sense our own self interest lies in cultivating compassion, kindness and the rest. We do not cultivate them to be good or worthy, but because satisfied mind is our central goal.

The second reversal is that any resultant <u>feeling</u> of compassion or kindness, if it arises, is secondary to the skill of putting ourselves in the appropriate frame of mind. We thus do not start with a feeling of benevolence, although if we try to cultivate this helpful way of looking at others and their actions the feeling will come. We may, however, have to "fake it until we make it". The feeling of compassion will follow if we persist in searching for the perspective which allows us to see others, however badly they behave, as like ourselves and not as aliens or enemies.

Language and belief: Story skills

Story skills are the way we deal with habits of language and belief which prevent us from achieving and maintaining satisfied mind.

Language and belief form the structural skeleton of the inner life. Negative emotion can sweep us away, shake our reason and make us heedless of consequences, but mistaken belief can warp our perceptions and distort what appears to us to be reality. Unless and until the external world offers evidence impossible to ignore or explain away — and the more attached we are to a belief the more reluctant we will be to accept any evidence at all against it — we will take our inner world as a mirror of the external world. We each live in the world of our beliefs and we depend on those beliefs being accurate in order to take effective actions.

Our utter dependence on the beliefs we happen to hold seems inevitable, for how else could we proceed? It would make no sense to act as if our beliefs were untrue. But we can and do get "locked in" to beliefs which misinterpret both the external world and our own inner lives. What we believe shapes in turn what we are capable of believing.

For example, if I believed in fairies I might interpret certain events as both a natural consequence of their existence and as confirmation of my belief. So to me the world will seem just as I imagine it would be if there really were fairies. Whatever happens, I may develop the detail of my belief so as to make it very difficult ever to reach a point where the evidence that I am mistaken is too stark for me to ignore or explain away. This is not just fantasy, for even scientific belief has often reacted like this in the face of contrary evidence in order to preserve important theories, from the geocentric universe to Newtonian motion.

More prosaically, if I am seized, say, by the belief that everyone who belongs to a certain group is untrustworthy, that belief is likely to influence how I interpret the behaviour of any member of the group — I may look for hidden motives, I may mistrust what they say and so on. It will be very difficult to disprove my suspicion or change my mind, because my prejudice will filter every word and action of theirs. We have only to imagine that this group is defined by nationality, ethnicity or religion to realize how dangerous that could be.

One immediate conclusion is that the standard model of empiricism which insists that all will be well as long as our beliefs take full account of the available evidence tells only part of the story. Evidence is itself belief, often shaped by prior belief just as much as by the external world. That, of course, is why it is so difficult to persuade people to accept evidence against cherished beliefs. We all think of ourselves as reasonable beings, but our existing beliefs determine what we find reasonable! So we continue to congratulate ourselves on our reasonableness well beyond the point where others have given up.

Our beliefs in turn are a complicated interaction between the world and the language we use to describe it. Language and belief are closely intertwined, we cannot have one without the other. It's not as if we fully learned a language and then set about applying it to the world to form beliefs: we learn language by acquiring beliefs and we acquire beliefs by using language. To the extent that we use language to describe — we use it for lots of other things as well of course but in the context of belief description is foremost — we can only describe in ways our language allows, which are again intimately entwined with our existing beliefs.

If, for example, you took up a new interest (say, collecting antique porcelain) you might learn many new facts (new beliefs) but with the facts you would learn an extension of language, so that you could describe a part of the world (the details and varieties of antique porcelain, in this case) in new and different ways. Language begets and refines belief, belief begets and refines language. When we think or believe something we can only do it with language. But descriptive language only works at all because it is selective, it makes distinctions, misses out some bits of information and places emphasis on others. This is not a defect, it is the only way language can work.

We could describe the relationship between language and belief (if rather pompously) by saying that perfect objectivity is impossible, because as observers we always bring something to the observation, even if it is only the categories we use and the framework of belief we work within. But that risks making the whole business of forming and confirming beliefs seem strange and mysterious whereas it is something we all do easily all the time. Again, this is just how language works.

Stories

The important shift we need to make is to appreciate that our beliefs, including our understanding of ourselves, other people and the world we live in, are not solid and unchanging "facts". They are an astonishingly complex interaction between the system that is us and the system that is everything else. We may not understand all the details of how this works, but an easy way to grasp and use the idea at a humanistic level is to think of all descriptive language as the telling of stories. Everything we know or think we know, all the everyday things but also all of science, religion, history, mathematics and all the rest, is story. We swim in a sea of stories, but stories (like language itself) are selective. They miss some bits out and draw attention to others to keep the narrative flowing.

Just so we might think of our beliefs. They are always partial, they are always selective, they are never complete for there are always other angles, other perspectives. But since these stories contain all that we know — our own sense of identity, everything we believe, everything we rely on to anchor ourselves in the world — they dominate our inner lives. Not surprisingly, then, they throw up at least their fair share of difficulties when it comes to achieving and maintaining satisfied mind.

Wherever a story is for example wrong, or ambiguous, confused or misunderstood, or just taken as complete when it can only be part of the truth—there is an error. But with error there is the possibility that satisfied mind is lost, for example, through worry, fear, even anger or hatred because of that story. In such cases ways to recognize, understand and correct the error may be vital to restore satisfied mind. Even when a story is true (as far as it goes) it can have the same disturbing effects. We may need in such cases to find a different perspective from which a true story can be faced with equanimity.

The story skills, then, are ways to deal with the effects of belief on satisfied mind regardless of whether belief is true or false.

Managing stories

Clearly this family of skills must be very broad. Some story skills are simply parts of what we might consider as rationality or reason—the ability to test one belief against another, to weigh probabilities, to spot inconsistencies for example. Experiments show that most of us are less able to do these things than we believe: for example, there are systematic biases in our attitudes to risk or chance in identical situations depending on whether we frame them in terms of the chance of a gain or the risk of a loss.[48] Anything that can help our ability to think clearly and calmly may be an advance towards satisfied mind.

The importance of reason and its skills is worth emphasis. There is nothing in the satisfied mind ideal which is anti-thought or anti-reason. Because we cannot describe the world except through language it is easy but mistaken to think that there might therefore be a hidden or numinous reality beyond language which we cannot reach, or even that language is somehow an obstacle to true knowledge. It is true that language or particular beliefs can lead us into many tangles and (among other things) destroy our contentment, but more careful thought, not less, is usually the remedy. There are also as we have seen states of deep inner peace (samahdi) in which the relentless habit of storytelling is left behind, but they are not different ways of describing or understanding the world, just different ways of being in it.

On the other hand there are many truths, many stories, which are bitter and difficult to accept—the loss of loved ones, for example, or our own limitations, our disappointments and ultimately our own mortality. These are not illusions, mistakes or misunderstandings and no amount of careful thought will allow us to think they are. The loss and sadness that may accompany them are also real. But if we are to achieve satisfied mind we must do so against the background of such stories, there is no other way. So we must ask: what else is true here, how can we tell the story so that this sadness is not tragic or overwhelming or destructive? What perspective is there from which we can accept this truth and still move towards or back to satisfied mind?

We have to dig deeper into any story which generates fear or sadness. Why does death distress us, for example, when we know it is the condition, the price, of living? Can we find a different model or look from a different viewpoint? Why for example do we resist the idea that some processes have an ending while being quite content with the ending of others? We can think, for example, without distress of the best meal we have ever had, even though it had an end, so why is it so distressing to think of our lives as having an end?[49] Then again, death involves loss and the pain of it comes in no small part from our attachment to what or whom we lose. Sometimes then it might help to think of grief as a tribute of love.

We will find no doubt in our thoughts and attitudes to death a tangle of biological instinct, fear of the unknown and mistaken stories about the processes which are us and of which we are a part. We may find that there are underlying stories we have accepted but never questioned, perhaps even helpful stories we have used to create our success in the world but which, because they stress the importance of our progress, cast dying as some sort of failure. Whatever we find we can gradually start to amend such stories, dissolve the knot and live with less sadness and fear.

Such an enterprise could never be easy. It is likely to require patience and great skill with story, a skill hard won and easily neglected. Sometimes we just have to find a way to let time pass and lend perspective. But we must sometimes deal with hard but inescapable beliefs if we are to live in peace. That is why we need the skills of looking into and around every story, looking for alternatives and reframings, finding different perspectives. This is what the story skills are for.

Letting go

Besides the roadblocks of negative emotion and the many dangers which can spring from belief, we have one further major obstacle to satisfied mind: desire, in which we include aversion, the desire for something to go away. It would be wrong of course to suggest that all desire is problematic, because desire is the main motivator of everything we do. Without it we might, for example, starve, not through the impossibility of finding food but through failing to want to feed ourselves! Difficulty only arises because we tend easily to attach ourselves to drives and desires, even to identify ourselves with them, so that we cannot be content unless we have our way.

The problem with desire and aversion is thus that we often do not know when to stop. We convince ourselves that we cannot be happy unless we have, become, do, achieve, get rid of — whatever it is. Thus we are pitted against the world in a contest on which we have staked our peace of mind. If we lose, satisfied mind is replaced by regret, recrimination or dissatisfaction. But even if we win our happiness is now firmly identified with this external goal, or perhaps the next one, or the one after that. We can so easily lose the plot and identify our happiness with achieving or possessing. This danger is not absurd or remote, it is the way our lives so often work, even the very engine of consumer capitalism.

The point is not that possessions are bad, but that our attachment to them, or to acquiring or retaining them, can overwhelm us. The dangers of attachment are a staple theme of Buddhism, but the King James Bible makes the point brilliantly: "The love of money is the root of all evil"[50] — not money itself of course, but our attachment to it. In our context, we could say that if satisfied mind is adopted as our central and most important goal then desire can be a danger because it sets up rival goals which can easily come to dominate our lives instead. Thus we forget our central goal — then we wonder why we have all these goods, for example, or all this success and are not happy.

As we saw earlier, it is hardly possible or even desirable that we should have no other goals in life than satisfied mind — of course we will continue to want and value, for example, possessions, experiences, relationships or achievements. Recognizing that one goal is central does not mean that all other goals need to be abandoned, merely that we must be careful not to abandon the central goal in our enthusiasm for a lesser one. If goals do not conflict we can try for as many as we like, but in practice there usually comes a point where they do conflict and we have to choose. If we choose to pursue something other than satisfied mind we can hardly complain if we are dissatisfied with the outcome.

Our usual trick of course is to persuade ourselves that achieving some external goal or other will make us happy. That is one reason why it is important to be clear about the link between the inner life and happiness and especially that external goals will not guarantee happiness. But if you can for example live with riches and not be attached to them, not value them above satisfied mind, not regard yourself as superior because of them and not fret about their diminution, then you have done something rather special.

Living in the flux

The skills of letting go address this problem of attachment to lesser goals. To be attached is very often to want to keep things as they are. (Or sometimes to make one last change and then keep things as they will be. "After this, everything will be fine.") So it is very useful to cultivate our awareness of change. Everything changes all the time and we ourselves are rapidly changing in lives which last only a few decades. Everything is process, not stasis.

We must learn not so much to live in the now (as the saying goes) as to live in the flux, to recognize that everything, including whatever and whoever is most precious to us, will change or disappear. That of course does not mean that nothing is important, on the contrary everything, every moment in its uniqueness, is at once precious and transient — precious because transient. To want permanence is like wanting time to stop, but that would be the death of everything.

Forgiveness

One very important aspect of letting go is forgiveness, both of ourselves and others. Forgiveness can be seen as letting go of anger or hatred generated by the past. (If you need an example, think of the actions of Nelson Mandela after 27 years in prison.) We have already suggested that anger is seriously harmful because it precludes peace of mind: we cannot be angry and happy at the same time. When someone injures or insults us we naturally tend to get angry, but in doing so we suffer a double harm, the action against us and the loss of our peace of mind. The first is not under our control but the second may be. If the injury is great we may carry anger for years and we grow bitter, we brood, we desire revenge as a substitute for reversing the harm perpetrated. In this way we can lose sight of the possibility of satisfied mind.

We have only to imagine (so far as we can) the plight of someone whose loved one has been killed by violence to realize how easily any kind of happiness might seem irrelevant or impossible. But if satisfied mind really is our central goal how can we afford to allow it to become lost or submerged like this? How can we allow any event, however terrible, take way the possibility of living happily?

If we think about how we might regain peace after such a terrible trauma (albeit from the privileged position of not being so afflicted) we can see that, in the first place, recovery might very well take a long time and require specialist, even medical, help. Grieving itself is a process which takes time. The ability to forgive may take even more time. We should not fall into the trap of thinking that forgiveness is in any sense a duty. But hatred is not a duty either and certainly no tribute to our lost loved one.

At some point anger or hatred must be overcome if we are to regain satisfied mind. If we cannot find a way to let go of the hurt it will quite simply remain with us. It may help to understand why the wrong was done — what did the perpetrator think they were doing and why, how did they come to think that this action was acceptable and so on. But such understanding may not help, because any reasons may seem insufficient. To forgive is not to excuse nor even necessarily pardon, if pardon involves accepting that punishment or the prevention of further harmful acts is unnecessary. Forgiveness is not primarily about the perpetrator, it is about the victim or the victim's family. It is about them restoring <u>their</u> chance of living happily by leaving the wrongful act in their past, where it belongs, and moving on.

Fear

If forgiveness is about the past, fear is about the future, about what is still to come. Fear is dispersed or prevented by confidence. In any everyday circumstance, if we are confident that we have the skill to deal with whatever is likely to happen we will have no fear, or certainly less fear, whether we face an interview, a work task, an examination or whatever else. Even when we fear pain, if we know we can manage the situation the fear is lessened, as when we sit in the dentist's waiting room.

Just imagine, then, if we had confidence that we could maintain satisfied mind in all circumstances, because our inner skills were polished and we knew how to maintain our equanimity. There would be nothing to fear and we would be completely free. By practising all the skills which enable us to deal with disturbances in our inner life we can move towards this goal, letting go of fear gradually as we strengthen our skill. Few people will get to the end of that road, but it is an ideal.

Even the fear of death might be overcome if we were confident that we had done everything to prepare ourselves for what we believe will happen. Perhaps letting go of fear to this extent is the ultimate prize, the last piece of the jigsaw of living happily, but it depends on living in such a way as to develop the confidence that our inner lives can deal with anything. Dying well is of a piece with living well.

For most of us, however, being free of fear remains an ideal, not a current reality. For that reason we need to cultivate another skill in this family, courage. Courage too is about letting go of fear, not to the extent that it disappears but to the extent that we can make our decisions and take our actions in spite of it. Fear remains, for if there is no fear there is no courage, but with courage we can live with and despite the fear.

Courage is cultivated in part by story techniques, convincing ourselves that the danger is not as great as we fear or that action is necessary whatever the danger. Getting used to a situation helps, showing ourselves we have the skill to deal with what we fear. The value, for example, of military training is not to convince young soldiers that there is no danger in combat, which would be stupid, but to impart procedures, techniques and equipment which will significantly lessen risk and increase both confidence and chances of success.

Enjoyment

The last of our families of skills is enjoyment. We can easily forget in the daily grind that enjoyment of the process of living is so important. We can even devote ourselves so seriously to altering the habits of our inner lives to achieve satisfied mind that we simply overlook the joy available to us as we proceed. We might even postpone happiness until the work is done, forgetting that our goal is not just to die happy, but to live happily along the way. Happiness postponed is in this context happiness lost.

In any case, there is nothing strange about encouraging inner skills which help us to enjoy life more, it is plain common sense. Among the key habits which enhance our inner lives are gratitude, patience and humour. All it takes to turn them into skills is to cultivate them as much as we can.

Gratitude

Take gratitude, for example. There may be circumstances in which we have absolutely nothing to be grateful for, but they are very rare. Perhaps we are biologically conditioned to focus on what is wrong or lacking in our circumstances—it is easy to speculate how useful that might be from an evolutionary point of view. In a harsh climate of scarcity and dangers such attention to negative detail might be invaluable. But even if this is so, it is an instinct which in more usual modern conditions can lead us to focus on the 1% of our situation which is unsatisfactory and neglect the 99% which is absolutely fine.

The habit of gratitude needs cultivation for precisely this reason, for it is a matter of appreciating what we have, what is going well, what is pleasant and enjoyable about where we are and what we are doing even if we would rather be somewhere else doing something else. It does not preclude action to remedy or perfect the external situation, if that is possible, but we can spend a lot of time and effort trying to order the world exactly to our specification only to find that something slips out of line just as we think we have finished. To learn to be grateful for what we have is not a matter of tolerating second best but of appreciating what is.

It is so easy, for example, to take basic comforts for granted. Why, I might think, should I feel grateful for having enough to eat today when I have enough to eat every day? Nothing special, surely? With this way of thinking we can ignore or undervalue everything which makes our lives pleasant and get on with the serious business of grumbling that we would like more, or that someone else already has more. Gratitude is the practice of being aware of what we have, what we can experience, and how it enhances our lives, ideally taking nothing for granted. It takes an effort sometimes to get into the mindset of being grateful for small things and aware that they could so easily be otherwise. Nevertheless, it is a worthwhile effort because through it our enjoyment and appreciation of all the details of life are enhanced.

Many religious people understand this attitude very well and make a point of "giving thanks". But it is not necessary to be a believer to be grateful or feel gratitude. The skill is to be closely aware of what it is we have reason to be grateful for, not necessarily that we can identify someone we should be grateful to. Attribute your comforts to fortune or luck if you must, or to nothing at all. Every comfort, every beauty, every pleasure, great or small, is something to be grateful for and in being grateful we stop and pay attention to the enjoyment it provides. Even the social background to our lives provides many opportunities for gratitude: merely to live in a society which functions at all, let alone reasonably well, is a huge advantage not enjoyed by everyone.

On the other hand, it is very temping to regard our successes and achievements as of our own making, particularly where great effort or creativity has been involved. No need then for gratitude, we might think, we earned this success by our own efforts. But even here the cultivation of gratitude can enhance our experience. The skills we used to create this success have only been acquired through opportunity and the natural gifts to apply ourselves to them. Opportunity might not have presented itself and our natural gifts (the clue is in the name) are certainly not of our own making. So while we rightly celebrate any success we might recognize that we are fortunate to be able even to strive for it.

We are certainly not solely responsible, for example, for our intelligence, or our agility, or our persuasiveness, or our ability to apply ourselves and work hard. By remembering also to be grateful we can avoid allowing ourselves to become self important or to look down on others. This is invaluable, for satisfied mind can be quickly lost if we slip into a competitive mindset which constantly requires us to measure ourselves against others. And when on the other hand things do not go well we can more easily cope with disappointment if we have avoided the habit of attributing every success to our own prowess but are skilled in looking for positives in any situation.

Patience and humour

Patience is another skill of the enjoyment family. Life is full of delays and waits, not to mention potential annoyances and irritations from others going about their lives in apparent ignorance of the importance of our own current projects! Without patience we can be constantly frustrated by daily life. We can throw away our time because we are so focused on some end that the time we have to wait is like a desert we have to cross. We are like children who cannot wait for a cake to come out of the oven. Worse, we can even turn to anger, for example when our frustration at traffic delays is vented as anger against some other traveller we see as transgressing our rights.

Patience is the skill of reminding ourselves that every moment has something in it that is worth valuing. If it is not a moment which provides exactly what we would prefer it still provides something and, more importantly, it is a part of our life, something whose quality is up to us but which forms a part of us. We push forward our projects, certainly, but not at the expense of satisfied mind.

Humour is a skill which helps us keep perspective on everything that happens to us. External circumstances, other people and the physical world may have little regard for our projects and designs and may constantly thwart or obstruct us. If we regard these setbacks darkly we can become bitter or angry, which does no good for our inner life. The same is true even of our efforts to acquire the skills of the inner life themselves, for the process of practice is full of setbacks and we can easily fall into being angry with circumstances or with ourselves.

We are rightly suspicious, I think, of anyone who claims to have achieved any degree of spiritual progress but who lacks humour, because humour represents a perspective from which life and its difficulties can be worn lightly. It is remarkable, for example, that when people are faced with difficult lives one of the most common defences is to develop humour which cuts their misfortune down to manageable size. We may take our central aim very seriously but that in no way implies that we should be solemn about it, a distinction which sometimes gets lost in religious approaches to satisfied mind. So humour, the ability to see the funny side of life's difficulties, or our own foibles, or the arrogance of power, is one of the key skills which keeps us from being overwhelmed and creates the space in which satisfied mind can grow.

Chapter 11

Satisfied Mind
as the Central Goal

External needs

We have already noted that satisfied mind, involving the cultivation of inner skills, is not the whole story of living happily. Some external conditions must surely also be satisfied. It is clear for example that someone who is starving, or recently bereaved, or suffering unremitting physical pain because of illness will find it very difficult to be happy. It would be unhelpful at best to say that the source of their difficulty is the level of their inner skills, even if a higher level of skill might indeed enable them to cope better. The real problem is the extraordinary demands made of those skills by external circumstances. We must expect in any case that most of us, most of the time, will face life with an incomplete level of inner skills. Satisfied mind is an ideal we move towards all our lives, not the attainment of a few weeks' or months' effort.

Yet if we look at each possible <u>external</u> source of unhappiness — even physical illness being external for this purpose — we find that it is at least possible for someone to be happy under those conditions. Severe hunger and thirst are obvious sources of unhappiness and yet we find examples of people gladly undertaking such hardships voluntarily because they believe they will gain spiritual insight or merit by so doing. Even pain which most people would find difficult to endure can be and is regularly overcome by brave and hardy people who find the resources in themselves because they must.

Although we can thus agree that both happiness and satisfied mind might often be easier to attain if external circumstances were more helpful, satisfied mind seems to be the only <u>necessary</u> condition of living happily — which is not of course the same as being a sufficient condition, or the only condition necessary. Moreover, it is the only condition common to all of us, since our external conditions vary widely. And as we have seen it is something over which we can all take action.

We could with some justification regard happiness in a more ordinary sense as a balance between external conditions and the inner skills of satisfied mind. Without satisfied mind no amount of external luxury will help, without a basic minimum of help from external conditions even the most skilful cannot survive or will struggle to achieve happiness.

Such minimum levels, although they may vary from person to person, include absolute survival needs. We do not choose these, they are imposed on us by biology. The ordinary satisfaction of these needs may require survival skills — like, for example, the ability to obtain food in the circumstances in which we live — and such skills may be highly valued by ourselves and those who rely on us. But for all the reasons we saw earlier about why survival does not act as our central goal, such survival skills are subordinate to values. For example, to sacrifice the chance of satisfying such needs — even to die to secure the survival of another — might be a supreme expression of the values we live by.

Even basic survival needs cease to have force once they are satisfied to a certain level. It is obvious that too little in the way of resources like air, food or water, for example, make survival difficult. But an excess of these things does not necessarily increase happiness. Where external needs are concerned, enough is enough, even if we find it difficult to accept that we really have enough if we see that someone else has more.

The precise definition and quantification of our external needs beyond survival levels could be disputed endlessly, and when we come to look in detail at politics, which is very largely concerned with external matters, the question of what constitutes "enough" for those needs will be important. Each of us will also have many secondary desires and goals which will involve external conditions and of course we will pursue our secondary goals to the extent they are compatible with our central goal. External goals whether real needs or secondary goals are not to be set aside or despised. But they are not central.

Other people

At first glance, satisfied mind may seem a selfish or self centred goal, but this would be a misunderstanding. Satisfied mind is intimately bound up with our relationships to other people.

It is said that you can link any person on the planet to any other by just six stages of connection. Whether or not this is strictly true it is a reminder that everyone is connected to us in some way, however indirectly. Hence there is at least the possibility that we could interact with anyone, anyone at all. In turn such interactions are influences, however remote or subtle, on our own inner lives. Every slight contact

—with the casual acquaintance, the shop assistant, the person passed in the street—is a pebble dropped into the pool of our inner life.

Not only does every encounter affect our inner lives to some degree but every memory, every imagining, every thought of another, every reflection entwines our inner lives with other people. Such decisions, thoughts and feelings are conditioned by existing habits, but those habits, reflexively, are strengthened or weakened by the interaction. A thought about how I should act in some given circumstance is likely to include how others will be affected, not only those directly involved but also those more remotely touched by my action. Thus my thoughts about my own actions involve thoughts about others, are conditioned by my attitudes to others and may affect my habits of thought about others.

When I think about what kind of society I would prefer to live in, what for example I would be prepared to have done on my behalf to help or thwart this group or that, I am considering myself in relation to the members of that group. The habits of my inner life are both given expression and changed or confirmed in the process of this thought, just as they would be if I was acting face to face.

No wonder, then, that those in search of religious versions of satisfied mind often withdraw from the world, reducing their close external relationships to a few (if any) governed by clear rules, as in monastic life. This simplification may be a good way to reduce the "noise" affecting the inner life and allow progress. But even recluses take their inner lives with them! Withdrawal from the world does not mean withdrawal from the emotions, the prejudices, the hurts we carry with us. Without new distractions the old relationships, desires and feelings may bulk even larger. Withdrawal at best clears an external space in which to work, it does not guarantee that the work will be done or will be successful. In any case, for most of us our lives are necessarily led out in the world and therefore it is out in the world that we need to create and maintain satisfied mind.

But for that very reason interaction with others is the heart of the enterprise. What we think, believe, feel, want or fear is crucially determined by what we think, believe, feel, want or fear **about other people**. We cannot achieve satisfied mind unless we can achieve it in our interactions with other people. There is no split. I cannot say: my inner life is something apart from the world, something which is mine to ponder and know about, but my actions or my politics are something else entirely. That simply cannot be made to work because they are all of a piece. The actions I take in respect of others feed back into my inner life, altering or reinforcing some habits at the expense of others. Those habits in turn shape my actions.

This of course is the mechanism we make use of when we consider any formal practice. We choose actions deliberately to reinforce habits we know to be helpful and weaken those we know to be harmful. So then, all of life is potentially practice and every interaction with or thought of another is part of practice. Interacting with others is as much an influence on whether I develop satisfied mind as my most secret contemplation or, say, the meditative techniques I might use to develop mindfulness.

To focus on the inner life is thus not a turning of the back on the world, it involves a recognition that everything we do and everyone we meet, brush against, even imagine is an influence on our inner life and our chances of living happily. The goal is impossible to achieve unless we align our actions towards others, through our ethics and even our politics, with the inner habits we want to encourage, not just because inner feeds outer but, more importantly, outer feeds inner.

The ideal of satisfied mind thus requires commitment across every aspect of our lives. Already we can see the potential for a very radical shift in particular in our consideration of politics. We will need to consider the effects of political actions and policies on our own inner lives, a hint that we must develop some sort of politics of satisfied mind.

Responsibility

Satisfied mind involves personal responsibility. I cannot make you happy, nor you me. For each of us, our happiness depends on our own careful cultivation of inner skills and this is work we must do for ourselves. Others can perhaps help, encourage or advise but they cannot do the work for us or deliver the end result. So our happiness and the direction of our lives is to that very large extent our own responsibility. But unlike objective or external understandings of happiness (based for example on possessions or power) this produces no conflict, because my satisfied mind — dependent as it is on my inner life and skills — in no way competes with yours.

Thus we take responsibility for our lives through taking responsibility for our inner lives. Small children, for example, are apt to take their feelings or desires as forces of nature: what a child feels or wants at any moment blots out all else. In such a case we distract the child if we can because we know that she yet lacks the trick of distracting herself and thus letting go of the desire. But as we get older we can often balance strong desires or feelings (though not necessarily all!) against other considerations.

Even in cases in which we are not able to change the world outside ourselves, we can learn how to adapt the world inside ourselves. Making these adaptations in a consistent direction to serve our own chosen purpose of living happily is, in a nutshell, what the practice of the skills of satisfied mind is about. So a commitment to developing these skills is the "grown up" option, as far from a childish commitment to our own whims as is possible. It is acceptance of responsibility for our own happiness.

This points towards a certain approach to living, a responsible approach. It does not of course mandate a particular lifestyle – it does not for example say that we must renounce the world to live on mountaintops or on the other hand devote our work to the welfare of others. But it denies that we can only be happy if we accumulate as many possessions as possible or gain power and influence in the world. In fact it is very obviously neutral towards the external trappings of life and all those external things which we normally spend our time worrying about.

The new stance is thus not that we should be passive about the external world, but that we should be far more active about and take responsibility for our own inner lives.

Religious central aims

Many people of course still base their values on religion. If they adopt some form of the legal paradigm we have seen that this is a mistake, but they may be committed to a religious aim as their central aim in life, thus following our argument in part. Because an important part of our task is to show how values could be shared and form the glue of society, it is important to consider what relationship such religious commitments have to a secular ideal and in particular the ideal of satisfied mind.

If you had a strong religious belief about the purpose of your life (and all religion is about the purpose of life) it would surely make perfect sense that such a purpose should be your central aim – salvation, enlightenment, paradise or whatever. The question of how your faith itself could be justified would remain, of course, but that question is quite separate. Secular people and everyone with a different faith would be convinced that you were mistaken in your particular belief, but given that you had that belief it would be rational for you to make the consequent aim central in your life and thus the basis of your values. After all, what could be more important in your world?

Such a religious central aim does not in itself preclude acceptance of satisfied mind as a secondary aim, maybe even a close second and maybe a step in the right direction. Not all religions find human happiness problematic! It is just that the religious aim would take precedence in the case of conflict. But we seem to be left still with a split between religious and secular central aims. Is there any way to resolve this problem?

Some religions — perhaps most at certain phases in their history — are apt to insist that anyone who disagrees with them must do so out of wickedness and that violence and killing are the only proper responses. There is no prospect of accomodation with such beliefs, only the need to contain the threat they pose. But most religious belief is not of this kind. While insisting as they will on their own privileged access to supernatural truth, most religions accept that they cannot impose religious hegemony by force, indeed that it would be wrong or point-less to do so. They may even accept that belief in their doctrines is a matter of faith rather than proof or virtue and that religious pluralism, including secularism, is therefore inevitable, however regrettable they find it.

They will naturally insist that for their believers religious aims are central. But if those aims are broadly compatible with the development of satisfied mind (by treating skills as virtues for example) they may be willing to cooperate with other "people of good will" despite disagree-ments over the supernatural. Perhaps they can even accept that there is a level of ethical thought and behaviour which is attainable without religious aims, so that the ethical and the religious ways of living are so to speak on different planes. In any case, such religions may be allies in the creation of shared values.

Any such religion might still have major ethical disagreements with secular society even if secular values were widely accepted. We might hope that such disagreements would be less marked than with a society based on material greed. But the formulation of a coherent secular basis of values offers a platform on which ethical disagreements can at least be discussed. The most widely shared values would be secular, because they would avoid religious disagreement. For religion, the challenge then would be to convince others that a proposal which, say, was objectionable on religious grounds was also objectionable on secular ethical grounds. A genuinely pluralist society after all cannot accept the argument: "<u>You</u> cannot do that because it is against <u>my</u> beliefs", just as it should not accept the argument: "You must do this <u>despite</u> its conflict with your beliefs."

Believers might prevail in a particular instance or they might not, but the outcome would not depend on an argument about religion. Instead, the argument would be about shared secular values, about the implications of a common secular foundation of values in a particular case. If those of faith did not win the argument, they could still live by their own stricter or different code while regretting that society had not followed their lead. But at least religion would share with secular thought a language, a way to conduct ethical arguments independently of religion and thus have a chance of convincing non-believers, believers of different faiths and society at large.

We do not need to show that religions offer nothing worth listening to about ethics or values — fortunately, for that is untrue anyway. But as we have discussed, common ground on ethics cannot be founded on religious belief because we cannot find common ground among religious beliefs, even leaving aside those of no faith. By providing a sound secular foundation for values we not only provide the basis for a value-based secular life but hold out the possibility that ethics can be rescued from a relativist shouting match. We can provide a context in which common values can be found across beliefs. That will not mean an end to ethical arguments, nor should it. But it might cure a structural weakness which might otherwise threaten pluralism and take us back to some form of fanaticism. Clarity about secular values may free all of us from that fate, religious believers and secularists alike.

Satisfied mind as "the real ideal"

We have now sketched out in some detail what is involved in the ideal of satisfied mind and what is required to attain it. We have seen how satisfied mind is essential to living happily and that it involves the encouragement or development of particular inner skills which together mandate a particular approach to life and our relationships to others, close and distant. Moreover, satisfied mind is something at which we can each aim through practice, something far more within our control than any external circumstance.

We suggest that we have thus constructed a viable central aim. Living happily, with the crucial understanding that it depends on the cultivation of satisfied mind, meets all the tests we suggested for a central aim in life.

It is a rational choice. It is consistent with all that we know about ourselves as human beings, both humanistically and scientifically. It is unconditional, depending on nothing more than that we are human beings living human lives. And finally, living happily and particularly the practice of satisfied mind is, we suggest, an ideal which can inspire us and which resonates with our aspirations and our humanity. It offers a vision of ourselves living as fully and as happily as it is possible to live, together with a vision of what it might be like to live in society with others motivated by the same ideal.

This goal suggests that we can be noble because we are human, because we have rich human inner lives and understand their uniqueness in nature. It shows us that there is more to life than getting and spending, without asking us to take the supernatural on trust. It gives us a direction to travel and a purpose for our brief enough lives. It tells us that being deeply happy is not a trivial undertaking but it can be done: we can build our happiness and the way forward is to cultivate our inner skills by one means or another.

We suggest, then, that living happily with satisfied mind is a rational and worthy goal for each person to put at the centre of their lives. Nothing is <u>more</u> important, perhaps not even continued life itself. That does not of course mean that nothing else is important. We will still have a whole hierarchy (jumble!) of desires and needs each of which we will naturally strive to meet. But living happily with satisfied mind lies at the centre, the overarching motive, our own reason for everything. And thus, by our own rational choice, the pursuit of satisfied mind can become the centre and foundation of our values. It is the real deal, the real ideal.

Of course other related ideas are to be found in existing moral systems, for example in the great religions. Some offer broadly similar formulae but offer them as a way to achieve a religious goal which they place at the centre of human life. You need faith in that religious vision —faith quite independent of the attractiveness of the ethical prescription—if you are to accept such paths otherwise your adherence is incomplete or insincere. Others offer much more simple formulae — love your neighbour, for example, or do as you would be done by. These are excellent summaries or slogans but how do we make them operational, how do we apply them in detail to the complicated business of living a modern human life? Satisfied mind, as we will see later, does not give us all or easy answers but it gives us much more to work with and it offers an ideal to which any human being can relate whatever their supernatural beliefs.

Regardless of what particular aim you choose, we have suggested that the choice of and commitment to a central aim is the only way viable values can be maintained at all. The legal paradigm is a myth, emotivism leads to value nihilism, nothing else works. Values have to be organized around a central purpose in life or they do not work. We must choose <u>something</u> as our central aim or we abandon values altogether.

Your choice of the central aim in your life makes that choice the basis of your values and the foundation of your moral and (as we will argue) political choices and actions. Living happily with satisfied mind, we contend, is far and away the best candidate, perhaps even the only one. But as with all important choices—and if we are right there are none more important—we should want to see the fine print. Before anyone could contemplate a commitment with such far reaching consequences it would only be sensible to explore what the practical implications are for their everyday life, their major ethical decisions and their politics. Answering those questions with regard to satisfied mind (as we will now often abbreviate the goal for the sake of brevity) is the task to which we turn in the second half of the book.

Part 4.
Satisfied Mind and Personal Ethics

Chapter 12

Moral Reasoning

Practice and action

We turn now to explore how personal values, in other words ethics or morality, might work if based on satisfied mind. We expect after all that our values will guide us in making vital choices across our lives and we have to look at how that can be done. But personal values are as much about small actions, our attitude to everyday living and our relationships to others as about great decisions. This sits well with satisfied mind because everyday life is where we practise and use the essential skills.

In this chapter we look at important aspects of moral reasoning, the way we think about ethical matters and how the process is affected by the adoption of the satisfied mind ideal. This discussion of moral reasoning in general will pave the way to look at specific moral issues in the next chapter.

Rules of thumb

Teleological or goal-based values, the tradition into which satisfied mind fits, offer a very different approach to ethics from the one with which most of us were brought up. That approach was about rules and injunctions, thou-shallts and thou-shallt-nots. But this radical change is already implicit in our rejection of "deontology", the technical name for the myth of law.

Now the basic ethical question or stance is not "What is the law?" or "What are the rules?" but "What will best foster progress towards the central goal?". In our case, whatever actions we judge will strengthen our inner skills and promote satisfied mind will be useful and good, while actions which foster unhelpful inner habits are to be avoided.

It does not follow that rules have no uses, but their status changes. The rules we use are summaries, convenient ways to use our own or others' experience to make quick decisions about what might be best in the current instance. Laws or commandments are replaced by approximations or simplifications, "rules of thumb". They are not binding ordinances but helpful ways to work out what is likely to keep us moving in the direction we have chosen without having to ponder from first principles every time.

Such rules of thumb are also a convenient way to transmit the gist of our values to others, including young children. The trouble is that we are apt to stop at that point and mistake the rules of thumb for binding laws, forgetting the all-important idea that there is an underlying reason why these rules of thumb work but that there might be cases which the approximation simply does not cover. In those cases we have to think matters out from scratch, asking what is most helpful to and consistent with our central goal rather than trying to squeeze more pre-cision from a rule of thumb which cannot help us.

For example, a general prohibition on taking what belongs to another without consent (stealing, to you and me!) is clearly a good rule of thumb. Any other course too easily leads us for example into lack of compassion for others (and their losses), hardness or indiffer-ence about what misfortune we may cause, preoccupation perhaps with indulging our desires for external things, etc. Stealing is wrong for many reasons but ultimately because it fosters the wrong attitudes which will lead us away from satisfied mind, quite apart from the probable external difficulties that may result.

But such a general prohibition is not and cannot be a fully detailed piece of "legislation" — even leaving aside the difficulty that no one legislated it. There might indeed be circumstances in which taking what belongs to another might be the better course. Imagine someone had a weapon they intended to use to kill thousands of innocent people but it was possible for us to remove and destroy it — who would say it would be wrong to do so? The detailed circumstances of course matter greatly but at face value there are instances where the argument does not stop at a prohibition against taking what belongs to another. Exceptions are not to be lightly or easily conceded or the rule of thumb itself would become useless, but they may happen and we should expect them to happen.

Again, take the general prohibition most of us recognize against telling lies. The greatest moral philosopher of the Enlightenment[51] suggested that such a rule had to be absolute and admitted no exceptions. So if a person clearly intent on homicide asks if the intended victim is at home, we dare not lie to avert the crime. This seems strange, for effectively it makes us accessories to murder. But if the rule is a rule of thumb, a summary of experience based on what the practice of useful inner skills requires, we have less difficulty. First, we can agree that honesty is a very good general rule, not only fostering respect and kindness in ourselves but promoting trust between people. But we can also accept that there might be exceptions in which the better course might be to lie. We may miscalculate of course but here as elsewhere that is no excuse for not trying to take the right course.

On a day-to-day basis therefore we might actually proceed pretty much as if we were bound by or chose to observe certain rules which experience (or our teachers or our culture) has taught us are generally helpful. The status of such rules, however, has now changed dramatically from being binding but mysterious laws. They are rooted in our practice of inner skills, in what generally works as a way to achieve satisfied mind through the development of those inner skills. The rules are not the final word and if we are faced with a complex or difficult situation where rules conflict or are unclear we must do what we can to choose a way which will preserve or do the least harm to our skills.

The "golden rule" and others

Specific moral rules are thus just guidelines. We should not place too much weight on their exact formulation nor wonder about their fine print – again a significant departure from any idea of morality based on detailed laws. In many ways the more general such rules are the more useful they become, for we can apply them widely using common sense to interpret how they should be adapted. Only where we find ourselves stumped by circumstances do we need to consider what lies behind such rules of thumb, but then we get back to considering the foundation of our values – our central goal of satisfied mind – and what effects different courses of action may have on our attaining or retaining that goal.

In this light we might very usefully for example adopt some form of what is known as the "golden rule". In a more demanding form it runs: "Do to others as you would like them to do to you", in a weaker prohibitive form "Don't do to others what you would not like them to do to you". The golden rule is at least at old as Confucius and is found everywhere, for example in early Judaism and ancient Greek thought.[52] It encapsulates a very high if approximate standard of morality and interpersonal behaviour in a simple formula. It is not hard to see how it reflects the practice of skills like benevolence, gratitude, forgiveness and so on, so it is without doubt in close harmony with our goal. It is such a good general rule precisely because it fosters so well the skills which underpin satisfied mind.

A broadly similar general principle is to treat other people as ends and not means, or in other words not to use or exploit others to meet our own ends ("Kant's rule"). Another is to love (which surely implies to think of, feel about and behave towards) our neighbours as we do ourselves ("Christ's rule"). All these rules are very useful and any of them might point the way more clearly given particular circumstances.

Since we are treating all of them simply as rules of thumb or summaries of experience we need not worry about which is more exact or which should prevail if they should conflict, however unlikely that may be. The real source of authority is not one rule or the other but the goal which lies behind them.

Equality and humanity

These very general rules also suggest another consequence of our focus on satisfied mind. They point towards treating everyone as we treat ourselves or as we would like to be treated and therefore treating everyone equally.

Since the same central aim fits every person, satisfied mind is potentially a common goal. Everyone is equal in at least the sense that everyone might reasonably adopt this goal and this equality is the result of no further qualification beyond being human. In fact it is probably true in much more ordinary senses of living happily that everyone wants to live happily and avoid suffering so that it is no stretch to describe such a goal as a fundamental characteristic of our species. In this central respect we are certainly all equal.

In addition, the practice of treating everyone we meet equally well is a strong and very efficacious practice for several of the inner skills we need if we are to move towards satisfied mind. Of course each of us has a particular interest in developing satisfied mind for ourselves, but as we have seen that interest does not compete with others' corresponding interest in satisfied mind. My progress (for example) is likely to be enhanced rather than hindered by any assistance I can give you in your skill development. Hence both the underlying condition of being human and the practice of the skills of satisfied mind support equality in at least this respect. The golden rule, Kant's rule and Christ's rule are excellent rules of thumb which express this equality in practice.

When we come to consider political values we will look again at equality because this moral equality, strong as it is as a guide to behaviour and action, does not imply equality in everything. We know perfectly well anyway that we are not all equal in our personal gifts — for example strength, athleticism, mathematical ability or artistic talent — and it would be nonsense to insist that we are or should pretend to be. So we should be clear-headed about what is and is not implied by moral equality. It is not a question of treating everyone as identical, but of treating everyone as far as possible from the same standpoint. To treat some people as less deserving of our compassion or forgiveness or even less than human, especially if that means that we are indifferent to their lack of basic necessities, is difficult to reconcile with the practice of the inner skills we need.

Predators

One of the factors which keeps many of us from embracing a way of life that embodies such ideals is of course the fear that to live in this way leaves us vulnerable to those who don't, whom we will label generally as "predators". To live in an open hearted, benevolent way for example is perhaps to invite exploitation; to remain unattached to possessions may attract the predatory interest of those who covet ours; to treat others with kindness and compassion might leave us vulnerable to those who prefer to live by force, deception or even just indolence.

These are of course real practical dangers. But if we allow them to deflect us from living so as to develop our inner skills we are implicitly accepting that living happily is impossible unless and until everybody reaches the same understanding about what is the most rational central aim to adopt. Since that state of affairs is probably not imminent this attitude gives up on satisfied mind and the life and values it allows before we even start. It amounts to accepting that living happily is the most rational central goal but is too difficult or too impractical. We are thus forced in effect to adopt the values (or lack thereof) of the predators and therefore those are the values which will shape the lives we lead and the society we live in. The bad guys have already won.

The existence of predators is a practical problem — but only that. It should not determine our choice of a central goal. However difficult, it is by no means an absolute obstacle to an ethical approach to life, still less a theoretical refutation of satisfied mind. If developing inner skills is the best way to live because it reliably takes us closer to true happiness, the existence of predators is a danger to be recognized and dealt with by whatever strategy we can devise. But the answer is to try and solve the practical problem, not to abandon the goal.

Any danger is a call for the exercise of ingenuity. Indeed many of the structures of complex social and political life, for example criminal law and law enforcement, are more or less ingenious attempts to solve practical problems about predators. Another solution of course is to live so simply and frugally that there is nothing to attract the interest of predators, as happens in some monastic traditions. Between these poles there are many different solutions and many more to be discovered, for appropriate solutions are very specific to circumstances.

If it helps, predators could be treated like natural hazards such as storms, earthquakes or volcanos — or as dangerous with or without malicious intent, like a monkey with a machine gun. They are real dangers and certainly not to be ignored. They will always exist, for it is unlikely everyone will be so convinced by our arguments that universal benevolence breaks out! Moreover, the skills of satisfied mind have to be adopted and cultivated anew by every individual in every generation, for there is no reason at all to think they have a Lamarckian tendency to become part of "human nature" — indeed if they did, we would by now no longer need to discuss them.

But the persistence of predators offers no good reasons for changing the goal and direction of our own lives. It is understandable that someone who lives surrounded by predators might decide that being one, even being more predatory than the rest, is the best and safest course. But to make such a decision is to choose a life in which greed, violence and indifference to the suffering of others are the norm. If we are right that the development of the skills of satisfied mind is the key to living happily, such a life is doomed to failure.

Moral certainty

We often have the feeling that we should be able to get an answer to any moral question with certainty. This feeling might even lead us to reject satisfied mind because it fails to give us the level of certainty we think we need in particular cases. But this problem to a large extent mirrors problems we meet in establishing everyday facts about the external world.

Take as a light-hearted example how I know that my front door is painted blue. Well, it was blue when I looked this morning but perhaps I have mis-remembered or my wife has painted it while I have been writing. If I am in doubt I could just take a look, satisfy myself that the door is blue and that would usually be the end of the matter. But if you wanted to make things difficult you could point out that there are all kinds of tricks that can be played with light and perhaps some such trick is being played here. I eliminate that possibility and you suggest that I might be suffering from some visual aberration, some kind of colour blindness perhaps. Rule that out, and you think of something else — maybe I am dreaming, maybe I have forgotten how this shade should be classified, whatever. The point is that it is quite impossible to eliminate every possibility of error even in the most ordinary situations. Nor do we have to, because a possible anything is not an actual anything and, in particular, a possible doubt is not a doubt at all.

We can establish facts "beyond reasonable doubt" without them being "beyond all possible doubt". In practice we don't bother, we are perfectly comfortable with being 90-something percent sure. That in practice is what we call certainty — it doesn't mean there is not even a theoretical possibility of error, just that we are confident that all likely sources of doubt have been removed.

Some people are of course more cautious than others and demand higher levels of assurance. But no one gets stone-cold certainty on any empirical fact even in the most rigourous scientific contexts. Occasionally we get caught out, make a mistake or get tricked, but as a rule we are fine. Ordinary facts can often be taken for granted, or in special cases verified as more likely than not, or even, when the issue is particularly important, verified altogether beyond a reasonable doubt. Absolute certainty is a mirage, a standard we never actually apply outside mathematics — which may be a false model of knowledge anyway. If we insisted on such certainty as the essence of knowledge we would struggle to progress beyond "I think, therefore I am".[53]

When we look at values while in the grip of this false ideal of certainty, we tend to want a fully specified, all-questions-answered method here too, a decision system which is never stumped, always gives an answer and can't possibly go wrong. But if we don't even have such cosmic certainty for the most ordinary facts why should we expect it in the field of human choices? We can always be wrong and we can always meet situations which are undecidable. Sometimes we just don't know what the right thing to do is, so we have to eliminate the obviously bad and do the best we can.

It is popular in moral philosophy to produce moral dilemmas, like the tramcar (trolley) cases,[54] to show that our ordinary ways of thinking about morality are flawed. Well, so they are. But we should not conclude that the answer is available from elsewhere, for example from better rules which high theory will reveal. If we are suspicious anyway of treating morality as a set of rules we will not regard such dilemmas as requiring us to decide which rule prevails or what the detail of the rules prescribes.

With satisfied mind, moral dilemmas occur not because we don't know the detail of the rules well enough, but because it is sometimes just impossible to work out what to do for the best. Sometimes we are put in a position — especially in specially constructed philosophical examples, the kind of insoluble moral sudoku in which the puzzle has been "fixed" — in which nothing we do is conducive to peace of mind or the development of inner skills. Such cases sometimes also occur in real life, though fortunately not often. They are the stuff of genuine tragedy, because there just is no happy outcome to be found and we are reduced to finding the least bad. In the most difficult cases we cannot escape the loss of our inner peace however we act and the question may become how we can retain some shreds or find our way back towards satisfied mind. But tragedy is not the norm and we should not be put off by hypothetical cases in which we cannot be sure of the answer.

Occasional moral uncertainty comes with the territory because the territory is difficult.

Moral judgement

We should above all not conclude from occasional uncertainty that we never know what to do, nor that we are always wrong when we make a decision. We make moral judgements in an environment in which we could always be wrong and we do well to stay alert to the possibility. Just as with empirical or factual observations we can be wrong, we can misinterpret, we can miscalculate—but most of the time we are fine. Sometimes the right thing to do is clear enough and we should not be afraid to back our judgement.

On the other hand, because we know we can be wrong we need, even when our sense of being right is at its height, to remain open-minded enough to consider evidence or argument that we might have made a mistake. This caution is particularly apposite when the answer has come easily from a rule of thumb, because the underlying question is always whether we have applied such a rule appropriately to the detailed circumstances we face.

It is no accident anyway that moral and empirical "facts" share this characteristic of fallibility. Once we have rooted ethics in a central aim of living happily by developing satisfied mind, particular moral judgements become largely empirical or practical, for the moral question in any situation is what action will best strengthen (or at worst, least damage) our inner skills.

There is no violation here of the "is-ought" distinction we saw earlier because the "ought" comes clearly from our commitment to satisfied mind. The moral question in other words is not a bare "What shall we do?" but has become "What shall we do given that living happily through satisfied mind is our central aim?". The question then is how best to advance towards or preserve satisfied mind, which is a practical question in any given circumstance. So moral judgement is founded on a non-empirical commitment to satisfied mind, but given that commitment the particular questions and dilemmas we face may largely be empirical or factual.

Practical moral judgements are thus to a large extent factual judgements, just because the central aim already sets the direction of travel. Hence whatever difficulties there may be come from the general uncertainty which attaches to our empirical reasoning about the world, not from trying to tease out the implications of complicated general laws.

We don't often know all the details of any case and we rarely know all the implications of all the details. We can be and often are wrong because it is sometimes too difficult to predict accurately what the effects of an action will be, especially on our inner lives and inner skills. We have to make judgements, or "judgement calls", and our judgements may be wrong. But the ethical enterprise is to recognize that this effort is part of the task we face.

The boundaries which our values set on a particular choice can be anything from tight to very loose and distant. A common form of moral argument is to show that such boundaries are tighter than we have supposed. If, for example, I knew that the conditions of farm workers producing tea were in every case much harsher than the conditions of workers producing coffee, the knowledge might affect whether I bought and drank tea or coffee (relatively tight boundary). But absent any such consideration this choice is no more than a matter of taste (distant moral boundary if any). Any appeal based on the consequences of such a choice (the effect of my choice along with millions of others on the conditions of distant workers) must depend on establishing very detailed facts and causal chains. But the form of argument is clear enough: the attempt is to draw tighter the moral boundaries of a given choice by showing that what might seem to be a matter of mere preference actually affects others in important ways.

Thus values can operate in many different ways on our choices. The central aim is not always directly in point but what matters is to consider whether and to what extent it might be. We can regard every choice and every action as a potential opportunity to practise our inner skills. This is itself a matter of mindful living, thus both a practice and an exercise of skill. Indeed, we might expect that as our skills grow so also does our "moral sensibility", our willingness to be mindful of the consequences of our actions. Moral clarity demands that we distinguish and give precedence to how we can approach our central aim, even if that is only part of the story of how we construct our lives. No one said it would be easy!

There will be times in moral debate with ourselves or others when the answer is obvious and times when the answer is totally obscure, times when agreement with others over the right thing to do is easy and times of furious disagreement. In committing to satisfied mind as a central aim we have set a direction for our lives and a life with direction is surely more satisfying than an aimless existence. But the best way forward will not always be clear and cannot be deduced like a theorem of mathematics. Ethical argument will always be part of and remain framed by the muddy, uncertain business of human life.

Particular cases and general rules

We have seen how there may be much practical usefulness and experiential wisdom in "rules of thumb", but that rules are not the essence of values. It follows that the particular case and not the general rule is the basic unit of moral decision. That is to say, when faced with a decision we have to look closely at the particular circumstances and decide what will best serve our central aim, given the current level of inner skills we possess, given the likely ramifications of one decision rather than another, given the effects of our actions on others and as much detail of the practical circumstances as we know or can take in.

These are seldom easy matters. In particular, they are not easy to decide from the outside or from the point of view of a spectator, however closely interested. But moral judgement is not like a judicial process where we must decide how the facts fit given rules. We could perhaps say that every judgement is about applying only one rule, something like "Act so as to advance towards satisfied mind, preserve it or at least minimise damage to it". But this distorts the nature of the enterprise for the sake of using a formal model which is really not appropriate. Moral judgement is better seen as empirical judgement about what will best advance us towards satisfied mind because we recognize that only thus can we live happily in the long run.

Thus the kind of high level moral argument which tries to reach moral generalizations is not really all that helpful. We do not need generalizations to apply to particular cases, we need to look closely at the particular circumstances of the cases. The trolley car cases for example and other constructed examples are indeed difficult, but that is because they were designed that way. We could perhaps take them as demonstrations of the difficulty or even impossibility of drafting rules to cover every eventuality. But the particular case is what matters and the particular case is often unique. Generalization may have its place as the attempt to formulate helpful rules of thumb so that we can reach particular conclusions more easily and quickly but we should not mistake it for the pronouncement of moral laws.[55]

The most difficult moral problems we are likely to meet in practice may in fact be of a very different kind. Such problems involve a clash between our other objectives and our central aim. The other objective is likely to be something quite powerful to set up the clash in the first place, perhaps ambition, material wealth, sex, even in extreme cases survival. The first and greatest difficulty is to recognize and acknowledge that there is indeed a real conflict between our central objective and another strong but inconsistent objective. It is always easy to deceive ourselves that we can have it all. This is of course an aspect of mindfulness which we need to cultivate. With the conflict recognized, we can look at how if at all possible the lesser objective can be reconciled with the central objective. If it can, the way forward is clear and the dilemma resolved. If not, morality, indeed reason, requires that we forego the lesser objective. But of course we often just choose wrong, abandon our central objective and then wonder later why we are not happy!

Chapter 13

Moral Issues

The best lack all conviction

In this chapter we will look at some issues which cause or have caused wide debate and perplexity as moral problems. The point of course is not to pontificate about answers but to show how reasoning based on satisfied mind might approach such problems. Bear in mind that if some of the suggested solutions are controversial it may be my particular reasoning rather than the whole approach which is wrong. If, however, you find yourself saying "Well, of course, we all knew that!", that may show the extent to which the satisfied mind ideal supports our (your!) existing moral intuitions.

The previous chapter, particularly the emphasis on the particular case against the general rule, should have prepared us for what some might consider disappointment. We will not be able to "solve" general classes of problems and discover general laws. We can only indicate how to approach cases and the sort of considerations which need to be looked at. Since the particular case is everything, each problem may have a different answer depending on the detailed circumstances in which it is posed.

It would be ridiculous, because ultimately impossible, to try and prepare a comprehensive handbook of detailed rules of thumb covering every possible eventuality. But whereas a legal-paradigm view of ethics might see this as a failure or maybe a lack of precision or clarity, in our framework it is only to be expected. Moral issues are complex, reflecting the complexity of life and circumstances. Simplistic rules won't work.

Telling lies and breaking promises

We start with aspects of verbal honesty, for example lying — deliberately trying to make others believe something we know to be untrue or being complicit in such deception. We also include keeping and breaking promises.

Social interactions obviously depend to a very high degree on people being able to trust that what others say is true and that promises will be kept. Such hopes are regularly disappointed in practice but if we could not rely on them being fulfilled most of the time society would be impossible — indeed dishonesty itself is only possible because we rely on honest behaviour so much of the time. So telling the truth is an essential glue of society and should be encouraged and fostered for that practical reason alone.

However, there is as we might expect a further, moral dimension which emerges when we question why someone might tell a lie or break a promise. If the intention is to harm or to gain an advantage at the expense of another then the deception will inevitably be at odds with the good practice of inner skills. It might foster inner habits of greed, perhaps, or malice, hatred or ruthless self advancement. It will be inconsistent with compassion and benevolence to the other person, or with non-attachment to whatever we seek to gain. In these cases, dishonesty has a corrosive effect on the inner life whatever its effects in the external world, forming or strengthening unhelpful habits which do not foster satisfied mind but on the contrary lead to a hardening of the heart. So dishonesty is not just an external or social problem but a threat to satisfied mind.

It is possible on the other hand that we might deceive out of compassion for another — to spare them bad news for example, or simply to make them feel better with a little mild flattery without intending to gain anything for ourselves. The motive here makes a huge difference to the inner consequences — we are less likely to encourage unhelpful habits and may well encourage helpful ones. We are being mindful of the effect our words have on others and trying to benefit them, make them feel better or spare them pain. We do not act out of (or encourage in ourselves) hatred, or malice, or greed.

In everyday life we may often tell such "white lies" to our friends and loved ones without causing or risking harm to them, to ourselves or to third parties, and in so doing we may indeed be acting well. There are nevertheless clear dangers in "white lies". If we encourage someone to believe falsehoods even with the purest of motives we must surely take responsibility for the consequences of our deception. If we depart from the truth even with good motives we have to be mindful that the consequences may ripple beyond what we expect. So we take a risk which we have to weigh carefully. In most ordinary circumstances there is little danger, admittedly, but being reckless of possible harm to others is not a helpful habit to foster.

Again it is easy to see from a satisfied mind perspective why keeping promises is generally a good practice. But, for example, a promise may be made in good faith but circumstances may change so that the promise may be impossible to keep, or the cost (by whatever measure is relevant) of keeping it may be vastly higher than expected, even threatening satisfied mind. It may not be dishonest to break such a promise, but it is hard to say that we have no responsibility for the consequences of so doing. Particularly if someone has relied on that promise it may be that we should at least mitigate the effects of excusing ourselves from it. Once again particular circumstances are of the essence, but we can see that while the keeping of promises is an essential rule of thumb there might be circumstances which excuse breaking a promise.

This brief discussion shows that the moral dimensions of verbal honesty turn out to be quite complex, involving awareness of the motives from which we act, consequences actual and foreseeable and an assessment of the risks of harming others. We should perhaps expect nothing less. It seems at least that the idea of satisfied mind as a central aim is up to the task of reflecting this complexity and avoids the temptation of jumping to simplistic conclusions.

Abortion

We look now at something much more difficult, the deliberate ending of a pregnancy for whatever reason. The subject is notoriously divisive, even leading in some cases to murder in the name of protecting the unborn. Broadly speaking religious ethics has tended to take the view that abortion is wrong in all circumstances, while secular views have tended to be more liberal, up to the point where some regard abortion as a morally neutral decision. But if we accept that there is no absolute law we can fall back on, how might we think about a subject like this given that strong emotions are engaged even in the abstract and even more in actual cases?

For the purpose of this discussion only we make the assumption that the law of the land is not an issue. This allows us to consider only the moral aspects of the primary decision itself without considering any further complications which may arise from law-breaking. Of course there is a separate and more general issue about the extent to which law should enforce or permit ethical results, but that is not the question we consider here.[56]

We start from the understanding that each person is responsible for their own satisfied mind and the development of their inner skills. The particular circumstances of each case are at the heart of the issue, which as we have noted makes generalization difficult and even unhelpful. The full circumstances are generally appreciated if at all only by the person who directly faces the decision, in this case the pregnant woman. In our framework, the decision is not a matter of construing rules nor of balancing rights, for example those of the woman against the unborn child, nor even the rights of the two potential parents. It is a matter of a particular woman examining deeply and honestly what course of action is most consistent with her living happily, with the added understanding that her inner life is what is paramount in her chances of living happily. This balance has to be found, often in difficult circumstances, under pressures of all kinds and often without disinterested advice, without any assurance that she will get the right answer or be free of regret about whichever course she chooses. But that is what moral responsibility entails.

To terminate any pregnancy deliberately is a responsibility likely to weigh heavily on the inner life of anyone who so chooses. Whatever else it may be, this decision is not therefore morally neutral but surely an issue of the greatest ethical moment.[57] Thus we might expect that a woman even considering such a course would be faced with major pressures, including reasons which make the termination seem to her one of two evils to be weighed. This is the essence of a tragic situation, in which no course of events leaves the inner life unmarked.

The idea that satisfied mind is central entails that the focus of the decision lies in the woman's inner life. A woman might thus honestly decide in all the circumstances that termination is more conducive to satisfied mind than continuation. For example, where the woman's own survival or capacity was threatened (perhaps by ill health, conflict or social circumstances) termination might seem to her the compassionate course, not least because compassion in this context as always includes compassion towards herself but also because the happiness or even survival of the unborn might be unlikely for the same reasons.

The often discussed example of a pregnancy created by rape might (again we cannot say in the abstract) be a case where the woman feels she is not capable of loving the child she will bear and that the inner life burden of that incapacity is too great for her. But a different person might come to a different conclusion. These are just examples, not "permitted categories". The decision in every case is very particular because it reasonably takes into account the inner skills, including the emotional state and resilience for example, of the woman making it. These are matters <u>only she</u> can weigh and judge. It is not so much a matter of the woman having the right to choose, as the old slogan suggested, as the woman having the responsibility to choose.

No two cases are identical, which is why general rules are not helpful and even broad rules of thumb break down in these most difficult cases. Individual cases are not about formulating or applying rules. Each of us faces ethical decisions from a unique perspective, namely our own inner life and the state of our capabilities and skills at the time of the decision. Even though we share the common aim of satisfied mind we have a unique responsibility to find our own way to that goal. To judge another person is always an exercise in ignorance. For those outside the crucible of such a major choice as this, the only helpful attitude is compassion.

Assisted suicide

Assisting suicide is still highly controversial in most countries but, to be clear, we mean to include only cases in which a person has decided and communicated that they wish their own life to end but are unable to end it without help from another. How this state of affairs should be evidenced and what safeguards should be put in place to prevent abuse, given that the principal party obviously cannot answer after the event, raises very difficult practical questions which legislators would have to solve. To write rules which at their heart are mostly about motives rather than actions is an unenviable task and might be so difficult as to preclude any change because of the risks involved. But in our discussion we can adopt the luxury of assuming the legal work is done and that whatever is ethically acceptable is within the law. So we consider only the ethical question of whether and when it is acceptable to assist someone who genuinely desires to end their own life.

Some people sincerely believe that a person has a duty to suffer until death overcomes them naturally. But how could such a duty arise if laws and rights in general are not part of our moral framework? On the other hand, to encourage a person to die or accept death because the "helper" stood in some way to gain, even if the gain was only the ending of a heavy burden of care, would not be in keeping with the practice of the inner skills. Such an act would be an act of selfishness, involve harm to another for personal benefit or at the very least involve a radical failure of compassion.

In some circumstances, however, for example if the person suffered from an incurable and progressive disease which had moved to the point where the person could look forward only to extreme pain or loss of dignity, the desire to die might be a rational acceptance of the facts. The test might broadly be, would the person kill themselves if they were able to achieve it and would it be reasonable for them to do so? Of course, anyone asked to help would want to be very sure, for example, that there was really no hope for the person to escape their illness or condition and that the request was not the effect, for example, of temporary fatigue, depression or a sense of being a burden to others. Any such factor which could be relieved in other ways would make the desire to die a mistaken response to the situation. But if the desire to die is itself reasonable and not the result of such factors then, however hard it might be, to assist them would be to show them the greatest kindness. Assistance would in fact be the hardest but best practice of compassion, putting aside our own feelings and discomfort for the sake of their release.

Nevertheless, even if it is clear that the desire to die is real and justified by the situation, it is entirely understandable that anyone might shy away from fulfilling such a request, not only because of our natural respect for life in general but because of emotional attachment to the person who wishes to die. Many of us would find it impossible to help for different reasons. Some tasks are beyond us at any stage of our lives, some requests are just too hard or too shocking to manage. If, for example, someone was asked for help but believed that to die when one chooses is always unacceptable, even if one accelerates the end by only a short interval of suffering, that in itself would be a circumstance which changed the balance of the situation.

So we should not assume a duty to help any more than we should assume a duty not to help. Once again we have a responsibility to weigh the particular circumstances with great care and to reach a con-clusion which seems to accord most with our own practice of satisfied mind. There is no guarantee that we will get it right but we cannot hide behind rules. To take responsibility for our own happiness, which properly understood is to take moral responsibility for our actions, is no light thing.

Sex

It says something not altogether flattering about our society that "morality" often means nothing more than the observance of rules about sexual activity. When newspapers for example question the "morals" of a public figure they usually mean that he or she has been caught in some sexual transgression rather than that their honesty or good faith are in doubt.

More distressing is that we also find a focus amounting in some cases to obsession with sex and sexuality from and within many reli-gions. Nearly all religions have strict rules about when and with whom sexual activity is allowed, and some seem to regard sex as a necessary evil which must be contained at all costs, often and unfairly by imposing particularly strict rules on the conduct and treatment of women.

The obvious reason why sex so concerns religious authorities is its sheer power as a motive for action. If any motive is powerful enough to distract people from religious observance or from a focus on the here-after, sex is right up there along perhaps with greed. Thus the powerful pleasures of sex tie peoples' attention to this world and undermine what religions see as a more proper focus. At worst the sexual motive is so strong that it can override every kind of self-restraint and lead to violence, dishonesty, broken promises, a complete breakdown of all rules of conduct.

A more sinister reading is that if this powerful motive can be controlled and regulated great power falls into the hands of the regulators themselves,[58] while the flouting of such rules can be cast as an act of rebellion against authority which the regulators may be glad to punish to show their authority, or perhaps must punish if they are to retain control.

For non-believers it is sometimes hard to grasp why a Supreme Being should be so minutely and specifically concerned with the bedroom antics of human beings, or with our unsuccessful struggles with desires which that same Being has instilled. But in any case a prohibitive stance against sexual activity depends on some form of the legal paradigm. When we abandon that paradigm the idea that there are preexisting sexual rules which must be obeyed regardless of circumstance or consequence is left behind as well.

Insofar as we can formulate any "rules of thumb" in this area they must surely concentrate on harmlessness. To harm another to satisfy any desire cannot be consistent with the development of satisfied mind, whether the desire is related to sex or something else. It is uncompassionate, it fosters contempt and other negative emotions, it fosters obsession with our desire at the expense of others and so on. Clearly non-consensual activity of any kind falls under this general heading. So does sexual activity with those whose consent is for any reason questionable, including those who are too young, lacking in understanding or coerced in any way. But harm may also involve knowingly exposing another to risk, very obviously of pregnancy and its consequences for example, or of STDs, but also of harm for example from family or community if their activity becomes known. In some cases harm may be so likely or foreseeable that the consent of the other person may not be enough to override responsibility for it. Kant's rule of thumb to treat others as ends and not means seems tailor-made for this area.

The sensitivity to consent which harmlessness implies also excludes dishonesty or deception, which might lead one party to engage in sexual activity based on a belief which the other party knows is false. Dishonesty is difficult to justify in any context as we have seen but it is perhaps the most common sexual fault. If we have a legitimate interest at all in the sexual activities of politicians, for example, it is surely because of what their behaviour tells us about their honesty and thus other aspects of their character.

As for contraception, still regarded in some quarters (rather astonishingly?) as a moral issue, we know that little humans need a great deal of care for many years. The quality of the relationship with parents is a huge influence not only on how a person develops but ultimately their chances of living with satisfied mind. Accidents happen, but to start a life out of recklessness seems to be the opposite of mindful. But insistence on the possibility of reproduction on the other hand seems to suggest a prejudice that sexual activity is somehow intrinsically unwholesome and needs the excuse of reproduction to justify it. Certainly sex and reproduction are biologically linked, but so are eating and nutrition and very few insist that food taken for sheer pleasure is unwholesome. A perfectly responsible attitude consistent with the practice of inner skills is surely to embrace reproduction when the circumstances are appropriate but to take reasonable precautions against it otherwise.

It is always unfortunate if a person's sexual life dominates their consciousness to the extent that sexual gratification becomes their central aim in life, because then happiness and peace are likely to elude that person. In particular, promiscuity is perhaps more likely to be harmful than commitment just because there is a greater risk of dishonesty, deception or carelessness in the treatment of others. But some people may scrupulously manage to avoid those risks.

It is not clear, finally, why sexual orientation should give us any kind of concern if we are free from doctrines about sexual activity being governed by specific laws. Desire, any desire, is a problem if it torments us, if we cannot find a way to be at peace because of it or if it drives us to inflict harm on others. But the nature or direction of that desire is surely irrelevant otherwise.

Thus the hallmarks of an approach to sexual activity consistent with a commitment to satisfied mind are honesty, consent, the avoidance of harm, caution about desire tipping over into obsession and responsibility about reproduction. In other words, as long as the activity is fully consistent with the inner skills and all that they entail, it is enjoyable and life-enhancing. But you knew that!

Violence

We know that humans are capable of great violence towards each other. We may hope that by fostering kindness and compassion towards others we may reduce anger and hatred and become less violent ourselves, in our minds as well as our actions. But realistically we know that not everyone will accept or live by such values so that occasions may still arise in which others are violent towards us – war, brutal authority and criminal activity being the obvious examples.

There is nothing in the development of kindness or compassion, or for that matter forgiveness, which suggests that one should submit or succumb to any attack. The point of such development as we have seen is to avoid or lessen hatred, anger and other negative emotions. Hard as it might be not to experience such emotions (and fear, of course) when under attack, our goal remains to minimize them. But that goal does not prohibit defence. Indeed, negative emotions are just as likely to arise if we do not defend ourselves.

Dealing with a natural disaster, for example, might test our external strength and external skills to the limit in much the same way as dealing with human violence, but without the same tendency to feel anger or hatred. Action involved in defending against, escaping or avoiding attack does not generally require hatred or anger and our response need not be weakened by their absence. Thus even with adrenaline flowing there is no intrinsic conflict between genuine self-defence and the ideal of satisfied mind. What matters is the attitude we take towards the attacker, so that we deal with the threat but try to avoid negative emotion, however hard that might be.

Furthermore if attack is inevitable, as for example in the case of war, a pre-emptive attack may reasonably be judged to be the best form of self-defence—it depends critically on the circumstances. In the right circumstances, honestly assessed, there need be no conflict between such an attack and values based on satisfied mind. However, to seek violent confrontation because of hatred and/or anger, even if faced with a brutal state or a powerful enemy, is a different matter. In such a case the negative emotions are encouraged and even harnessed and the ideal is abandoned. The real motive for an attack is thus crucial to its consistency with values based on satisfied mind.

It sometimes happens, again war is the example, that harm to innocent people is the only way to save many more lives. Such a situation is genuinely tragic, in the sense we have already met that there is no answer which can leave the decision-makers without regret if they are fully mindful of their responsibility. Satisfied mind might be hard to reach for someone who must take such a decision, for rules cannot take away their responsibility and there is no good answer in such cases, only the least bad. That in itself may be a good reason for avoiding both positions of power and violent conflict, because values may be early casualties in both cases. For this reason and others the person who seeks satisfied mind will accept power reluctantly and only for the good of others. Sadly, this rules out most professional politicians.

Extreme scarcity

Every day in some part of the world survival itself is threatened by extreme resource shortage. Such shortages have always occurred and blighted lives but as the population of the world grows many believe such shortages may grow also, particularly shortages of water. If climate change simultaneously were to make agriculture more difficult in some areas perhaps food would also become more scarce. Mere survival might then become problematic for many individuals and even whole societies.[59]

We do not have to accept this as the most likely future scenario to take it seriously as a possibility. Such a scenario might call into question many of the rules and arrangements we take for granted in modern life, for example the rules surrounding property rights. If someone is starving to death or must watch their family starve, the idea that property rights forbid them to take food is likely to carry far less weight with them. Thus increased violence between haves and have-nots might be inevitable. Again, what in times of plenty may be accepted as minor injustices of property distribution, not worth disrupting or challenging society over, might appear insupportable if they became matters of life and death in times of scarcity. This indeed is why wise governments resort to rationing in such times. But what if the unacceptable distribution is between states or regions? Force and violence of many kinds, including war, are highly likely to be the result.

What have values to say about such a fight for life? In practice perhaps values and reason would simply be replaced by force. Under such pressure we might just become savage predators, grabbing from those unable to protect themselves. In our fear we might well forget compassion. We might tell ourselves that compassion is for times of plenty but if we did, that would be to abandon values and accept a basic struggle for survival, competition to the death. It would be natural enough, but such a collapse of values would be precisely the collapse of civilization and a descent into barbarism.

But this is not the only path, we would still have choices. It would still be true that satisfied mind is of central and paramount importance for any human being. There are moreover many practical adjustments which could be made, if we were willing, to meet changed circumstances rather than descending into valueless anarchy or (more likely) a ruthless oligarchy of some kind. It is one thing for example to take a share of something which leaves a neighbour (whether a person or a state) with sufficient, even though his property rights are infringed, quite another to take an amount that condemns him to starve. The task, difficult as it is, would be to devise new practical rules about property and distribution which could hold some kind of balance between the strong and the weak and which at the same time respect our deeper values. That of course would be impossible for those who think of existing property rights as the deepest values.

Thinking about such an extreme scenario in the abstract is not even remotely likely to produce practical answers to all the issues we might face if it came about, but it is useful to illuminate our thinking about values today. Two points stand out.

In the first place, it becomes even clearer that survival is not in itself a value and may even run contrary to living by values. This does not mean that survival is not a strong instinct or even an important aim, but if it becomes our central aim and determines how we behave toward others it may actually be dehumanizing. How we live is ultimately more important than how long we live, and a commitment to this idea is at the heart of all thinking about values and maybe even of being human, living with awareness of our mortality.

Second, thinking about extreme scarcity raises questions about our attitudes to property, possessions and the needs of other people which may help us think about how we live in easier times. This is a subject to which we return when we consider political values in later sections.

Blame and evil

For many people culpability and blame are at the heart of morality. If, however, morality is about adjusting my own conduct to develop the habits of my own inner life it is hard to see why blaming others and particularly labelling them as evil is important. In most cases blame is nothing but an emotional reaction I direct against the person responsible for an action. This is understandable perhaps but not helpful to my own satisfied mind. It is rather as if we said: "I do not understand how they could have done that and so the only explanation I can fall back on is that they are somehow alien."

It is of course practically important to identify threats, for example from people who are dangerous or not to be trusted, but such warnings can be treated as factual and do not have to carry implications of guilt and blame. To say someone has behaved or is likely to behave in a way of which I need to be wary is a practical judgement: to go further and blame that person requires a great deal more information about their motivation and why they behave as they do. In any case, anyone who behaves so badly that they compromise their own prospects of satisfied mind is acting against their own true best interest, whether through misguided choice, ignorance or lack of skill. Hence compassion as well as forgiveness may often be more relevant in these circumstances than blame.

A related question is whether it is useful to retain evil as a category. We might note that our secular values generate no "problem of evil", the difficulty which some theologies encounter in explaining why a benign and omnipotent god allows evil to exist at all. There is no prior presumption that humans will be benign and the natural world may be presumed to be indifferent or value-neutral. But still, are not some acts, or some people, so far removed from what we have identified as the rational central aim and the necessary means of pursuing it that evil is the only proper way to describe them?

Certainly there are actions which are so harmful or so difficult to understand that no other category seems adequate. There are even aims people adopt (like the extreme political ideologies of the twentieth century) based on or supported by hatred for some group. These views may entail such harm or cruelty that most of us struggle to understand how their proponents could possibly believe them. There are strategies of destruction or cruelty which people adopt (like terrorism) because they calculate these methods will further whatever aims they have adopted. There are goals which may not be harmful in themselves (for example wealth or power) but which people pursue so obsessively and ruthlessly that they cause misery. There are also doubtless people who just like harming others, who actually enjoy cruelty, perhaps because it makes them feel powerful, although we can often regard that tendency as pathological. There is no reason to think we can eliminate such behaviours or beliefs or that they will ever disappear from the world.

All of these instances certainly involve people who are best avoided or contained and their actions prevented if at all possible. If that is all we choose to mean by "evil" it is to that extent no more than a synonym for "highly dangerous", and we can easily agree that there are many people who qualify for that label. Such people distort external circumstances to such an extent they make it difficult for all but exceptional levels of inner skill to cope, so that the danger posed may be a general threat to satisfied mind as well as a physical danger. The process of dealing with the threat, especially if it occurs on a large scale, may even make some compromise of our own values inevitable, giving us a tragic choice.

But the label of "evil" usually carries more baggage than that, a definite exhortation to blame and condemn. To categorize actions or people as evil is usually to encourage ourselves and others towards hatred, a defensive hatred in this case but still an emotion which makes satisfied mind more difficult. The label is at best an expression of disgust and of course we need ways at least to express such negative emotions. But the label tells us nothing useful beyond warning us away.

It may also be lazy from a story perspective. Having labelled someone as evil it may seem we have finished, we need make no further effort to understand their motives or the other causes of their actions. At best, the different examples we have listed (and no doubt there are many more) are not all the same and it may be important to distinguish between them. At worst, the label may tempt us into declaring such people inhuman, thus excluding them from ethical concern and reducing the issue to one of pest control — itself a classic move of "evil" regimes. Of course we may understand much and still conclude that we and others need to be protected from the danger this person presents, or we may gather every fact we can and still be mystified by their actions. But we can rarely claim that the label "evil" adds much to the story and it never tells the whole story.

Part 5.
Capitalism Is Not Enough

Chapter 14

Values and Economics

The revenge of Marx

Today, after the centrally planned economic system of the Soviet Union has collapsed and consumerism fed by private capital has become an accepted model of economic organization even in the remaining communist great power, capitalism rules the world. Despite the occasional and severe disruptions capitalist societies experience, this form of economic organization is unchallenged except for the marginal protests of the dispossessed.

The reality of everyday Western politics for example is that the needs of businesses prevail, maybe as long as the most extreme predatory behaviour is kept either within decent bounds or at least hidden. It is taken for granted that politics is largely about economics, that what matters most politically is indeed the organization and mobilization of money, goods and labour. The success of every society is measured by its economic success or even more crudely by its economic output. All other political goals, despite the occasional piety about tradition or religion or "higher values", are secondary to economic success.

We might regard this in one sense as the revenge of Marx. Marxism itself is widely (and rightly) discredited, not only for its economic failure but for its failure to predict accurately how societies would develop and even more for the crimes committed in its name. Yet it seems now to be accepted on nearly all sides that economic success is the supreme political value and thus that the organizing principles of society are and should be economic, precisely as Marx insisted.

Almost any behaviour can now be justified on the grounds that it leads to a favourable economic outcome. Social and educational opportunities are judged by their contribution to economics and economic opportunity. Even people become valued primarily for the market value of their economic contribution. The values that stem from taking economic success as the central aim of society filter down into personal behaviour so that personal values also become organized around external material goals, for example around professional

success, the accumulation of wealth, or the attainment of specific consumption goals — house, car, status spending, et cetera.

In Marxism personal values were downgraded and subjected to the
service of the cause. But something of the same has happened to us
with capitalism. If we are not careful personal values become little
more than manners or conventions while actions taken to secure profit
and growth are justified whatever their human cost. The world is per-
ceived as an economic jungle where it is simply natural that the predators survive and the weak perish. This is not the attitude of every
business, of course, but it happens often enough.

Yet in the first place it is surely obvious, as we have discussed, that
the organization of our <u>personal</u> lives around economic aims is a huge
mistake. If we put economics at the centre of our lives we lose our
humanity and take risks with our happiness. This is not as we have
seen to deny the importance and validity of personal economic aims,
simply to question whether it is rational to install such aims as the
<u>central</u> guiding principle of our lives.

Economic outcomes or the attainment of specific material goals
depend so much on circumstances beyond our control that we must
always be prepared to reshape our economic aims in accordance with
what is possible. For example, the goal of owning and paying for a
home, for many people the cornerstone of their material ambitions, can
easily be thwarted by natural disasters, financial crises or personal
tragedy. No single economic goal can be sustained through every
possible eventuality. Even more clearly, we all respond to certain key
events in our lives by reassessing and changing our economic priorities.
If we or someone close to us suffer an accident or a major illness, for
example, or even if by contrast we have some life-changing piece of
good fortune, our priorities change and what seemed previously to be
of the utmost importance to our financial and economic well-being may
suddenly pale into insignificance.

Capitalism and social values

Economic goals thus do not work well as the central aim of individual
lives. But could they still make sense as the central aim of societies or
perhaps governments?

In practice businesses collectively — "Business" if there is such a
homogeneous constituency — are often powerful enough to set the aims
of society just by insisting on the pursuit of their aims. They set the
stage for so much of our lives that it is hard to evade their influence.
But while Business may in practice be powerful it is far from clear in
principle why it should be allowed to set the goals for society as a
whole. A business is no more than a subgroup within society with no

intrinsic right to dominate other groups by setting the aims of society. If such groups are able to dominate it is perhaps because we have had no coherent alternative goal to set against theirs.

As for governments, we might assume that government is in principle pursuing goals which are thought to be of benefit to the people. This is obviously not always true but is generally taken to be the foundation of a democratic government. Any such government must surely align its goals with the common goal of the people, if such can be found.

This is a subject to which we will turn in detail later, to explore the political consequences of satisfied mind being a widely held individual goal. But if the people ask for nothing more than bread and circuses, in other words the pursuit of material success and diversion, that is all they are likely to get. Values will take a poor second place. If the people had a better idea, an idea about values and the basis of human existence which could stand up to consumerism and materialism and show how and why they fall short of offering us the essence of human life, such values might stand a chance of pervading government and harnessing power.

We might begin to see capitalism—and for that matter, other economic systems—not as systems of values in themselves or even systems which generate values, but just as more or less practical ways to organize the making of things. Values as we have seen have a different origin in our common humanity and our search for meaning and fulfilment in our lives, which is embodied in the ideal of satisfied mind.

We suggest, then, that economic success, consumerism and material well-being have come to be accepted as the central aim of society simply because a secular common goal, based on a rational, secular central aim which gives ethical direction to the lives of individuals, has not been properly articulated. Once this task is even attempted the absurdity of economic goals being the dominant, central goals of society becomes obvious. Again, this does not imply that economic goals or material success are irrelevant or unimportant to the lives of societies or individuals, simply that they are not central. They do not "trump" all other aims.

The other leg

We certainly do not need, or even wish, to argue that, for example, private enterprise, economic freedom, efficient resource allocation and other beneficial elements of capitalism are to be avoided or proscribed. Capitalism is still the best system we know, certainly it contains the best elements we know, to secure for everyone the benefits of innovation, efficient use of resources and potential abundance. No other known way of organizing economic life comes close.

But economic life is not the whole or even the centre of human life, that much we hope we have succeeded in reinforcing. Thus capitalism on its own is not enough, unless we are after all willing to say that producing and consuming goods and services are all or even the centre of what we are about. If something else is at the centre of our concerns then our economic needs should be balanced against, indeed subordinated to, the needs of this central goal. As individuals we will still strive and work to secure our economic security and even comfort, of course. But we can recognize that, important as this goal is, there is a more important and more central one. As members of society we will likewise seek progress, innovation and growth where appropriate, but with the recognition that if there is more to our individual lives, there must be more to our collective lives.

It is a mistake, then, to think that the demands of economic life in general or capitalism in particular should determine the values of individuals in their personal lives. It is equally a mistake to think that capitalism provides some overarching values for society. Capitalism does not set values at all, it is a tool for getting things done – powerful and brilliant when wielded successfully, but no more than a tool. We would be foolish to throw away such a tool, but equally foolish if we allowed it to dictate what we should want or how we should live.

At the very least we might say that society needs another leg to stand on, a balance for the organizing influence of economics in general and capitalism in particular. That other leg needs to be provided by our values. Capitalism on its own is not enough.[60]

We start now to look at what this might mean for society and specifically for the two activities which dominate it, namely economics and politics. For economics the main point is already made, that values must stand outside economics because economics tells us how to get things done, not what we should be doing. In the remainder of this Part we consider some further aspects of how values might affect our economic life. We will look for this purpose at work, enterprise and markets. Then we go on to consider the vital question of political values and how they relate to personal values based on satisfied mind.

Chapter 15

Work

Alienation

Work, for most of us and for a large part of our lives, is how we spend most of our waking hours. For a lucky few work is a vocation, something we might do for its own sake even if it brought no material reward. But for most of us it is simply what we do to obtain first the necessities and then perhaps some of the luxuries of life.

But if my central and paramount aim in life is the development of satisfied mind I must surely pursue that aim in or at work just as much as in any other sphere of life—no other course makes any sense at all, especially when work takes up so much of life. Satisfied mind does not preclude having separate, subsidiary work goals but if I leave my central goal at the door of the workplace it is as if I had two separate lives with different central goals.

It is simply no use spending my leisure time practising mindfulness and kindness (for example) only to spend my working hours in activity so frantic that I became angry and upset at the slightest provocation, or beating down those around me to gain preferment or advantage. Half a step forward, two steps back. Work is so important a part of our lives that we need to find ways to make it part of the practice and application of inner skills. Satisfied mind must at least be sought in our work, otherwise any commitment to satisfied mind as the centre of our lives is hollow.

But, for many, "satisfied mind" does not come close to describing their experience of work! Whether it is the nature of the task itself (arduous, monotonous, dirty, stressful) a consequence of working arrangements (bureaucracy, seemingly pointless rules, the arrogance or stupidity of authority) or simply our own dislike of what we find to do, many people do not enjoy or find fulfilment in their work.

Thus we find the phenomenon of <u>alienation</u> from work and more broadly from a life based on work. Many people feel that work is wasting their lives and their talents, that they pay a high price for their cash—and they are the lucky ones! Others live under the stress of worrying about whether they will have any work today or in the near future, so that their ability to pay their way is always under threat. Still others live with the cold certainty that they have no job and therefore no way to earn what they would like to make their lives more comfortable.

Alienation is a common experience in the modern world and there have been many attempts to explain it, the best known being the Marxist view that it arises from the theft by capitalists of the value workers create.[61] But in the context of satisfied mind alienation can be simply explained as a separation or even conflict between the goals we set or accept at work and our central goal of satisfied mind.

This may come about because we have not formulated or are not clear about a central aim at all, let alone satisfied mind. The pressures and goals of work then force us to question what our lives are really "about". But it can also occur because we recognize satisfied mind as our central aim but forget or must put it aside when we are at work. Work thus becomes meaningless in the context of what really matters to us. Because work dominates our external lives, those lives themselves may come to seem meaningless and we become alienated both from work and perhaps from life itself, losing ourselves in distractions as mindless as possible.

What, however, is the alternative? What might it be like to live so that our central aim remains relevant in our working lives, so that the time we spend in our work is not divorced from the development of satisfied mind, so that we both practise and apply our inner skills at work?

It cannot mean, for example, that we waft about at work in some sort of benevolent trance, or that we give away the goods we make or sell because that seems the kindest thing to do! Such a caricature is a misunderstanding about how a central goal relates to other goals. The central goal precludes only lesser goals which <u>conflict</u> with it. Earning our keep, being useful, performing necessary tasks well and efficiently (for example) do not in themselves conflict with satisfied mind and may well help us towards it. It is only when (for example) efficiency or gain or workplace politics become central and override our concern with satisfied mind, or lead us to treat other people as things, that they become harmful or alienating.

"Normal" work

Thus work, like all other external activities, is part of the context in which we pursue our central goal. At the same time what we do at work must be driven and bounded by the values we know to be essential to that central goal.

Work is part of the context because whether it's hitting a rock, a nail, a ball, a sheet of metal or a keyboard, work is an opportunity to pursue satisfied mind by looking for and taking advantage of opportunities to practise our inner skills. Productive work which takes care of our external needs and those of our dependents is not in itself a distraction from pursuing satisfied mind, it is an opportunity to practise. Indeed, since it is an acceptance of responsibility for meeting our own external needs, work is an excellent practice in itself.

Among other things work relieves others of any burden in supplying our needs, whether through kindness and good neighbourliness or through a welfare system. There may of course be unavoidable reasons why it is impossible for us to contribute — illness, age, lack of skill or opportunity — but in the absence of such reasons, to refuse to work is to make demands on others, making their external conditions that much more difficult. To refuse to work for no other reason than disinclination is to place a burden on others incompatible with being fully compassionate and mindful of their welfare.

Work is bounded, however, by the demands of our central goal because there are actions we cannot take without the risk of eroding our essential inner skills. The vigorous pursuit of work-related goals is fine as long as what is required does not conflict with our central goal. But if that point of conflict is ever reached the central goal should prevail — because that's what being central means.

Pursuing satisfied mind may obviously cause us to shy away from certain types of work because of the adverse effects on our inner life and skills. But for the most part it does not dictate what job we should do. We do what we can or what we must depending on the external opportunities which present themselves. For the most part our values will dictate the <u>way</u> we do what we do, the motives we have and the way we choose to act when we have a choice. In particular they dictate the way we deal with other people, whether employees, employers, customers, suppliers or neighbours.

Our attitudes to other people are the essence of business ethics as well as the key to avoiding alienation at work. With work, as with all external activity, it's often not what you do, it's the way that you do it.

Work and hardship

Sometimes, however, the only work available to someone involves real hardship — it is disproportionately dangerous perhaps, or degrading, exhausting, poorly paid or run by people who lead through aggression and instilled fear. How can such activity be combined with the development of satisfied mind?

With great difficulty, surely, yet this is the plight of millions of people. In the worst cases the question might even be asked whether life without the resources this work provides is really worse than enduring the work itself. But sometimes the only choice is an inner one, between hating and resenting the work on one hand, or on the other finding ways to make it as close as possible to being tolerable. We might cultivate an attitude which finds what positives there might be in doing the work, including importantly the satisfaction of providing means to sustain life and family. This is not only a way to advance satisfied mind but an approach to enduring the hardship the work imposes.

This will sound glib of course, especially from someone sitting comfortably at a computer, but it is not meant to imply that such a task could possibly be easy. We might add that it is hard to see how profiting from requiring others to work in such conditions could be in tune with practising satisfied mind, which suggests that expecting people to work in such conditions is unethical or immoral. But that is not the issue we are considering at this point.

Satisfied mind as we have seen is not about a passive approach to external conditions but an active approach to the inner life. Like slavery, which it may closely resemble, harsh work imposed by economic necessity can at best be endured, and even to endure it requires a high level of inner skill. But this is how the world is, until we change it.

The worst external circumstances call for the highest levels of inner skill, which is doubly unfortunate for such circumstances often fall on those who have been given the least opportunity to develop such skill. That is why we should all be concerned that such conditions exist at all, rather than simply being thankful if they do not apply to us. But even if circumstances make satisfied mind remote or difficult to achieve they do not make it irrelevant or impossible. Satisfied mind remains the most rational central aim even in the harshest conditions. To maintain the goal may even be in itself an act of defiance, a refusal to abandon humanity despite conditions which threaten to degrade us.

Chapter 16

Business and Enterprise

Enterprise and profit

Enterprise is a form of work, a rather special form which creates rather than accepts an opportunity to provide for material needs and which may also benefit others by providing them with work opportunities. For both reasons, and absent any particular reason to the contrary, enterprise is to be welcomed and even applauded as a wholesome and helpful aspect of human activity.

A commercial enterprise needs to make a profit and without it cannot remain viable for very long. Even if an enterprise is not commercial ("not for profit") a surplus of some kind, however small, is the only way to avoid perpetual subsidy — and subsidies we know tend not to be perpetual. We can easily conclude therefore that there is nothing intrinsically unethical about profit. It is simply a necessary condition for the continuation of any self-sustaining economic activity.

It does not of course follow that enterprise or the making of profit are free from ethical restraints. On the contrary, since enterprise like any work is a key human activity we would expect it to conform to values based on satisfied mind, so profit seeking should always remain ethical in that sense. Profit making is good if — but only if — it remains within the bounds set by our values.

However, an enterprise itself obviously cannot seek to develop satisfied mind because it is not a human being and has no inner life. But any enterprise is the work activity either of an individual or people acting together, so we can specify as the boundary of ethical behaviour in business that the enterprise should be so conducted that everyone involved can behave in a way consistent with satisfied mind. Any other standard after all would require someone in the enterprise to compromise their own inner lives. It would be very strange to say that although it would be clearly inconsistent with good inner practice for someone to act in a certain way, they should do it anyway because business requires it, or even that such behaviour is excused because it leads to profit. To accept such excuses would simply be to free business from ethical restraint altogether.

Profit thus becomes problematic and unethical in certain circumstances. It might be obtained by activities or practices which are wrong in themselves, in the sense that they require someone to ignore or put aside satisfied mind. An obvious example of such malpractice would be dishonesty, for example deception of customers, failure to keep promises or corruption. But we could also cite examples like the deliberate or reckless sale of something dangerous to the buyer; deliberate or reckless cruelty in production; or forcing workers to accept disproportionate risks. Satisfied mind suggests that (those involved in) an enterprise should not inflict harm or damage deliberately or recklessly, even if indirectly, in the pursuit of profit. This obviously mandates concern for the safety of customers and workers, but is also relevant in terms of the environment and the externalities of production. In cases which fail this standard there is a failure of compassion and a cultivation of greed.

Many such practices are not only damaging for the reputation of a business but forbidden by law, of course. If nothing else, such existing restrictions confirm that we intuitively expect profit objectives to be bounded by ethical considerations. It is, however, partly a function of our lack of clarity or agreement on ethical matters that we cannot agree where the boundaries of ethical business lie. But we can now translate this intuition that profit making should be bounded by morality within our framework of satisfied mind.

All profit seeking, then, should be governed by the requirement that the people involved should not compromise satisfied mind and the practice of its skills. In fact, they should seek wherever possible to develop satisfied mind through their business activity. As with all ethical considerations, what this entails in practice is highly dependent on the circumstances of individual cases. But the underlying imperative is clear enough.

Competition and compassion

Competition is a key element in the world as we know it, both because we live in a world in which resources of all kinds are and always have been scarce and because competition is built into the market processes we have embraced. So we live with competition for available jobs, competition for sales and profit in the marketplaces of the world, competition between firms wanting to provide similar kinds of product or service, competition between countries each of which wants to secure resources and prosperity for their citizens and so on. Economic life, which is to say any kind of life in the real world, draws us ineluctably into competition.

So, we have no choice but to compete. But by competing it seems we are inevitably "doing down" our competitors, or at least trying to. The whole point of competition is that we want to win and although there may be no personal animosity our success inevitably means we must ensure that others lose. This seems at first glance to be the very opposite of compassion and kindness and thus at odds with our central objective. At the very least, we need to understand and reconcile this apparent tension between competition and compassion for it seems we cannot have both.

As a preliminary, we should perhaps recall that satisfied mind itself does not involve competition. Since my happiness (satisfied mind) depends on my inner life and yours on your inner life we can never be in direct competition for happiness. I cannot access your happiness nor you mine, we cannot trade or steal or borrow satisfied mind, neither can we donate or confer it, for without my own inner skills developed by my own efforts I will always be at the mercy of my own emotions, desires, beliefs and so on—and you at the mercy of yours. Satisfied mind is in that sense beyond competition.

"The law of the jungle"

Still, the situation may be bad enough. There may be no conflict over inner skills but we still have possible—probable—conflict over external resources and aims. Hence there is in turn potential conflict between actions designed to gain advantage in competition and actions based on the practice of inner skills, particularly compassion. To put it bluntly, competition just seems like a very unhelpful practice as far as inner skills are concerned.

In part, however, this may involve a misunderstanding of competition. We may instantly think for example of ruthless corporations or oligarchs putting profits before people, overriding the wishes of communities, etc.—and of course that happens a lot. But what we tend to think of here is the power of enterprises which have already escaped or destroyed serious competition. These are most commonly examples where competition is over or never began and the victors are left to exploit a clear field.

In real competition there are winners and losers, certainly, but not a single winner dominating the field and always the chance for winners and losers to change places. That is why competition as a mechanism can for example help to allocate resources so that people can make the most of them, which indeed is the social and economic value it provides.

Real competitors do not destroy each other or even seek to, any more than weekend sportspeople seek to destroy the people they regularly play against and without whom they could not play. Economic competitors rather keep each other honest and up to the mark, by for example preventing anyone charging too much or offering poor quality —better perhaps to think of adjacent market stalls rather than the power of a giant supermarket chain. It is mistaken therefore to represent competition as essentially predatory, a manifestation of the so-called "law of the jungle". Sometimes those who wish to excuse predatory behaviour may encourage such misrepresentation, but if there is real competition there is little opportunity for predatory behaviour.

The "law of the jungle" metaphor for competition is a distortion, then, of reasonable business practices. It is probably for the most part even a distortion of what happens in jungles (or savannas). When lions compete for prey they certainly do not prey on each other and when a lion hunts another animal it is not a very good metaphor to call it a competition. The lion's hunt is more like an attempt, successful or not, to exercise overwhelming power, which is more like what monopolies do. A lion which is sick or old and cannot hunt may of course starve, but even the most vigourous free market enthusiast might think very carefully before accepting this as a model of human society.

More common in nature is competition within very clearly defined limits, for example competition over mating rights. In the case of creatures other than humans the limits are generally set by natural instincts and drives which operate to prevent powerful animals of the same species from killing each other and thereby risking the extinction of the species.

Rules

Among humans, leaving wars and economic life aside, competition is usually similarly confined within strict limits by explicit rules as in the case of games. Even if we are more cruel than other animals, Roman-style gladiatorial competitions to the death are no longer considered acceptable or entertaining and appear only in fiction. In any game the competitors must play within the rules and winning and losing are determined by performance within those rules. The rules actually define the game: pick up the ball in the field and you are no longer playing soccer.

In the economic sphere, competition is also generally bounded by rules, in fact often by enforceable laws. Business would scarcely be possible if this were not so—agreements, for example, must be enforce-able other than by violence or commerce would literally be war. Certainly, some people assume that competition is a justification to do anything which the law does not explicitly ban, or even in some quarters anything that might escape successful prosecution. This, how-ever, is simply to argue that ethics or values do not apply in the world of business, which is to demote values to some quaint form of private manners.

But we have already seen that, since work is a vital part of living for everyone, whatever values apply in life must also apply in work or they are without meaning. Since business is but one form of work, the same reasoning applies. Someone who claims that ethics do not apply in business is thus implicitly claiming that ethics do not apply in life, a nihilism of which we would be wise to be wary and should certainly not allow to shape our society or our world if we can help it. Competition can and should be conducted within the bounds of everyday values, which means it should not be an excuse for greed or oppression. But if this condition is satisfied, competition and compassion are not in conflict.

Understanding competition and indeed enterprise in this way as integrated into life and bounded by the same values as we observe in other spheres is surely possible, even if it tends everywhere to be corrupted by greed. It was for example the basis of the business practices of the Quaker entrepreneurs of the nineteenth century, many of whom were immensely successful. Compassion does not require that an enterprise is run inefficiently, or that for example one should defer to competitors, pay too much or charge too little. It does require that one behave with humanity, decency and honesty towards employees, customers, suppliers, competitors and others. But that is generally the foundation of a healthy business anyway.

"Greed is good"

This line of argument—that the same values by which we guide our private lives should apply to business—may seem hopelessly naïve, or at least it may seem like a fine prescription for an ideal world but hopeless in the real one. The obvious reason is that some may "play fair" but others may not. The marketplace, it will be argued again, is a jungle and unless we claw and fight and if necessary cheat our way to victory (profit) we will inevitably be destroyed by less scrupulous competitors.

We must behave as dispassionate, even dehumanized economic agents, this argument runs, and should treat others either as dehumanized "factors of production" or even as potential victims of our cunning and power. If we give way to compassion our competitors will prevail while we go broke. This line can even be pushed further, claiming for example there are no prohibited practices and no limits on what we make and sell. All business is good business for if we do not supply weapons, or diabetes-inducing foods, or tobacco or narcotics, someone else will.

Sometimes ruthless practices are justified by invoking a duty to the owners of the business, the shareholders, who (it is said) invest expecting that everything will be done to provide them with the best possible return on their investment. But why should shareholders be entitled to expect others to act unethically in their name, bearing in mind that in our perspective to act unethically is to compromise what is most important in a person's life? Corporate managers would simply not accept such a task if their own central aim was satisfied mind.

But in any case, why should shareholders trust managers to act unethically in their name while expecting the same managers to hold sacred their duty of trust to the shareholders? It is surely more likely that if managements were prepared to act unethically <u>for</u> the shareholders they would also be willing to better their own position <u>at the expense of</u> the shareholders — with overgenerous benefits packages for example.

There is often a perverse romanticism attached to the most ruthless business practices, as if those involved somehow saw themselves as swashbuckling pirates of the Hollywood variety. But more like real pirates they are simply cruel, violent and deceitful. (That "law of the jungle" thing is of course another piece of misplaced romanticism.) The choice any management has is to carry on their enterprise with respect for values because enterprise is part of life — or play pirates. There will always be business pirates just as there will always be predators in private life. But they should not be allowed to set the agenda for values or for economic life — and certainly not for society.

In practice of course we generally do not accept that "anything goes" in business. We do not tolerate certain kinds of behaviour and corporations which behave in seriously unethical ways usually take great care to conceal their behaviour from the public and their customers for that very reason. We limit business practices by law, just as we protect business rights (contracts, for example) by the same law, which those who chafe at legal restrictions on business behaviour sometimes forget. There is a wide, difficult and probably perpetual (because the ground and the possibilities shift all the time) practical debate to be had on where the legal boundaries should or can be drawn but the ethical boundaries are indicated by the practice of satisfied mind.

The great difficulty is of course that because huge financial resources may be involved the unscrupulous in business sometimes have real power to affect competitors, customers and society itself. Because they are unscrupulous and powerful they may do serious damage. But we should be clear that this is a practical problem for the rest of us, not something which should cause us to question our values.

If we find such power objectionable, which we surely do, we must seek ways to contain it. Containment involves legal and democratic controls and we should not accept that such controls are an interference with "the efficiency of the market" or "the ability to compete", provided they remain focused on the restriction of unethical behaviour. Rather, such controls set the rules of the game, they are the means by which business activity is integrated into society in a way which reflects the values of society. This is no easy task, but it is a practical, intellectual task. Changing our values to accommodate bad behaviour instead would be absurd, although that is often the garden path up which capitalism seeks to lead us.

Even if an enterprise has to struggle against the unfair practices or power of others, there is still a choice between ethical and unethical responses. Such a struggle is a test of which values we make central in our lives. Our argument throughout is that there cannot be a different set of values which emerges when we go to work. We cannot neglect the development of inner skills if satisfied mind is our central goal, and if we feel compelled to do so at work then our real central objective has shifted to something different, something external and material. The values of satisfied mind do not change because we are working, nor even because we are directing the work of others.

Chapter 17

Markets

The working of markets

We have suggested that enterprises should always operate in a way which is bounded by ethical practice, that is to say by the principles and practices of satisfied mind. But most enterprises operate within or around markets of one kind or another. The questions then arise, how do values interact with markets and what part should markets play in society?

There is today a fashionable idea, even a modern myth or romance, that markets know all the answers. They are held to be somehow omniscient, perhaps even offering a supreme expression of the will of the people. Therefore, the argument runs, the more decisions are left to market mechanisms the better, for society will become more efficient, perhaps even more democratic.

No one who has worked in or with markets, certainly financial markets, could sincerely believe such a thing. Markets can be crazy places where waves of emotion are amplified as everyone tries to anticipate what everyone else will do next. Quite apart from such excesses, there are many well documented flaws in the way most markets work even under normal, everyday conditions. Access is restricted, for example; some participants have more power or better information than others; and at the worst the rewards for manipulation may be so great that the temptation to manipulate can prove too strong, to say nothing of the temptation to cover up mistakes. We have seen all of these problems emerge repeatedly as scandals in recent years.

That said, what every market sets out to do is something harmless, simple and useful. Markets are designed to bring potential sellers and buyers together in a way which allows information to be revealed to both about the price at which items should be valued and exchanged. Thus bargains can be made which, at least at that moment, are fair and reasonable for both sides.

There can surely be no intrinsic harm in such a simple process. Indeed it has an obvious social usefulness whether the traded items are fruit and vegetables or financial instruments. In the simplest case something I have (which may be money or goods) is exchanged for something of equal value which you are willing to part with. The strength of an open market mechanism is that we can both assure ourselves that there are no better terms available on either side: no buyer is ready to offer more, no seller is ready to deal for less. I may get what I consider a bargain if you do not value what you are selling as highly as I do or are perhaps under some duress to sell. But the normal case, the reason why markets work at all, is that we are both satisfied at the time with the bargain we make. Notice the key point here: if there is no duress or mistake we are exchanging items of equal value, though obviously of different usefulness to each of us. Markets in these circumstances do not create value, nor do they, if working properly, alter the distribution of value: they merely alter the forms in which value is held among participants.

Thus Jack arrives with a cow and goes home with magic beans. Unless he has been reckless, foolish, lucky or cunning (he was of course both foolish and lucky) he has neither lost nor gained. What happens later may make either side regret or rejoice in the trade but at the time we must be satisfied or we just wouldn't do it. If someone makes a profit by buying or selling in these circumstances it may be because they have tricked or cheated someone into trading at the wrong price, but the advantage of open markets as opposed to private arrangements is that this is in fact quite difficult. More likely, one side has better information, or they have just guessed right.

Market failures

But there are many things which can and do go wrong here. A common problem for example is that sellers find there is more of what they are selling than they had hoped. This is the classic bind in which farmers all over the world often find themselves. If the growing has been good for one it has likely been good for all, but buyers do not want more just because produce is plentiful and if one farmer will not offer a reduction in price another will, so the price tumbles. Conversely, when the growing has been hard the prices may be high because the buyers must scramble to get what they need.

Curiously, rich governments which otherwise are very respectful of market forces often regard agriculture as an exception and try to devise subsidies, stockpile schemes or price guarantees to protect their farmers, while poorer governments can do nothing. Our point for the moment though is not whether such government intervention is good or bad. It is that even in this very basic, simple application markets do not necessarily get an answer which meets all the needs of society. Finding a clearing price (a price at which everyone who wants to sell and everyone who wants to buy can do so) is not always a terribly useful social function. Sometimes it leaves producers (in the case of a glut) poorer than they expected and perhaps unable to meet their commitments and function properly, while buyers and maybe consumers get an unexpected bonus they did nothing to create.

The market has in such a case redistributed value, or perhaps more precisely the growing conditions have redistributed value and the market has simply endorsed or expressed that redistribution. If this happens on a sufficient scale, the whole structure of society, dependent as it usually is on gradations of wealth, may ultimately be governed by weather, soil and insects! The beneficiaries of these forces at any one time will no doubt declare the process to be just and reasonable but it is not obvious that it is so.

So there are problems even for simple produce markets, but in financial and capital markets the setting of prices may become a subsidiary function. The main social function and usual justification for financial markets is not just to provide reliable prices by which financial assets can be valued and exchanged but to provide a mechanism for enterprises to raise capital. This is indeed a valuable function and societies which lack the means for capital to be orchestrated in this way often struggle to create enterprises at all.

But in well established financial markets this capital-raising function itself easily becomes secondary to various forms of short-term trading whose usefulness is much less obvious. Jobbing, principal trading and arbitrage—that is to say buying and selling not out of any desire to acquire or dispose of an end product but simply to take a profit out of the working of the market itself—become primary activities. In principle these activities can perform a moderately useful function by eliminating accidental market distortions and creating volume for other participants. But when they become the main event, so that the market redistributes value towards successful traders, the market is increasingly detached from any social usefulness.

The limits of "the invisible hand"

We have seen, then, how markets may transmit the effects of essentially random factors into the distribution of wealth and power in society, as in the example of produce markets reflecting the effects of weather. We may not care about this, or we may indeed prefer such random effects to the manipulations of officials, however well meaning, who think they know what is best for us. In the simplest agricultural societies there may be no alternative anyway. But it is strange nevertheless to imbue this process with some kind of wisdom or proclaim that markets know best about the organization of society. We may acquiesce in the distribution produced by markets but it seems an odd thing to claim that such essentially random effects represent the best possible arrangement.

It is sometimes argued that one of the principal values of markets is that they provide signals to producers to guide their future decisions. But even this guidance is limited because some of the most robust economic activity comes through radical innovation, as in all forms of technology, where there are by definition no signals available in advance.[62] Nobody knew they really wanted to spend their life on social media sites, for example, until someone invented them.

In more complex examples, financial markets can redistribute wealth based on trading activities out of proportion to any useful function they provide. Again, this may not matter at all—sport and entertainment also provide many examples of wealth being accumulated out of proportion to the social usefulness of their product or activity. But to accept that this is just what happens is very different from accepting that it is the best thing that could happen, still less that the "winners" in this game are morally better or more deserving than those who are not involved.

The reputation of financial markets has of course suffered anyway in recent years because reckless trading was allowed to get out of hand, to say nothing of fraudulent trading, imprudent bank lending and incompetent regulation. Governments then felt it necessary to step in with public money to limit the damage and prevent widespread destruction of savings. This only emphasized that while the rewards for trading successfully are vast, the penalties for failure are often borne by someone else.

The system hardly gives an incentive to prudence at any level, but the necessity of government bailouts also shows that society as a whole is implicitly underwriting the attempts of a few to get rich by trading. It is hard to think of any other sphere where a massive risk to the well-being of the majority would be tolerated in order to allow a few the chance to become incredibly rich. It is as if a country imposed heavy taxes but made the tax revenues the prize in a lottery. Or as if some giant scheme risked poisoning the inhabitants of a whole country if it went wrong, but would benefit just one powerful family if it went well. No one would suggest, we may hope, that this would be a good way to run things.

One of the causes of the financial crash of the "noughties" was that regulation failed or was evaded. This should not surprise us, with all due respect, for if the rewards for senior traders and their managers are in seven figures (for example) and the regulators are paid as public servants, which occupation is likely to attract the most eager candidates? But it is revealing that we even try to regulate such markets, which we do precisely because market mechanisms are so easily abused and the rewards for so doing can be so high. We already recognize, in other words, that markets can have dangerous effects and should be treated with caution. It is disingenuous then to declare that markets are all-knowing or that they should be allowed to guide society with their wisdom.

It does not follow at all that markets or indeed trading should be banned or criminalized, but there is certainly no evidence here of a mysterious, wise and providential hand which we should allow to shape the way society and all our lives are organized. Markets often produce crazy results and even when they work well we can recognize that their functions are limited. A market is only a limited mechanism which does a limited job moderately well. It never pays to under-estimate the sheer power which may be exerted in or through a market, but that power is either the disguised power of those who dominate the market or, if the market is genuinely open and free, it is a blind power no wiser than the forces of nature. If we invest market mechanisms with a social authority they cannot realistically live up to we should not be surprised if they disappoint.

The market society

But now we come to the deepest fault with markets as a way of organizing society. Most people anyway have little to trade except their labour and work skills, so treating society like a market reduces people to commodities, "factors of production". Such a society is already and intrinsically light years away from one in which people relate to each other as fellow human beings striving to live skilful lives with satisfied minds.

Furthermore, if someone has nothing to trade they cannot even enter the market and so they remain with nothing, for we have seen that redistributing wealth is not generally something a well-functioning market is meant to do. A fair bargain is an equal exchange of value. Thus, even when they work well and there is no abuse, markets reflect an existing balance of power and wealth, which in turn reflects no more than the accumulated accidents of previous market conditions.

Power does of course shift within markets, so that mighty players can fall while new powers emerge, but as we have seen such trans-formations are generally not the work of the market itself but of forces which bear on the market, like the weather on our farmers. Thus markets can do little in themselves to relieve poverty or deprivation, for example, other than to provide a place to buy and sell when value is produced elsewhere. If society itself is regarded as a marketplace injustices are likely to be unchallenged and be perpetuated. A market is therefore a crazy model for society, and a truly "market society", if that meant a society whose structures and functioning were left to markets, would be a nightmare.

None of this should be taken to mean that we can do without markets or that bureaucrats or "experts" or anyone else can do better the things that markets really are good at. But we should be very cautious indeed about the magical powers sometimes claimed for market mechanisms. We should be prepared to recognize that they are not the whole story of human life or even of economic life and are unlikely by themselves to organize a society any sane person would want to live in. We should use markets for what they are good at, but not let markets use us, still less bow before their wisdom.

Part 6.
Politics as if
People Mattered[63]

Chapter 18

Politics

Politics and political values

Politics and political activity are usually and very obviously about large scale external matters, for example about how society is organized, who has authority over whom, about macroeconomic relationships or the public rules which govern our behaviour towards each other. It is not immediately clear what part anyone's inner life plays in such matters, yet our argument has been that sound secular values can be based on satisfied mind and the taking of responsibility for our inner lives. So the first question about politics is how values and politics can connect at all.

This is not a question of any split between external activity and inner development. We have already seen that the development of inner skills crucially depends on how we act and behave towards others, so that external action and behaviour are part of the process of practice as well as being the forum in which inner skills are used. Satisfied mind is not a matter of isolated interiority, not least because the mind or the inner life is not like that. All human activity has its inner and its external aspects, they are sides of one coin. What is different with politics is just the scale and perhaps the collective nature of the action. Nevertheless, when we think about "political values" we are apt to think that they are something different, larger, grander than the values which we recognize in our individual lives – we even use a different range of terms like justice, freedom, fairness, equality and so on.

On what basis though can any particular political values be justified? Often they simply depend on a conviction which defies further explanation. As with the emotivist position on private values – in which as we saw it is accepted that a person's values are not open to discussion – the conviction which underlies such political values is also effectively closed to rational discussion ("You are either with us or against us"). But again as with personal values, if there are no reasons we can give to others to justify political values, there are none we can give ourselves. They are inherently unreasonable.

So we face a crucial question about politics. Are there identifiable political values which can lay some claim to being universally applicable? For, if not, political values might either be illusory altogether or simply statements about the convictions of an individual or group.

Means, ends and everyday politics

Before we consider this vital question however, we have to recognize that we will get little help from examining everyday politics. However we justify collective values (if we can) and however important values might be in politics (if they are) they would still be very different from politics as it is practised.

Sadly, most political argument in practice involves partial truths charged with unhelpful emotions.[64] People from any point of the political spectrum tend to believe what they want to believe and argue what they think others want to hear. How rare it is, for example, that anyone changes sides on an issue because the better argument is actually with those who are usually opponents. Raw emotion—envy, anger, disdain, greed—plays a huge part in the decisions of both politicians and electors. Even without emotion, most of what is argued about is empirical or factual, but since the facts are complicated and the connections obscure there is often no real clue, let alone clarity, about what actions will lead to what outcomes. Emotions fill the gap when facts are scarce.

Then again, talk of political values is often a thin veil for material self interest. Everyday politics is often about about determining whose interest will prevail. If none can prevail outright, then politics is about seeking compromise. In this sense politics does not often aim at a common goal so much as at somebody getting what they want, even when political values are expressly invoked. Equality for example is naturally more appealing to those who feel they would gain from redistribution, economic freedom is more appealing to those who already have enough to exploit it. It is not always obvious in practice that any values at all—as opposed to interests—influence political decisions and policies. But we should not give up, because in politics as in private life examples of bad behaviour do not show that there are no values, still less that there could be no values.

We can recognize many other elements which go to make up "political reality"—any or all of which can seem to be the essence of politics depending on the circumstances and context. Take for example the (often insalubrious) business by which individuals get and keep power, which is what our media present daily as the essence of political activity but for which we will here use an old fashioned word, politicks. In different contexts this could for example be a matter of trying to get others to support a seizure of power, jostling for the favour of an autocrat, trading favours and support with other powerful players or, in what passes for democracy, using the arts of persuasion, presentation, spin and media coverage to win votes.

In every case, however, gaining power is the clear end of the activity and success is what matters to the players. Politicks is a means to that end, at best a game, at worst a form of combat. In democratic contexts it is about tactics and presentation. In the best cases it will be bounded by the personal values of the players but personal values, sadly, are often a casualty of the process. Because it is only a means to an end (power) and even the end is not central or desired for itself (but for what it can achieve or bring), politicks generates no collective values of its own, even if much of everyday political activity is taken up with it.

Again, most underline policy goals are generated by practical problems which need to be solved before the next problem appears or is addressed. As such, even the most important policy goals are fleeting and transitory. Consider, for example, the conduct of a war which actually threatens the integrity of a society. Achieving victory may be so overriding a goal that people may forget that victory itself has a purpose, which in the best cases is to defend the people and the values by which they live. Indeed the war effort may even challenge values and choices may arise in which values may hinder victory. Winning the war is a practical necessity, of course, but not the purpose of people's lives or the basis of society. When the war is won the next problem appears.

In similar vein many people believe or have believed that the most pressing problem in politics is to destroy existing forms of social or political organization, a belief which has drawn more than a few blood-baths. But even allowing that such fundamental change might be the most pressing practical problem in particular circumstances, it cannot be the final end of politics. What happens when this goal is achieved? People may believe or be duped into thinking that a utopia will automatically result, but it never does! All that happens is that one pressing policy goal is replaced by another.

Practical underline policies are what much everyday political decision-making is about: what actions will reach the political goals we have set? But what will work in a particular case is usually unclear because the issues are generally complex and the evidence rarely sufficient. Politicians usually see it as their job to exude certainty even when there is little certainty to be had, perhaps one reason why politicians so often appear insincere. Nevertheless, policies are about questions of fact and practical solutions, if there are any, are always empirical, with their roots in economics, social psychology, history, comparative government and all the other disciplines which attempt to study the workings of people and society.

Effectiveness in solving a practical problem is the real test of an empirical policy. We might hope that policy choice would always be informed by and bounded by values, so that for example some policies might possibly be effective but are ruled out because they contravene our values. We surely would not tolerate slavery, for example, even if it could be proved that it increased overall wealth. But within such value constraints, the choice of one policy over another is an empirical prediction (or guess!) about what will work. Neither policy goals nor policies generate values, but presuppose their existence.

Structures of power

Power is clearly the essence of political activity. It is why politicians seek office, it is what makes it possible to change or conserve or lead society. We might describe it as the ability to get others to accept decisions, whether by persuasion, from respect for structures and institutions (such as the law or democracy in advanced societies), from loyalty or regard for the standing of a leader, from fear (whether of legal sanctions or of violence or arbitrary retribution), or in the worst cases from the violent elimination of opposition. But it is immediately clear that all power is instrumental. Power is always the power to do something, but it is the choice of what is done which reveals the values of the powerful.

In every society and community there are many structures and mechanisms which determine how power is exercised and by whom. So the state (or "the system") in practical terms is simply a collection of such structures, a different collection in each state. An advantage of thinking about power in terms of such multiple structures is that it breaks down any tendency to think of "the state" ("the system") as a monolith.

Some of these power structures are visible and some hidden. Some of them work well at any given time and do what they are designed to do, some don't. Each may work in harmony with other structures or in opposition to them. Depending on what kind of society we examine, the structures of power may include formal constitutional arrangements (for example a way of deciding who has executive authority), the informal ability to influence those who legitimately make decisions (for example media influence, funding, personal or family connections) or simply the ability to threaten or use violence (most obviously in criminal cultures and totalitarian states, but to some extent in every state). They thus include the obvious institutions and constitutional arrangements which describe "the government" of any community, but they also include mechanisms behind the scenes, often unwritten and fluid, which represent the real workings of any institution.

The power structures of the nation state are generally pervasive and crucial in everyone's life. But in particular cases the power structures of a locality or community for example may be more important, because more immediate. In some countries the structures of the state are weak compared with religious leaders, local warlords or those who use violence to command obedience. Similarly, we know that the structures of corporate and commercial power often have just as much influence on the shape and quality of our everyday lives as the more formal structures of government.

For many reasons, people often become very loyal to structures in themselves and frequently adopt the survival and aims of a particular structure as important aims of their own. Power structures can thus seem to become ends in themselves and even to determine values, in extreme cases overriding the values people ordinarily seek to live by. For example the protection of a particular institution, perhaps a Church or a form of government, may be taken as a value-creating end in itself, justifying actions which normally would be regarded as unacceptable.

But there is no power structure which is not created by human beings, sometimes painstakingly by slow evolution over centuries, sometimes by immediate fiat backed by force as in the case of a coup. Thus every power structure is there to serve the purposes of some human being or group. The preservation of any particular structure cannot be an end in itself, however desirable its preservation may be.

By contrast, people sometimes decide that particular power structures are the root of major problems and that they must destroy these structures to improve their lives. Since most structures, however imperfect, serve some purpose and support other structures the difficulty in such cases is always how to destroy without inviting chaos. No doubt occasionally destruction will be the only way. But whether the aim is to preserve, reform or destroy a structure such an aim is always a subsidiary aim, not a central aim and still less a value, for any structure can only be a means to some end.

The test then of structures, like policies, is effectiveness: do they do the job they are intended to do and, if not, how can they be improved? They are means, not ends. They do not generate values in themselves — that would be a sort of institutional idolatry. If we hold certain structures dear it is often because they are thought to embody or support certain values while the proposed alternatives seem to negate or deny those values. But the structures are not the values and sometimes with changed circumstances they may begin to work against the very values they are intended to support.

Values from outside politics

Both the activities and the structures of politics then, important as they are both in the life of any society and as activities, can potentially be conducted with different underlying values and do not themselves provide us with values. If politicks, policy goals, specific policies or power structures are driven by values at all they depend on there already being values which inform and constrain them. In itself, each is empirical or instrumental, a means to some end.

Thus if we are to discover a sound basis for political values we must look outside these activities, which means in effect that we must look altogether outside the activities we generally consider to constitute politics. Broadly, people bring pre-existing values into politics. This hardly comes as a surprise but it is important. So now we have to consider what the source of such political values might be.

Chapter 19

The Unity of Values

The Common Good as the good we have in common

If power were used at a given time simply to serve the interest of some group which controlled power and dominated other groups, the obvious question would be why everyone else would tolerate it. The answer would have to be that they were oppressed or deceived in some way, which may often happen. But if politics can find an alternative and more acceptable aim we might hope it would be to serve or aim at some common good.

Just as with individuals, we can imagine a great variety of collective aims and goals, some more important than others, susceptible to some kind of ranking by importance however loose. So what might lie at the centre of this ranking, what collective aim matters most? Such an aim, if only by analogy with individuals, might be the true source of political values. That central collective aim would be the Common Good, justifying its capital letters.

But here there are two broad possibilities and only two. Either this central aim is something uniquely social or political, something which emerges at the level of collective goals but differs from the goals which individuals set themselves. Or, alternatively, political or collective values are based on or derived from the values and thus the central aims of individuals.

In support of the first view we might note again that in everyday talk about politics we often use different terms from those we use in thinking about (say) a personal moral problem – for example we might talk about social justice, or liberty, or prosperity. But there is one great problem with following this line.

If there are public or collective values with a foundation independent of our private values, how do we link up the two kinds of value or (as an example of the kind of difficulty we must face) which type of value takes precedence if they clash? It seems very strange to say that when we think about some of the biggest public issues – what is best for our society, whether we should go to war in certain circumstances or even who can be trusted to take important decisions on our behalf –

we must put aside our private values. For in our framework those private values after all are based on what we have rationally chosen as the central aim of our lives. At the very least, if there is such a source of public values independent of private values, we need to be clear what it is and from whence it derives an authority which overrides the central aims of our individual lives.

The second alternative avoids this conflict between the two sorts of goal — it doesn't preclude there being purely collective subsidiary goals but it places the central goal of individuals, their chosen life purpose, at the centre of public as well as private life. The main obstacle to this is the thought that everyone is likely to have a different central aim, so how could we combine them into a collective aim?

But this problem disappears if there is something like a shared central aim for everyone, namely to live happily through satisfied mind. Everyone in a society which shared this aim would be focused not only on attaining it for themselves but on helping others to attain it. This common private aim would thus also be the overriding collective aim in such a society, for it would not make any sense for collective decisions to diminish or thwart this shared private aim. Public or political values therefore, whatever subsidiary political goals might be pursued at any one time, would rest on observing and encouraging the practice of satisfied mind, and policies would be bounded by those values. Private values and public values would be in alignment.

The Common Good in these circumstances could thus be interpreted as the good we have in common. The central, most rational and resonant good we have in common is satisfied mind, moulding our own subjectivity into getting the best out of what we experience. If public values are based on the recognition that this goal is paramount in collective actions precisely because it is central in the actions of individuals we will have unified values in public and private life which are both rational and shareable.

A very radical idea

If this is right, political values are exactly the same as personal values. There is no divide but a unity of values across personal and collective life. Our deepest collective aim is for each of us and all our fellows to achieve our deepest private aim, to live happily with satisfied mind.

Of course arguments about what subsidiary aims are in everyone's best interest (or more likely, whose best interest they are in) will continue as the stuff of everyday politics. But these arguments are, as now, about what will work (empirical arguments) or power struggles about whose interest should prevail (however well disguised as something else). Genuine appeals to values in politics must appeal to what conduces to the broad development of satisfied mind and more important, ethical policies and politics should be bounded by the practice of satisfied mind.

This is in its way altogether radical. It is radical because of the implication that satisfied mind is more important even at a collective level than any economic, material or external goal, displacing economic goals and aims as the heart of society. It is radical because it subordinates the large or grand decisions of the political arena to the private pursuit and practice of satisfied mind. And it is radical because it explains the shallowness and moral vapidity of most politics as we know it.

The unity of values across the private and public spheres helps also to explain the intuition we all have that there are boundaries we should not cross in pursuing political aims, actions which betray our values and in doing so betray what we are about. We cannot practise cruelty in the name of the greater good, for example, if the greater good depends on compassion. Again, to ask that a citizen give up their personal central aim for the good of the state or even for the "common good", a common trope from both ends of the political spectrum, cannot be right. Such a demand might be justified for lesser aims – it doesn't preclude someone having to compromise their economic or material good, for example, for the material good of others. But the central aim of the state should be to promote the shared central aim of the people and therefore the citizen owes no duty to subordinate his or her central aim to any aims of the state.

Just as we have "rules of thumb" to avoid having to scrutinize every personal action, because we can identify large classes of actions which are generally helpful or harmful to our central goal, so we may have political rules of thumb, rules which we can apply to collective action. Equality, fairness, justice, freedom and so on might qualify as such, but (as with rules of thumb in personal morality) there are circumstances in which we should be wary of such simplified norms because of the sheer complexity they hide. We need at the very least to see how such rules arise and to understand that they are not absolute laws but only summaries of experience, approximations. Ultimately we must judge the moral or value integrity of political action by the same standards as personal action.

Our key contention therefore is that political values do not stand apart from private ethical values. The same ethical values apply in the sphere of collective action as with personal action. "Political values" are not exactly empty categories but they are not generally values at all, they are likely to be interests, ideologies or wishes about how society should be organized. At best they are rules of thumb to remind us how politics should follow the shared central aim of the people.

Is a common good authoritarian?

The very idea that we might all come to the same notion of what our private central aim and values might be, especially if it entails a notion of what our public values might be, is likely, given the temper of the times, to incur the charge of authoritarianism. The suggestion that we might share an ideal of the common good, it might be protested, is an attempt to impose values. Closely related is the even stronger if rather adolescent charge of moral fascism, that we are trying to impose standards on everyone against their will. It is worth briefly addressing these charges if only to rebut them.

Values would be imposed if someone were to insist that everyone should adopt them whether they agree or no. But that is not what is happening here. We simply suggest that there are strong reasons why anyone who thinks about the matter will be drawn to adopt a certain idea about what matters most in their life and any human life. From that idea certain values inevitably flow. We suggest, for all the reasons we have been through, that there are very few candidates for a universal ideal which can underpin our values and that satisfied mind makes the most sense.

That's not imposing values, any more than someone who suggests that the Earth is a spheroid is imposing geography. If there is a case that another aim makes more sense and does the job better, let us hear and consider it. Our ideal might be said to be imposed by a common desire to make sense of our own lives but is certainly not imposed by anyone else.

Some people might even fear that to use rationality as a key test of whether we accept a central aim is to allow some hidden authoritarian ideology to dominate us. It is true that appeals to "reason" (usually incomplete or bad reason) can sometimes be used to bully rather than persuade. But surely it is not authoritarian to suggest that rationality should be one of the factors which guide us in the choice of the central aim of our lives. We need only ask, why would we prefer irrationality? Irrational, remember, simply means "doesn't make sense". If you want an irrational life, a life that doesn't make any sense, that is up to you. But why would you want such a life?

The key point, however, is that it is not actually possible to impose the satisfied mind ideal on anyone. We started from the assumption that the key to our own happiness and fulfilment in life lies with the habits which govern our own inner lives. It is the attempt to mould these habits and align them with our central aim of living happy, resilient and fulfilled lives which gives rise to our values. But this is a matter of individual commitment and, much more, individual effort. It simply cannot be imposed from outside.

If we start with an ideal which recognizes that the inner life is the essential basis of values, we may do our best to explain and persuade others but it would be both pointless (because we couldn't do it) and a betrayal of the ideal itself (because even trying would involve actions inconsistent with developing our own inner lives) to try and impose it forcibly on others. Thus even if we imagine a society in which the satisfied mind ideal was the majority view or the accepted orthodoxy, it would make no sense to impose it on dissenters. This ideal, properly understood, is actually the least susceptible of becoming authoritarian.

The end of ethical neutrality

But imagine now that those who recognized the satisfied mind ideal became the majority in a society which then, through the normal processes of democratic pressure, reflected the central aims of the people who made it up. Policies would try to take society in a direction which people believed (rightly or wrongly only time could tell) was most conducive to the realization of their central aim.

There is of course no reason to think that everyone would agree on the highly complex and empirically uncertain business of how best to go forward on practical issues. But if we knew that everyone else shared the same ideal and that disagreements were only practical opinions about what might work best, we might hope that society would be more cohesive and more tolerant.

However, in these circumstances it would surely follow that the state or its structures would not and could not be morally or ethically neutral. Recognizing that the common good and the common goal shared by the majority lay in a certain direction the structures and policies of the state would surely be oriented accordingly.

This, however, is completely at odds with recent liberal orthodoxy in which the state takes no stance on values and merely provides a democratic framework in which the different values of citizens vie for expression.[65] But if it is, after all, possible to identify a rational shared common good, what is the merit of a neutral stance? Of course the state would be guided by democratic processes in all practical matters but the acid test of what practical aims the state pursued and what policies were permissible in pursuing them would rest on the common values of the people. The institutions of the state would share the values of the people, based on the satisfied mind ideal.

This conclusion may be difficult for many liberal-minded people to accept because it seems to go against the idea of a pluralist society in which, potentially, everyone has different values and the state remains like a neutral referee. But, despite the theory that the state should be morally neutral, the state today rarely remains so and its institutions and structures reflect whatever ruling orthodoxy holds sway. Surely it is better that the moral stance of the state should be both explicit and, more important, in tune with the rationally held values of the people.[66]

In any case, value diversity is precisely where the most insidious danger to a pluralist society lies. Moral confusion is not something to be cherished. Diversity of opinion is often a good thing but not always: not, for example, when found in the medical opinions of surgeons about to operate on you or in the calculations of engineers constructing a bridge. Diversity of opinion on values may be harmless, but may become equivalent, as we saw earlier, to moral nihilism. We need shared values to live together. But if we have them, on a basis we can all inspect and agree without being required to take anything on trust, surely our society and institutions should reflect them?

Chapter 20

Traditional Political Values

Political rules of thumb

We have argued that political values must be based on the same foundation as private values, so that the common good is no more or less than the good we have in common. But the notion that there are specifically political or public values and virtues, which do not or even cannot appear at the private level — justice, freedom, equality and so on — has a strong historical hold and politically committed people are often strongly attached to them.

We do not deny of course that such specifically "public values" may be important in appropriate contexts, for example in helping to mobilize support for some needed change or indeed to resist a proposed change. Our suggestion is rather that they are derived from private values and that any ethical force they have can be traced to that source. If they matter it is because they follow from the pursuit of private values — from the practice of satisfied mind — or are useful to help people achieve their common but privately chosen and privately important central aim. As we suggested earlier, they are not values in themselves but at best rules of thumb. In this chapter we look very briefly at several such ideas and how they fare in our framework.[67]

Universal laws and rights

For example, we rejected at the beginning of the book the idea that the values that govern our personal lives and behaviour derive from some sort of natural or divine laws — laws which are not made by people through any of the processes which usually promulgate laws. But when we come to collective values somehow the idea of natural laws twitches back into live. At the political level there seems to be a recurrent belief that government laws and policies, at least in certain important fields, somehow reflect or record a pre-existing natural law. Thus for example the eighteenth century talked of "The rights of man" and today we have "human rights", with the idea in both cases that human laws should not deny or conflict with these natural laws.[68]

However, the idea of natural laws or natural rights runs into exactly the same difficulties in political contexts as at the individual level. If people don't make these laws, who does? How are they made, how are they adapted to changing circumstances? How do we find out exactly what they are, where can we consult the "fine print"? We quickly get lost, because unfortunately the familiar metaphor of law simply does not work.

The idea of "human rights" as values is the modern manifestation of the tendency to invoke natural or non-human laws. As a codification of the rights which citizens <u>ought</u> to have in relation to the state in which they live—a state which is inevitably vastly more powerful than any particular citizen—the various treaties and conventions on human rights serve important political and diplomatic functions. Few states are entirely comfortable to be seen going against the tide of international opinion, so the invocation of human rights may be a powerful tool to protect people who would otherwise be crushed by the power of their own state.

But these conventions on human rights as we saw earlier are essentially aspirational. They are the best that could be done by lawyers and diplomats from many countries meeting at a particular time with particular political objectives. In no sense can these conventions be interpreted as the reading or transcription of some pre-existing natural or supernatural law, nor as the product of some process which generates law independent of the activities of human beings. (Nor, to be clear, would their authors generally make such a claim.) They are produced by people—good people with the best of intentions but still just people—trying to codify their shared ideas about the desirable relationships between citizen and state.

They do not therefore represent an independent source of political values. They are in themselves a political structure, in the sense we saw earlier. They may invite us to agree that we share the aspirations set out but they are not self-evident or self-justifying. If someone disagrees, for example, how can they be persuaded if not by appeal to some underlying values? We cannot persuade by referring to the conventions themselves.

In particular, the massive political achievement and agreement they represent should not lull us into thinking that they are underpinned by non-human laws to which the convention-writers somehow had access. In part this craving for natural law is simply a response to the observation that governments are routinely capable of making appalling laws —not just incompetent, inefficient or petty laws, but oppressive, inhumane, cruel laws. The idea that some human laws are wrong despite being lawfully enacted and should be resisted is hard to disagree with but does not need the underpinning of non-human laws.

To decide that an ordinary law clashes with our values there must indeed be some standard or touchstone we can apply against which we judge the law in question, but values based on satisfied mind provide that touchstone in themselves. The kind of laws which would be most objectionable would require those who enforced them, for example, to violate ethical standards based on satisfied mind. So if we apply that standard, the same standard we would apply to our own behaviour, there is no need to invoke anything else. The demand is simply that the actions of government and the laws governments impose should be consistent with those personal values. Human Rights may be a useful structure and even embody or express our values, but they are not values in themselves.

Equality

The notions of equality and fairness have been fundamental to Western political thought, particularly on the left, for centuries. Even today, many politicians would describe their fundamental political value as the struggle for "fairness" or perhaps "social justice". So perhaps here at least we might have a basic political value which we must recognize alongside the personal values we have described based on the ideal of satisfied mind.

A moment's thought, however, suggests that unless the ideas of equality or fairness are understood within an already agreed ethical framework they are little more than slogans, perhaps adopted because of their undoubted historical and emotional resonance. Unless we already have values based on a foundation we can understand and share we cannot apply these notions. We deal first with equality.

Of course no one wants to feel that they are regarded or treated unfavourably compared to others — it's like asking whether you prefer good-tasting food or nasty food. But giving substance to the idea is much more difficult. Few if any have ever advocated absolute uniformity between individuals, an idea beyond the worst totalitarian nightmare. People are different one from another and differences imply inequality — better at sport perhaps, or legal argument, or medicine. But how if at all should this translate into differences of reward or power? To turn the question around, what sorts of unequal distribution of goods, wealth, income, power, opportunities, services and so on should we oppose on ethical grounds and why?

Most people would agree that there are <u>some</u> cases of inequality which are highly objectionable. But agreement that certain cases or certain extremes are objectionable is completely different from agreement that <u>all</u> departures from equality are objectionable. To pick out the types of inequality we think are wrong we need some basis which enables us to advance rational arguments about why they are wrong, otherwise we end up like small children merely shouting "It's not fair!" at anything we dislike or disagree with. But that immediately suggests that the basis for objecting to certain inequalities lies outside the simple fact of inequality itself. If some inequality is unacceptable but some acceptable something else, not inequality, must make the difference.

We can easily suggest, for example, two categories where inequality is morally objectionable, without ruling out the possibility of others. First, the inequality may have been created or sustained by means which are themselves unethical, involving perhaps a lack of compassion or the indulgence of greed, for example by exploitation or expropriation. A common and important subset of this category is where the inequality is based on hatred or dislike of a certain characteristic, as in cases of discrimination. Many modern political demands for equality can be recognized as belonging to this subcategory, for example demands for rights available to some but denied to others solely on the basis of a dislike or prejudice against anything from gender to race to sexual orientation. In such cases it is the basis of the inequality which is unethical and that is why the inequality itself is unethical.

In a second category, which applies particularly to certain cases of inequality of wealth or income, inequality is ethically objectionable because it entails that some people do not have sufficient for a dignified and secure existence. But here it is not the inequality itself but the plight of those without enough that is objectionable on grounds, for example, of compassion. In the happy if unlikely event that everyone had more than sufficient, for example, why would it be an ethical problem if some had a greater surplus, leaving aside cases falling into our first category? Or again, if a particular society was very unequal what good would it do to address the inequality by impoverishing the rich without improving the condition of the poor? Merely to confiscate resources from the rich and destroy them, for example, would certainly make society more equal but would surely be pointless.

Setting aside their undoubted emotional resonance, therefore, it is difficult to accept that there are fundamental political principles based on the idea of equality which are <u>independent</u> of general moral arguments. If a particular inequality is wrong, it is wrong because it is unethical not because it is an inequality. Conversely if a particular inequality occurs without any wrongdoing nor any moral failure in allowing it to persist, it is hard to insist that it is wrong. Clearly we must look to our values more generally to decide the issue in particular cases. Quite simply, some inequalities are wrong, others are not.

Fairness and justice

As a matter of usage, "fairness" is different from equality because it already carries a moral charge. It can make sense to say that certain conditions are unequal but acceptable—for example that the best sportspeople win more tournaments. But it doesn't really make sense (or if it does, it is contradictory) for example to say "This is unfair but right". The same could be said for "justice": "Unjust but right" is nonsensical or contradictory. Thus where "unequal" can be purely descriptive and involve no moral judgement, "unfair" or "unjust" cannot.[69] In order to decide that something is unfair or unjust—as opposed to tragic or unfortunate for example—we need <u>already</u> to have applied some moral standard.

In the previous section we saw that we must look to our general values or ethical foundation to decide specifically whether an inequality is ethically acceptable or not. Surely, however, it is those same values we use to decide whether any injury, detriment or disadvantage is ethically acceptable or not. If in a particular case the situation or action is unethical it may usually be described as unfair or unjust. This suggests that "unfair" and "unjust" are broadly proxies for "unethical", perhaps more appropriate in certain contexts but carrying essentially the same charge.

To say that someone has suffered unfairness it is probably necessary not only that they should have suffered some injury or detriment but that the damage should arise from an action or omission of someone else which is itself unethical.[70] If someone is injured by an unforeseeable accident, for example, it is not clear that they have suffered unfairness or injustice. (It may be unethical that we know about their plight and are indifferent, but that is another issue.) If this is right, we have to distinguish between harms or lacks which arise from natural causes or unforeseeable consequences of another's actions, which are unfortunate but not in themselves unfair; and harms or lacks which arise from the culpable or unethical actions or omissions of another, which are unfair. But that means the concept of fairness needs an existing framework of values to decide its applicability, rather than supplying one.

In the case of justice the same argument can be applied. In addition, we can distinguish injustice for which there is a remedy at law from injustice which still offends our values but which the law will not touch. Likewise we can make sense of the idea of an unjust law—simply, one which goes against our values. But we can do so only because we already have values.

None of this should be taken as arguing against equality, fairness or justice. It is simply that they do not represent independent principles we can rely on to guide public action or social organization. They are embedded in, rely on or are even identical with general values, the same values we apply in our private lives. When they are clear at all and not just slogans they may be rules of thumb such as we saw in a personal context. Such rules can be very useful but they can also be dangerous if people forget that they are little more than shorthand and that they depend on an underlying ethical foundation. If we do not refer back to that foundation in unfamiliar cases we are in danger of getting the answer very wrong.

Noble ideals can become tyrannical when they are taken out of the ethical context which gives them their meaning — so for example people have committed fearful atrocities in the name of equality or the righting of social injustice. But the more important general point is that the foundation of ethical social and political action and judgement should be no different from the moral or ethical framework we adopt in our personal lives.

Independence, freedom and liberty

Liberty, freedom and independence, terms which we will use virtually synonymously, are all "relation" terms. We do not know what they refer to until we have specified what it is we are or wish to be free from.

Freedom from servitude or slavery, for example, lies at one extreme in a spectrum, the minimum condition of liberty so to speak. Lack of freedom in this sense is obviously unethical by our standards (hence unfair and unjust) because it can only be sustained by violence or the threat of violence. But there are as many other forms of freedom as there are things or people from which (whom) we might wish to be free. Different people in different circumstances find irksome or even intolerable the impositions of governments, bureaucracies, public opinion, the media, ruling elites, bullies, their neighbours, their families or any number of others. There is no doubt a good case to be made for many such particular freedoms, but absolute freedom is not an idea which makes much sense — we cannot be free of all ties.

All life is led under constraints of some kind, even if only the constraints of our own natures, the relationships in which we engage and our particular environment. With good fortune and sufficient determination we can perhaps address and remove any one given constraint but we cannot remove them all at once. Perhaps it would generally be clearer to talk of "freedoms", rather than "freedom" as if it were absolute and indivisible.

This point is obvious but nevertheless important. Freedoms frequently must be traded or balanced, particularly in our complex societies. I may rail against some particular irksome imposition of government but life without any government would be intolerable, because it would simply expose me to the yet more arbitrary impositions of anyone strong enough to enforce their will. We frequently acquiesce in the authority or power of others, implicitly trading that freedom for some other advantage.

In addition every freedom, like every power, is instrumental, a means to some other end. If I am not free, I might for example be prevented in the worst case from living my life as I choose and as others are allowed to live. But even in such cases freedom itself is not my ultimate aim: my real aim is to do whatever I would want to do if indeed I were free. In any case, freedom can be co-opted in almost any cause, for almost anything can be described as freedom from whatever prevents it.[71] Rhetoric apart, freedom, however important, is at most a step along the way, the removal of a constraint which keeps me from some other aim. In this sense, freedom is always a means or an inter-mediate goal rather than an end in itself. It follows that freedom itself is not a central aim such as might serve as the foundation of a system of private values.

At a collective level freedom from some particular constraint or form of authority may at times be a crucial political goal. It may even be the most important and pressing practical problem of the day, occupying all our attention and effort while it lasts. But such struggles do not elevate freedom to the position of a value. Rather like the con-duct of a war, with which it may indeed coincide, when any struggle for freedom is won the real task, the pursuit of the aims for which free-dom was sought, has only begun.

Chapter 21

Sufficiency and Poverty

Enough is enough

A little while ago we posed the question of how politics, concerned as it is with external and collective matters, can interact at all with values, concerned as they are with the individual development of the inner life. So far our answer has been that politics like any other human activity is governed and bounded by the human values which stem from the goal of satisfied mind.

In itself this is an important step. It suggests among other things that politics, so far from being the grandiose moral enterprise it often purports to be, is an activity whose real importance is and should be subsidiary in our lives. Politics is useful only to the extent that it supports the real Common Good which frustratingly politics itself can do little about, the individual development of satisfied mind.

But we can go further. As we have seen, the external conditions in which we live and particularly our consumption and possessions are secondary in our lives if our central goal is to live happily. Important and even delightful as such external things may be, they are not the essence of living well. We need sufficient to prevent our material needs from being an obstacle to the development and enjoyment of satisfied mind, but we do not actually <u>need</u> more. We may well crave more, but it is not essential to our happiness or well-being and the craving itself may even be an obstacle.

This suggests the possibility that in material terms there may be a point where enough really is enough. This thought may be astonishing to our consumerist mindset and a profound shift from the way we now think but it is not, let us be clear, a call to personal austerity or asceticism. What we suggest is simply that beyond some point of sufficiency (leaving aside for the moment the important question of what that point may be) accumulation or additional consumption may be fascinating and enjoyable in much the same way as games are fascinating and enjoyable, but it carries the same relatively low moral and even practical importance.

How much then is sufficient? This is a complex question. There is first of all no reason to think that "sufficient" represents a quantity (of anything) fixed for all time and all cultures. We also have to allow that material security for the future is likely to enter our calculation of sufficiency, so that we cannot necessarily rest content with "enough for today". To take a simple example, if a hunter/gatherer lived in a land where food was readily available all year round there would be no need to accumulate, but if the supply of food was highly seasonal it would be foolish not to provide for the barren season. In our more complex world, we are all familiar with the idea of saving for future needs, including for example life in retirement.

But even if enough is enough, sufficiency (along with the external aspects of inner practice) is also the key objective of our external lives, the external complement to satisfied mind and a second requirement of living happily. There can be few external questions we can consider about our society which rank higher in importance than what sufficiency means for us and how we can secure it. Thus a key range of questions which our political and cultural life needs constantly to address is how much of anything is enough in our time, place and circumstances. We might even regard the answers as the framework in which our practical political and social activities take place, but it is a debate without end, a constant reforming and remaking of a consensus about what is possible and desirable. What is sufficient for us, here and now? The answers each culture and each society arrives at may be indeed the way to define that particular culture or society.

Sufficiency as the external goal of politics

But suppose that we <u>can</u> find a consensus on what is sufficient in one or more important areas — it is not far fetched to think we can, for we do it already with, for example, government advice on what constitutes a healthy diet or minimum housing standards or even a minimum wage rate. Such consensus is a specification which applies to everyone in our society, taking into account what is feasible and necessary for our time and culture. That level may not strictly be a need, but in practical terms it acts like one. If there are people in our society for whom this level is not met they are therefore by our own definition denied the chance to live happily because they are living in hardship. They may of course have chosen to live with less for some reason or perhaps are possessed of better than average inner skills so that they can endure hardship and still live happily. But generally speaking they are likely to be living more difficult, less happy lives.

Any such situation is a challenge to <u>everyone's</u> values and practice of inner skills. We have assumed here that the standards set are feasible, obtainable minimum standards for our society. So it is not as if there were a basic overall lack which causes the hardship, as might be the case for example if we were in the midst of a famine. Certain people, then, lack the minimum external conditions of happiness which we think are attainable in our society. How can this be consistent with the general practice of compassion, say? How can we live comfortably with surplus and excess if we are aware, to take a stark example, that some do not have enough to eat? We might be tempted to turn a blind eye but how would that be consistent with mindfulness?

Satisfied mind and sufficiency are the inner and external conditions of living happily. Just as it is part of our own good practice to help and encourage the development of inner skills in others, it is part of good practice to help others towards external sufficiency. Sometimes it may be appropriate to help certain individuals directly but such help can (probably) realistically only play a small part in society overall. But many of our most important external actions are collective, social and political. We can all encourage, vote for, assist in moving the society in which we live towards a situation in which no one is denied happiness because they are denied basic sufficiency in one respect or another. That goal, sufficiency for all, becomes the natural aim of our collective action, indeed the only aim truly consonant with satisfied mind.

Here, complex and shifting as the idea of sufficiency may be, we have a second touchstone of political values. The first and primary touchstone is of course that they should be based on the good we have in common, satisfied mind. But within that framework, politics is about our shared approach to external conditions. What we all require of external conditions is sufficiency to complement our inner develop-ment. Hence securing if at all possible this same sufficiency for all is the function and justification of politics, where politics comprises all the actions which are taken in our name by collective structures. If politics were conducted as if people and human values mattered such actions would be guided and shaped by satisfied mind above all. But beyond that, the most important political aim would be to help secure sufficiency for everyone.

This does not of course mean that sufficiency is the responsibility of the limited activity called politics alone and that other forms of activity can ignore it, still less that government action is the only means by which sufficiency is to be sought. On the contrary, it suggests that sufficiency is the key external aim of society, of social or collective activity as a whole.

It is a touchstone of socially responsible action in every field.

We already know for example that bureaucracies are not good at creating wealth or adapting to rapid change — and yet both qualities are probably essential for creating sufficiency. Government may thus in principle be able to stand back and allow private activity to create sufficiency on its own. But this is not the usual case, prosperity does not seem to "trickle down" to everyone as was once hoped. We might expect that governments and other political structures would have to intervene in the distribution even if not the creation of external goods to ensure widespread sufficiency.[72]

Sufficiency and equality

Sufficiency is very different from equality. If everyone had enough, it would not generally be wrong that someone had more. Material inequality, as we discussed before, may still be deeply unfair if it is caused by unfair actions and it is unacceptable if it entails insufficiency for some. But it would not be an ethical problem in itself absent such aggravating factors. At most the problem, if there were one, might be a problem about the inner lives of those overly attached to material goods, or on the other hand those afflicted by envy.

Sufficiency, we suggest, is the right ethical measure to apply to external and in particular material goods both for individuals and society. External surpluses (whether of goods, income or social standing) may be harmless and even life enhancing or they may be obstacles to satisfied mind, but they are not essential to a happy life.

Material inequality may still be an issue in society for other reasons. It has been strongly argued that it is empirically correlated for example with social tensions and instability, although if sufficiency were the standard it would presumably be necessary to remove the effects of insufficiency from these correlations.[73] Gross inequality might also be expected to make it more difficult to find an acceptable consensus on what is sufficient at any given time, because it is difficult to accept that you have all you need when great riches are being flaunted in front of you. Indeed we might anyway expect constant "creep" in the discussion of what constitutes enough in any dimension, as the less well off try to use the political process (or others use it in their name) to redefine society in their favour. This is understandable although it involves a constant catch-up process, so that the real objective of such politics can become an equality for which there is no ethical justification. Our central point remains that sufficiency for all is the right social goal.

Wealth and power

Material inequality may also be a problem because wealth and power are broadly correlated in society—not perfectly, of course, because there are forms of power which do not depend on wealth, but broadly. The wealthier you are the more power you have, even indirectly for example in your ability to command better education for your children or better health care. Even the moderately well-off are free of aspects of state power which can bear hard on those who for whatever reason depend on the state for the basic means to live. The very wealthy can buy the best legal help against both the state and other citizens, secure themselves from whatever aspects of interacting with others they find disagreeable and even, if they choose, dominate the lives of others through their economic activities.

Wealth, in other words, is not simply a matter of access to consumption, material goods and possessions. It also confers power, and the consequent imbalances of power in society can be a far more serious problem than imbalances of consumption. However irksome it may be that a wealthy man or woman lives in a bigger house, drives a big car, wears better clothes or eats expensive foods, such luxury would hardly matter if everyone else at least had sufficient of all these things. If the wealthy, however, are effectively subject to different laws (for example because they have better access to expensive legal advice and hence the justice system) or can impose their will on others because of their wealth, that is potentially a danger both to the external circumstances under which other people live and to the inner lives of both wealthy and poor.

It is easy to jump, as many understandably do, to the conclusion that more equality in wealth would automatically lead to more equality of power. But enforcing greater equality of wealth tackles only one sort of power imbalance at the expense of creating others. It usually works by increasing the power of the state and its bureaucracy for example, leading to a different distortion of power. Wealth redistribution as a cure for power imbalances is at best a blunt instrument and the history of nearly every revolution with that aim in history is that one set of abuses is replaced by another. Revolution is like adjusting a clock with a sledgehammer.

But just as, for example, those who live near the sea are wise to construct sea defences because to ignore the power of the sea is to invite danger and challenge, so it is wise to do what we can to restrain the exercise of excessive power wherever it arises. Power after all always involves an unequal relationship with others. It can lead to hubris and contempt, driving out compassion and making the powerful believe so much in their superiority that in the end they overlook their common humanity and connection with others. This may appear, for example, as indifference to suffering, willingness to make (or recklessness about making) already difficult lives still more difficult, or more insidiously as the temptation to meddle in the lives of others because one can. Anyone who wields power of any kind should be deeply aware and concerned about this danger to their own inner life. But the danger to their inner life is at the same time a danger to the external lives of others.

It makes practical sense, if we have the chance, to arrange society to minimize such abuses, just as coastal dwellers build sea walls. Our political and legal structures should be explicitly designed to protect others against the power which wealth confers, because that power is far more corrosive and damaging than material excess. For example, there is a strong moral case for "levelling the playing field" in civil legal disputes, whether by providing funds for poorer litigants or restricting the amount wealthier litigants are allowed to spend. But the issue in such cases is inequality of power and it is that specific inequality which needs to be addressed, not the underlying inequality of wealth.

We do not say, then, that inequality is never a problem, just that insufficiency is always a greater and more fundamental one. The two should not be confused although they often are. The primary focus of social and political action should be insufficiency.

Absolute and relative poverty

Insufficiency in this context is the same as poverty, in an absolute sense. There is a relative sense in which the word "poverty" is often used, a sense in which I can be considered poor if I have less than those around me although I still have sufficient for my needs. This sense, however, is only a slightly disguised version of equality and gives rise to the same mistaken tone of politics.

The mistake arises perhaps from the false assumption that the changeable nature and cultural dependence of sufficiency — the fact that what is sufficient varies in different times and places — means that sufficiency for a given individual is best defined in relation to what everyone around them has. For example, even after allowing for inflation what was enough to live with dignity in Western Europe a century ago is not enough, in character or quantity, to live with dignity today — if nothing else we need, for example, certain minimum pieces of technology to be properly integrated into today's world. ("Dignity" might possibly be used as a synonym for "sufficiency" in many contexts, although we will not pursue that idea here.)

But while absolute poverty is certainly a moving target, relative poverty is a false one. A norm which changes is not the same as a relative norm. For example, petrol (gas) stations sometimes set prices by matching local competition — which is a relative norm. But petrol (gas) prices change anyway and a station may simply change prices by reference to the wholesale price (for example) — which is a changing norm but not a norm set relative to the local competition.

On the relative view of poverty if we both have sufficient but you then gain more (for the sake of argument not from me or others, but by some act of discovery or creation) I am impoverished by your increase alone, by being left behind even though I still have just as much as I did before. If poverty is relative, any attempt to create wealth automatically creates poverty. We are thus trapped on a social or political treadmill from which "poverty" can only be eliminated by total equality. In fact, defining poverty as relative poverty covertly reinstates equality as the collective aim, rather than sufficiency. It may indeed happen in certain cases that the poverty of some is actually caused by the greed or afflu- ence of others, but that connection needs to be established on the facts and is by no means necessary.

Inequality or relative poverty, then, is a target which misdirects our efforts. But on our view absolute poverty (insufficiency) in all its forms is the most serious external issue for both individuals and society and its elimination is the heart and purpose of politics based on values, the heart and purpose of politics "as if people mattered".

Sufficiency and responsibility

If I have more than enough and someone else does not have enough it is *prima facie* good practice (compassionate, for example) to offer help, although that help may be channelled in many ways. There may be good reasons why I should not help in a particular way, for example the help I can offer might not benefit the other person, as when a drunk asks for money for drink. It is likely also that I must prioritize in some way between many calls on my (usually limited) surplus. But notice how my values, my commitment to practice of the inner skills, have shifted the burden of proof. I am not looking for reasons why I must help, only discounting possible reasons why I should not, or why help would be for example inappropriate, useless or harmful.

It doesn't follow in our framework that others have a <u>right</u> to demand help of me, for we have left behind the language of rights. It is for me to decide what the development of my own inner life requires so the moral "duty" my surplus imposes is at most a duty to consider how best I should behave, not a duty which confers specific rights on others.

Helping others as part of good moral practice is not an idea which in principle is bounded by geography, since every human being strives for a happy life. Appropriate sufficiency may be differently specified in and for different cultures, but the problem of poverty itself is a global one. Thus poverty in far away places is not something I can dismiss.

Good practice demands that I should at least consider what I can do about it, privately or politically.[74]

Of course, the practical consequences of actions can be complex and unexpected. Large scale publicly funded development projects, for example, were once thought to be the answer to poverty in less developed countries, but time has not been kind to that idea. Even if I were phenomenally rich it would generally be true that I could not cure all the material needs of the world even though I reduced myself to wretchedness and became in my turn a burden on others. It would be unhelpful anyway to expect anyone to give away their own sufficiency (as opposed to surplus) to help others. The practicalities of relieving poverty on a large scale are naturally immense. So a practical answer to global poverty will not magically appear as a consequence of our values. But the need to search for solutions is a clear consequence.

A separate issue is that it matters <u>how</u> I acquire sufficiency and still more how I acquire surplus. This applies both to individuals and societies. Values come before sufficiency because values are about my central aim. So I should abide by good practice and not (e.g.) cheat, steal, exploit others, deceive or behave without compassion. Sufficiency, still more surplus, obtained immorally is immoral, however keenly I may feel it is my due. So poverty confers no right to take arbitrarily any more than does the power that may come with surplus. Violence or dishonesty in acquisition would always be wrong, whatever the starting position.

Sufficiency and motivation

Some may fear that to advocate sufficiency rather than, say, the maximization of wealth as the measure of our material needs would destroy the incentive for people to work hard and achieve things in their lives which may benefit others as well as themselves. But why should this be? If I (and for the sake of argument my family and loved ones) have sufficient why does this mean I should stop trying, stop working, stop striving? In the first place, it is likely that continued effort is required to maintain sufficiency and security for the future, let alone the capacity to help others. Second, surplus is not at all prohibited by our values unless for some specific reason it stands in the way of others achieving sufficiency.

This aside, sufficiency may indeed mean that I can focus on other aspects of my well-being and inner development to the extent I might have pushed them into the background to reach sufficiency. But I may just enjoy what I am doing, or for example enjoy exercising the work skills I have acquired even if in a different context, so why not go on? If people do whatever they do for enjoyment, that is an enhancement of their life which may only incidentally be connected with creating wealth, for example. All that is entailed in advocating that enough is enough is that beyond the point of necessity continued drudgery and slavish insistence on acquiring more and more is unhelpful to a person's well-being.

Only a fortunate few in practice in any society reach such a point anyway. But because we tend to applaud or be mesmerized by wealth, it is worth noting that the pursuit of wealth beyond sufficiency is not necessarily socially or individually useful. It might be useful because, for example, it helps others to achieve sufficiency, or because it allows philanthropy. Equally, it might be an instance of a habit out of control, compulsive behaviour, greed or self aggrandizement. Each person in that position might look carefully at their own behaviour and motivation.

By the same token, perpetual economic growth and increase are not necessarily a sensible collective aim. We tend to assume automatically that growth is good and anything else is bad, although sustainability arguments are increasingly challenging this assumption. But this assumption may be just a product of our conditioning and the social and economic structures within which we live.

Whether growth is good must surely depend on circumstances. If there were insufficient to allow everyone even basic needs, as for example in some developing countries, growth would be a highly sensible aim. It might be sensible even if there were strictly enough to go round but because distribution was imperfect (as it generally is) not everyone had sufficient. Growth might then be better than the social disruption which significant redistribution would cause. The causes of why existing wealth has not spread to everyone in such circumstances are usually quite persistent, however, so that more growth on its own may be too simplistic a solution anyway. But that is a practical matter rather than a matter of values.

There must surely come a point, however, where more growth and more consumption add little or nothing to the well-being of individuals or society — we can easily see how this might be true of individuals but seem to forget it when it comes to society. If growth were free and potentially unlimited that might not matter much, but there are now obvious concerns that continued growth may be neither free nor unlimited, in fact it may be catastrophically harmful. The satisfied mind ideal suggests anyway that quite apart from these very practical concerns we should not assume that endless growth is the only sensible goal of policy, nor that it is synonymous with endless increases in well-being.

Chapter 22

Poverties

The many faces of poverty

Access to money or goods is not the only dimension of poverty. In this chapter we touch on a few areas where basic insufficiencies present serious external obstacles to the development of satisfied mind. We will call these lacks "poverties" to recognize that insufficiency is a multi-dimensioned problem. In these areas and no doubt in many others the values of satisfied mind suggest that policies are needed to alleviate that particular kind of poverty. Compassion alone suggests that we should work to redress these lacks just as much as bare material poverty.

In every case, private efforts to improve opportunities may be as important as public measures. The privileged arguably have a greater moral obligation to consider how they can help others — simply because they can and because their inner practice is set in the context of their external privilege. But if we all shared the objective of living ethically the choice between collective (or public) measures and private efforts would be a matter of efficiency and efficacy, in other words a practical matter.

The scale of many of these issues dictates, however, that some collective measures are probably required and in any case most of us can only contribute through our political support for collective measures. Hence we have here the beginnings of an approach to a practical politics of satisfied mind, a politics as if people mattered.

Sufficiency of power

Our discussion strongly suggests that power, like wealth, ought to be so distributed that everyone has "enough". To be powerless in a political sense, for example, is to be at the mercy of whoever has power and thus in a position where external circumstances are likely to be difficult and satisfied mind more difficult to practise. But power is itself multidimensional, a "relation" term (like freedom) about which we must specify what it is we have or need power to do, or we have said nothing. So although political power is perhaps the most commonly

encountered example, similar things could be said about many different sorts of power.

How much power is "enough" is of course highly dependent on
context. It is nonsense in most cases to suggest that everyone should
have equal power. Of course there are contexts — for example two
people in a relationship — in which equal or at least balanced power is
the optimal distribution, but in contexts involving numerous people
some will inevitably have more power than others just as some may
have more wealth or income than others. This inequality of power is no
more a problem, we suggest, than economic inequality provided it is
not so great as to threaten the stability of society and provided everyone has sufficient power to live peaceably and cultivate satisfied mind.

For example, some purposes of even the most primitive society
require us to "pool" power, which may take the form of some structure
of government or the law or it may be a private enterprise, a group of
individuals acting together. We then need ways to control the
enhanced power thus created, but also to exercise it and decide what is
to be done. We can devise forms of democratic accountability, for
example, or other mechanisms. But except in small groups it is not
usually feasible to take every necessary decision by referendum. Someone must therefore take or sway collective decisions in all the contexts
in which collective power arises, so it is inevitable that some people
have considerably more power than others. We may hope to ensure
that such people are subject to accountability and to mechanisms to
relieve them of their "extra" power in certain circumstances, and anything we can devise in that regard is at least a partial safeguard against
the abuse or excessive concentration of power. By such means power
can be concentrated to an appropriate degree which benefits us all
while everyone retains, in this respect at least, sufficient power. As
soon as joint power, whether public or private, is used oppressively
within the group or outside it the balance has been lost.

Thus there are direct parallels between wealth (income) (which itself
can be seen as a power or potential) and power of other kinds. A
person with too little is in a difficult position and their condition may
even be wretched. A person with too much may be subject to many
kinds of dangers to their inner life and its development, as well as
being a danger to others. But equality of power for its own sake makes
little sense. Sufficiency, difficult as it may be to pin down quantita-
tively, is a useful concept and a useful guide to how power should be
distributed.

Sufficiency suggests, for example, some form of localism or sub-
sidiarity in political decision-making. If important decisions are taken
by a national government, for example, when they disproportionately

affect some regions or localities more than others, then it could be said that the regions or localities do not have sufficient power. As ever the particulars are all-important. Perhaps the decision is simply not one that can be taken or which it makes sense to take locally – a decision on monetary policy for example. But still, such factors apart there is some sense in not aggregating power beyond the level necessary for the power to be exercised effectively, always assuming that the power is necessary in the first place. If that level is the individual, leave the power with the individual. But if a decision must mobilize the resources of a nation sufficiency requires that someone has executive power to do just that.

Work and welfare

Developed societies, if not all societies, use work not only as a way to produce what we need in material terms but also to distribute the products. We work to earn so we can pay for what we need – this is one of the foundations of our society. We usually make arrangements for cases in which people cannot work because of age or sickness or temporary dislocations in the economy but the norm for centuries has been that work not only produces but distributes material goods through the purchasing power wages give us.

Certainly, some are able to avoid work through the "rent" available from their ownership of capital. It has been suggested that this rent (return on capital) is a destructive force in society because it leads inevitably to gross inequality. Apart from the generational saving required to provide pensions, it is suggested, high capital returns ensure that further savings ultimately accumulate in the hands of very few.[75] Whether this is true or not, the reality for most people is that work, or the lack of it, determines their purchasing power and hence their standard of living.

This long standing pattern may today be threatened by a combination of factors which include globalization (freely moving capital with excellent transport links), technology which requires fewer workers, population ageing and the ease with which millions of people can now migrate across continents. Unemployment levels are already considerably higher than would have been tolerable only a few decades ago. One way or another, the idea of work as the basis of the way society is organized is under challenge.

This of course is not a problem solely about values. It is a frighteningly complex practical problem.[76] Any solution is likely to have many parts and need help from many disciplines. But the problem challenges our values and how they are expressed at the social or collective level.

If there is insufficient work to employ everyone of working age it is hardly consistent with our values to brand all those who do not have work as lazy, scroungers or second class citizens.[77] They are more likely simply to have been unlucky in the game of musical chairs which assigns a lower number of jobs to a greater number of workers. Such displacement has often occurred in the past when the lack of work was due to a temporary slump, but it is an even greater problem if the lack of work is structural for some or all of the reasons already suggested. Among other things, our values suggest that a solution is needed which is motivated neither by envy or hatred of success nor by contempt and indifference to the difficulties of those who struggle to find employment.

One great obstacle is that it is unfortunately inevitable that any system of transfer or welfare payments will not only be used by those it is intended to help but by others who, bluntly, take advantage of it to be lazy. An unlikely perfection of human nature would have to occur for this parasitism, which is unethical in itself, to disappear, although the size of the problem is often greatly exaggerated for political effect.

Thus any welfare system needs tests and safeguards, without doubt. But if the tests and safeguards become the substance of the system, or if the genuinely needy are left at the mercy of bureaucracy with no clear legal rights and no speedy recourse if they are denied, the system is not fit for purpose. That is sadly the direction in which welfare benefits are often being driven currently by "austerity" measures and it is the opposite of a system driven by genuine human values. An attitude which tries to punish the jobless with onerous bureaucracy and penalties is unethical.

The other major problem with welfare is dependency, including the infamous poverty trap which withdraws benefits as other income is received so that the poorest cannot profit from taking work. In effect the withdrawal of welfare benefits acts like a tax on income and those on very low incomes pay this "tax" at far higher rates than those on high incomes. Ironically, high tax rates for high earners are now avoided by most governments precisely because they are thought to act as a disincentive, but the logic seems lost where the design of benefits is concerned. This problem has an inescapable arithmetic which suggests that only by withdrawing welfare benefits sufficiently gradually as income increases can "poverty supertax" be avoided. Such gradual withdrawal of welfare benefits is, however, a very expensive business and implies large spending cuts elsewhere. But if spending cuts are acceptable to allow tax cuts for the rich, why not for the poor also?

Health care

Any society in which sufficient resources are available will decide, implicitly or explicitly, the extent to which it will allow suffering due to illness, disability or frailty to continue.

If the choice, for example, is that ability to pay will be the only criterion of medical assistance, we have a society which recognizes no goal more important than money. By our standards of course this is a fundamentally anti-ethical stance. Inability to pay for otherwise available health care is a particularly cruel form of poverty which, so to speak, kicks a person when they are already down. An ethical society would consider how to address health care needs regardless of individual ability to pay.

This is not an area, we might note, where a market mechanism alone is likely to produce an ethically acceptable result. Access to the market is the first problem. Since need bears no relation to ability to pay, the market is distorted before we start by an incomplete representation of need. An effective market could work only when demand and effective demand (demand that can be satisfied by paying a market price) had been brought into alignment, which is to say that the problems of how to provide services for the poor had already been solved.

But even if everyone were sufficiently wealthy (or subsidized or insured) so that everyone potentially had access to the market, most people don't have the expert knowledge to judge what they need. Buyers generally know only that they desire a return to health, but health is not on sale. The selection of a specialist, for example, itself depends on first tier professional expertise about which buyers (patients) already know too little to gauge whether the advice is sound. Everything depends on blind trust. Markets on the other hand work best on the assumption that informed buyers face informed sellers, which just cannot happen in this sphere. In any case, everyone wants the best practitioner and the best treatment so that market signals are of little use, unless we regress again to making treatment dependent on ability to pay. It is of course possible to create something that looks like a market, but the essentials are not there.

In the end, it seems likely that to provide care services for those who cannot pay requires some measure of either public subsidy or direct public provision. Neither is without drawbacks. Subsidies, if they involve the public payment of the going price for a given treatment, leave the overall cost uncontrolled, threatening public finances. Direct provision on the other hand involves immense problems about control, management, allocation of resources and the balancing of political with health care considerations. It is likely indeed that there is no universal answer which satisfactorily balances ability to pay and need – if there is, no society seems yet to have found it. A dream of perfection, however, should never be allowed to stand in the way of improving what we have.

Ensuring by one means or another (and in all likelihood a mixture of means) that there is a system which, however imperfectly, addresses health care poverty should be a key concern for a value based society. A society which does not care about the health of those who cannot afford to pay for health care has lost its way.

Education

Market mechanisms, it could be argued, are even less suitable in principle in education than in health care. The majority of people cannot afford the full cost of education for their children and therefore a system based on payment cannot work except by excluding the majority. That is of course why some education is publicly provided in every country with the means to do so.

Still, what matters in education is still sufficiency, not equality. In this field in particular, however, sufficiency is a bar which should be set as high as a society can possibly raise it, because although educational resources can be wasted it is hard to think that there can be such a thing as too much education. It is still important that each person has the best education available (sufficiency) than that every person should receive the same education (equality).

Education can make a huge difference to anyone's external life and their opportunities to achieve material sufficiency or surplus in a wide variety of circumstances. At the very least, such material success is likely to make pupils' achievement of satisfied mind easier. So the teaching of practical, economically useful skills is important, but it is not enough. If values are the basis of private life and society everyone should also have the opportunity to understand and develop the skills of the inner life.

If, however, we are not bound to a false norm of equality we can tolerate diversity in educational opportunities above the level of sufficiency. Thus we need not be troubled about selection by ability or aptitude for more intensive education as long as we can ensure that the "standard education" available is of the highest quality, which is where selective education has often failed. Selection also often creates hard cases and even injustices at the margins of selection but this should not deter us from trying to provide everyone with the best possible education. The question is rather whether that goal is better achieved in a system which includes selection or not – and that is a practical question, not a question of values.

Again, with sufficiency as the norm we need not necessarily be concerned about the availability of private education for the wealthy provided it sits alongside and does not preclude excellent education for all. In such a "supplementary" private sector it may be that we can actually rely on the market to ensure standards. But if the market standard is set by access to limited higher education opportunities there may be a problem of fee payers effectively buying such access at the expense of others. Some practical measure like a handicapping system might be needed to solve this problem.

A different problem of course is that private schools too often become a mechanism for perpetuating social divisions. But policies could attack this issue separately. For example, such schools could be required to accept a reasonable proportion[78] of children of low income families selected in open competition whose education was paid for by the state. If practical details could be worked out, such policies could potentially ensure that the private resource could be harnessed not only to raise educational standards generally but to erode privilege and social stratification over time.

Futures

The preservation of their particular society has been a preoccupation of people throughout history. This conservative concern is generally a doomed rearguard action because every society changes, evolves and eventually falls in response to changing circumstances so that over time very little about human society is static. Not all change is good, not all change is progress, but nevertheless change is relentless and largely unpredictable in its effects, simply because the variables are so many.

Today, however, we have, for a number of reasons, challenges to the future of the human species as a whole. These challenges arise, as we all know, from the sheer numbers of human beings and more specifically their material aspirations. We do not <u>have</u> to respond to these challenges, they will work themselves out in their own way whatever we do and we could just go on living in ways which were perfectly harmless when there were far fewer of us. But we might not like the world we get.

It could turn out to be be a world of extremes, a world of shortages and famines outside pockets of affluence sustained by force, a world of resource wars and the regular breakdown of social and economic systems, a world of lawlessness and violence.[79] Thus far, you might say, it sounds like a densely populated version of most of the world throughout most of history! But it might also be a world of crashing population through climatic disasters, famines on vast scales, wars and diseases which overwhelm our capacity to contain them. It would be a world in which insufficiencies of all kinds would be amplified until they drowned out all else. It would not be a world in which people could easily foster and develop the values we have talked about, but if they did not it would ultimately be a world of barbarism.

A society taking seriously the values of satisfied mind would see the issues of resource use and climate change as pressing, even if the worst imaginable outcomes were thought unlikely. The forces involved have the potential to unleash misery on a scale we can hardly conceive. But these are problems which by their nature no local society can hope to solve alone. They require consensus and cooperation on a large if not global scale. Perhaps that requirement (together with the sheer complexity of the issues) makes the situation hopeless, but we simply do not know. Since the alternative is to prepare ourselves to fight all-comers to get and keep resources including food and shelter at others' expense, a society concerned about values would expect its government to go to any lengths to find and build the consensual and technical solutions such a challenge requires.

Chapter 23

A Good Servant
but a Bad Master

Power and values

At the beginning of this book, we suggested that a key reason for looking closely at the foundation of values was to provide a secular counterweight to the dominance of consumer capitalism in our world. Capitalism, we said, is only a way to organize the making and distribution of things but it is so powerful that we too easily take it as the foundation of our society and way of life. At least with values which are shareable and firmly based on our humanity and what matters most to us we can pose better questions about how our interests are served by this or that economic action or policy.

In the real world, though, the answers we are likely to get to such questions — stripping aside the spin and gloss — is that things are done because they are in the material interests of those who have enough power to do them. The powerful may simply not be moved by human values however rational and firmly based, and may continue to put their material interests first. What good are values then against sheer power?

It is worth reiterating that this is not an issue about our own central goal and values, unless we are tempted to join the pirates and predators, but about how the world around us is shaped, whether predominantly by power or by values. The point of values is that they show us how to live, how to direct our own actions towards what matters most, our central goal. The fact that other people cherish other goals — wealth or even power itself — should not deflect us. If such goals are not acceptable as central goals we need not abandon them but they should be secondary to our central goal. If we place wealth or power at the centre of our lives, it is a mistake or at best a gamble with our own happiness. We should not, in other words, give up on satisfied mind because of predators and pirates.

But we will always be faced with the power and the actions of others, just as we are always faced with the power and vagaries of nature. The actions of the powerful may not affect our progress towards satisfied mind if we are sufficiently determined but they may certainly affect our external conditions in ways which make happiness difficult to achieve.

To meet power with power head-on is, however, a doomed strategy, not least because sooner or later we will always meet with greater power than our own.[80] The structures of the state, for example, have generally if imperfectly evolved to contain power in many of its aspects, but they are constantly circumvented or subverted because power shifts and evolves faster than such structures can.

For much the same reason, there is no panacea for keeping power in check in any other context, whether political or economic. It is a matter, among other things, of constant vigilance and effort. But just as this is not a counsel of despair it should not be taken as a licence for anarchism or cultural destruction in the name of limiting power. Although it is open to abuse, power is not only potentially benign but necessary in any society. It is abuses of power against which we must be vigilant, power exercised beyond the boundaries of values. The stronger, clearer and better established are our values, the easier the task will be.

Human power after all differs from the power of nature, the other external force which shapes our environment and our lives. For one thing, we can change human behaviour by discussion, not only by direct persuasion but by changing the social climate which sets what is socially acceptable and influences both the choice and the effects of actions. For another, power and its actions are always set in a context of social structures and constraints. Even if these constraints are not enough at a particular moment to prevent a particular harmful action they can be changed and adapted so that power can be removed or tempered by collective or political action.

Power and the social climate

We should not accept, for example, that business leaders or the wealthy have no obligations to society other than to make more money for themselves. Whether in politics or business, whoever acts without regard to values behaves like a spoilt child and we should regard with suspicion anyone who adopts this attitude. Now that we can see the possibility of rational secular values, ruthless profit seeking for example or amoral capitalism of any kind should be abhorrent. A transformation of public opinion, manifested for example in consumption choices, democratic processes and social acceptance, would be needed to bring about that capitalism accepts such moral responsibility, but the power of such a transformation should not be underestimated.

Openness and public scrutiny, simply to bring dubious practices into the light of day, is essential to this process. It is not the whole of the answer but it is a large and vital part: we should all be much more active in scrutinizing (and encouraging those that scrutinize) the way businesses and the structures of the state operate. Some secrets are of course legitimate but if a business for example requires that its every-day operations must be mysterious, the chances are the business is acting unethically. The law should everywhere assist enquirers and resist secrecy.

We are not suggesting that agreement on values will settle all problems. The rich and powerful are unlikely suddenly to agree that they share a responsibility for others just because they are rich and powerful. More likely, many will reject values based on satisfied mind because things as they are suit them better. But rational values give us back the opportunity to rebut arguments based on the assumption that economic life is all that matters. We can begin to discuss other ways in which society might be structured, not just argue about our places within it. And the protections on which a better society might be based can grow out of a recognition that better human life requires that economic and political power be restrained by shared values.

"Realpolitik"

Machiavelli, the author of the first and perhaps most durable manual about power, was quite explicit that a leader (the eponymous "Prince") may sometimes have to put aside whatever norms of ethical behaviour there may be in order to be successful in preserving the state and his own position in it. Thus a Prince, according to Machiavelli, may dissemble, break his word, deceive the people, use pre-emptive cruelty, ruthlessly crush enemies and even blame lieutenants for following their orders to avoid being hated for unpopular actions, all in the name of power. A Prince should avoid being hated by the people, but it is better to be feared than loved.

Such, after all, is often the way "the real world" works and Machiavelli's instructions may indeed be the best way in certain circumstances to achieve and retain power. But they are not (they were explicitly not meant to be) a system of values. They are a plea that values have no place in successful politics or statecraft. This is a claim still heard today, not only in politics but in business. Ideals are all very well, it is said, but to get things done we must "get real".

Clearly, an approach based on satisfied mind must utterly reject this view of power, whether in politics or business. To rule without values is to enshrine power itself as the central goal and hence to lose direction. To conduct business without values is similarly to enshrine power or profit or both with the same result. Whatever ideals the Prince (or the business leader) may start out with will soon be corrupted by expediency. Worse, the inner life of the Prince (like Charles Foster Kane?[81]) will be warped away from any habits which incline to good intentions, until there is nothing but the desperate need to hang on to power and profit.

Machiavelli's observations, sadly, may be accurate as observations of what often happens but we should not take them as prescriptions, nor should we trust anyone who does. If we begin from the question of what kind of society each of us would like to see given our central aim of satisfied mind we would surely choose a society free from unscrupulous lies, greed or violence. The fact that these evils may enjoy success does not recommend them, it shows us how far we have strayed from values in business and politics and from a society based on ethical principles.

An analogy (yet another!) with professional sport is perhaps helpful. Suppose a player achieves success by consistently cheating without being caught. They might reach the top of their sport, just as a politician might achieve high office through lies, corruption or creating fear, or a businessman might achieve great wealth and success through ruthlessness and double dealing. As long as the cheating remained hidden we might admire the player for their achievements because we like to see our sport played at the highest level possible. But this player is not really playing our sport, they are playing a very different game, indeed they are exploiting the sport we follow. If and when he or she is found out, do we still applaud their false achievements? And yet such a player is doing no more than applying a muted version of the recipe for success which was advocated in Renaissance Florence.

Defensive structures

However strong and well established values might become in society, predatory behaviour of different kinds would still occur. Such cases can only be dealt with by appropriate practical measures, much as we would take precautions to mitigate and deal with the effects of dangerous natural phenomena. Restraining the behaviour of commercial interests by legislation, for example, surely falls into this category. To use the law to protect those in a weaker position, be they workers, consumers or even the environment, is surely sensible and even inevitable, especially as long as business leaders see themselves as focused on profit by any means.

We would need the protection of law and other social structures to restrain occasional excesses even if we generally rejected that model of capitalism that suggests that each of us should seek to maximize economic advantage at the expense of others. If capitalism conducted itself within a framework of human values, the "piratical" model of how economic life should proceed would have no honour. But some would always prefer money to honour so that realistically some protection would always be needed.

The question of what specific protections we need is, however, a practical one, not itself a question of values, although it is a practical question fraught with great difficulty. We have suggested for example that law (legal action and judicial intervention) offers some protection against executive and corporate abuses, but law itself is a locus of power which can be abused like any other, for example by impeding legitimate uses of democratically controlled executive power.[82] Again, the better access to legal advice and action available to the wealthy means that the power of the law can in effect be captured by wealth.[83] There is possibly no such thing as power without danger, only power held in check by other powers – which is only a parsing of Acton's famous dictum.[84]

In any case, many multinational businesses (for example) have, in their way, as much or more power than any particular government or legal system. Globalization currently puts business in the ascendant. Partly because governments have come to see economic success as central to their own activities, the power of businesses to make or withdraw investment, create or destroy employment, choose where (or in some cases whether) to pay taxes gives them immense intrinsic power. Add to that the sophistication of lobbying and public relations which businesses can command, and it becomes highly doubtful that governments or democratic structures are in any sense in control.

It becomes apparent that we are looking here for a point of equilibrium which is particularly difficult to find. We do not want business corporations, say, or the wealthy in general to have excessive power, but we do not want the state to have excessive power either. In either of these cases, the people lose and our lives are made more difficult. Serfdom comes in many forms.[85] If capitalism is dominant we will be oppressed by economic decisions on which we have no influence and our democratic freedoms will be subverted because the state is in thrall to capital. But if the state is sufficiently powerful to prevent all abuses, it is sufficiently powerful to command rather than obey the people. Again, basic freedoms will be threatened but in this case economic sufficiency may falter because wealth creation will be stifled.

So the struggle is absolutely not to overthrow one side or the other, it is to find and constantly readjust the balance – many balances – so that neither side can bear down on those trying to craft happy lives through satisfied mind. Neither state nor business is likely to be enthusiastic about such an equilibrium because both prefer their own dominance. But this precarious and constantly adjusted balance is the essence of a successful state and society.

Capital and the state

We will look now very briefly at what may seem like a strange issue for a book about values. We use it as an example of where state and capital collide, because it will be helpful to see what contribution our values can make. The issue is tax avoidance.

First we must set some background. Taxation is the absolute heart of the democratic process, the trigger for revolt in contexts as different as Magna Carta and the American and French Revolutions. For this reason among others modern taxes are generally very strictly governed by the rule of law — you owe precisely what the law says a person in your circumstances should pay, neither more nor less. The alternative is arbitrary, lawless confiscation, the sort of thing that got the Sheriff of Nottingham a bad name.

Some people and companies evade taxes by fraud, secrecy and deception. "Evasion" is the term used for what is always a crime and if detected will generally result in criminal prosecution. We could argue it is also unethical because of the deception involved, because it makes greed and accumulation central and perhaps because it denies funds that are needed to help others and thus lacks compassion. But there may be instances where these motives are not present. If an evil regime needs money to persecute a minority is evasion still immoral? Could tax evasion have been a form of resistance in Nazi Germany, for example? There is still scope as always for the particular case to dominate the general rule. But in safer times we can surely agree that evasion is unethical. Nevertheless many people practise tax evasion in small ways and others practise it on a massive scale, a form of organized crime.

Tax "avoidance" though is different. If a specific exemption from tax is prescribed by the law (for example, if personal income is not taxed until it has passed a certain level), to refuse the exemption amounts to making a voluntary donation to the public purse. Nobody does that and there is no reason why they should since the amount each needs to pay has been taken into account in the design and rates of the tax system. But taking things a step further, if there is a choice of ways in which a particular transaction or arrangement could be carried out and one way involves lower taxes than the others, few would say it was unethical to choose the low paying route or morally incumbent to take the highest paying route.

For example, there is currently in the UK an inheritance tax ("death duty") on capital over a certain level left after a person dies. But there is no inheritance tax on any capital given away seven years or more before the donor dies. So a person with sufficient wealth can give their children money to buy a house or help their career, for example, when the donor is relatively young and healthy. If all goes well the children will have no burden of inheritance tax. What a particular individual decides to do probably depends more on their relationship with their children and their money than on the tax consequences, but the law-makers are clearly indifferent to the outcome or they could change the provision. Nor is there any particular moral virtue in a person hoarding their wealth until they die so as to pay the greatest possible amount of tax. In general, there seems no reason why we should look for ways of paying more tax than the law tries to exact on ordinary transactions and it is hard to see how it could be unethical to do so.

But any law is made of words and there is always a way round or through words. People may look for paths through the law to reduce tax in situations which the lawmakers did not intend and maybe did not even envisage. For example, income or transactions may be routed through a number of companies in different jurisdictions without there being any economic or commercial justification for so doing but just to exploit errors ("loopholes") in the rules. Or transactions may be entered into which deliberately result in artificial losses because there is some tax advantage from the losses, while profit is postponed or transferred perhaps to another jurisdiction with lower taxes.

This is "artificial tax avoidance" and tax authorities are usually very active in trying to combat it by litigation, changing the law and even by introducing "catch all" rules against it. But it is not generally a crime. If it is found not to work as intended in a particular case, all that happens is that the tax has to be paid after all.

Tax avoidance and values

To make blatant cases of artificial avoidance a crime might seem to be the best and obvious practical solution to the problem it presents. It would not be technically difficult as long as the definition of "artificiality" in tax avoidance was sufficiently robust. Such a measure would make people think very hard before using blatantly artificial schemes. But that is not our problem here. The question for us is whether such activity is unethical. Our suggested answer is that it is.

The usual argument to the contrary is that this activity is just a continuation of using tax legislation in the way it was intended — like sensible tax planning, as in the inheritance tax example. The intention, it is said, must be apparent from the words of the law and the artificial scheme has done no more than exploit the words, just as we all do when we gratefully do not pay tax on the first part of our income. But this is highly disingenuous.

First, apart from the fact that secrecy is often required to conceal aspects of the transaction or scheme, there is generally a pretence that the scheme is <u>not</u> designed principally to avoid tax, because otherwise the tax authorities might be able to challenge the artificial arrangements. Second, the actors know perfectly well that the tax advantage they are getting is not what the lawmakers really intended and they are deliberately exploiting a weakness in the drafting or foresight of those lawmakers. From a legal point of view it might be said that they are just playing a game with the lawmakers which the quickest player is entitled to win. But values are not about games. Third, the intention is quite deliberately to avoid paying the amount of tax which society expects a person in those circumstances to pay and to shift the burden onto others perhaps less able to afford it. The motive for this action is simply greed. So there is deception, greed and lack of compassion at the least. This is not ethical behaviour.

A related defence is the grey area argument: "Where do you draw the line?" We are challenged to say at what precise point sensible tax planning tips over into unethical tax avoidance, with the implication that if the boundary is not sharp there is no real distinction to be made. This type of argument may be a practical barrier to criminalizing tax avoidance if the boundary cannot be made sufficiently clear, but is nearly always specious where values are concerned — and it is so here.

There are many concepts where no clear boundary can be drawn and yet there is clearly a distinction to be made. Away from the boundary cases can easily be told apart even if there are grey areas in the middle. Everyday examples include "tall" or "bald" or "fat" — exactly at what point someone is rightly described by each adjective is hard to say but we can all tell when they clearly apply, or don't. In fact, in everyday language concepts with boundaries which admit of no ambiguity in any context are probably exceptional. Clear conceptual "tipping points" are rare and it is more common that one meaning shades into adjacent ideas. Thus the fact, if it is a fact, that we cannot pick the exact point at which avoidance becomes objectionable does not mean that we cannot spot blatant tax avoidance or distinguish it from innocent tax planning. Still less does it mean that avoidance is ethically acceptable because we cannot properly mark the boundary.

A third defence where corporations are concerned is that they have a duty to their shareholders to maximize profits and they can only do so by minimizing tax. Hence not to avoid tax where possible by whatever means available would be a breach of trust. Tax avoidance is not only ethical, it is a duty, on this view.

This argument too is specious. Reasonable tax planning rather than carelessness or inattention is of course something shareholders have a right to expect. But shareholders have no right to expect unethical behaviour of any kind, as we have discussed before. If tax avoidance is unethical (as we have argued) there is an ethical duty <u>not</u> to use it which is not overridden by any economic duty to maximize profits. Maximizing profits may be an important aim but it is a secondary aim which cannot override our central aim or our values.

Here we have a good example, then, of where the capitalist instinct to pursue profit gives us the wrong answer unless it is contained by values. But only with the help of clearly established values can the error be argued against, for the argument that profits must be maximized will otherwise prevail however queasy citizens may feel. The point of balance may be difficult to be precise about — and some will be more scrupulous than others. But the principle is that any economic aim is secondary and a secondary aim must give way at some point to the central aim. In that way, capitalism can work for us rather than the other way around.

Chapter 24

Politics and Progress

The story so far

We can summarize the position we have reached on political values as follows.

Political values are identical with the ethical values which apply to individual life, just applied to larger groups. Those values are based on commitment to an individual central goal and the aggregation of individual goals into a common goal is possible because the most rational and satisfying goal for everyone is the same — the goal of living happily driven by what we have called satisfied mind. The ethical demand we make as individuals on collective action is simply that what we do or allow to be done collectively should be directed by the same considerations as what we do individually.

The extent to which this congruence is achieved — the extent to which politics meshes with our private values — we could regard as a measure of the moral integrity of our political system. There will still be many subsidiary goals and aims at the collective level just as there are in our individual lives. But such collective goals and the measures and policies used to achieve them must be at least compatible with our shared private central goal.

Capitalism in some form is probably better at production and distribution than any other economic system available, although that is a practical question best left to economists. But capitalism is not and never could be the source of our private values and it follows that it cannot and should not be the source of our public or collective values. On the contrary, capitalism without strong rational values from another source will distort our individual lives and our society because it will pass off economic and material goals as the goals of human life. We may be materially enriched by that process, or at least some of us will be, but in every other way impoverished. A healthy society needs strong rational values to stand alongside, to contain and challenge capitalism. Those values need to be secular to be genuinely shareable in a pluralist world. That is what the ideal of satisfied mind seeks to provide.

We have to recognize, however, that political action can and per-haps should do little directly about furthering the inner skills of citi-zens. This being so, the next aim of a value-driven politics is to make everyone's lot easier or better by addressing external needs which otherwise, for whatever reason, are not met and which stand in the way of some or all of the people being able to develop satisfied mind. In other words, beyond observing the principles of satisfied mind in all public actions, the function of politics in a society based on satisfied mind is to address external poverties or insufficiencies of all kinds. This applies not just to material necessities but aspects of power, security and personal development. The task, strictly speaking, falls not to politics alone but is the overall aim of a value driven society. But politics is there to redress balances and pick up or cure what other activities drop or get wrong.

Values and vision

Clearly, these conclusions do not offer a blueprint for any kind of perfected society or utopia. But they are none the worse for that for utopian visions rarely approach what they promise and have a dangerous tendency to oversimplify complex situations. Among other factors, there is no reason to suppose that there is only one kind of society which is consistent with these ideals. The same central goal is consistent with very many different subsidiary goals, leading to as much cultural and organizational diversity as anyone could wish.

Getting clear about our values does not in itself give us a manifesto for collective action either. Some will see this as a defect — "What good are values if they do not tell us what practical steps we should take?" But manifestos are about policies and specific actions, values are about direction and aim. There is no blueprint here for what policies to adopt, partly because values may have to operate in varied and different circumstances, partly because values have to be supplemented in practice by empirical content about how certain actions may or may not lead to certain goals. We have to edge forward, testing what works and being ready to change course if it doesn't, or if circumstances demand a different course.

But all policies follow this tentative empirical path anyway, what-ever ambitious economists or politicians tell us. At least with values grounded in satisfied mind we have some inkling of what matters most and how we will judge success. As individuals we know that practice of the inner skills will improve our lives and we can use that know-ledge to shape our individual choices. Similarly, we can start to frame collective goals and make collective choices with that knowledge as the context and aim. We can have no certainty that we will get it right, but it is the only way forward which preserves our focus on what matters most.

Values and progress

Progressive politics, broadly the political left, used to represent itself as the champion of values and principles, challenging the status quo with a vision (often brave but not always accurate) of a better, fairer, more equal society. Today it is often the right which is able to present itself as upholding values, suggesting that there are fundamental (often religious) values which modern society is at risk of abandoning. That those values often happen to favour the interests of the affluent may be a coincidence, or it may be that the rewards of virtue are actually thought to be material, or it may simply be that material issues are part of this world and therefore values based on a vision of an afterlife have nothing to say about them. The left on the other hand too often relies on technocracy and empiricism to engineer society towards what it hopes will be a better future, without much idea how this connects with values.

But we have suggested that human values, both private and public, can only be based on the development of the individual's inner life. In many ways, this cuts across old "left–right" divisions. If our values are not based around the ownership of capital and material goods, it should not be surprising that old political attitudes based, across the political spectrum, on the supremacy of economic matters are displaced. What we might hope to see is a transition to a politics in which the quality of individual lives matters more than the quantity of goods, a politics as if people mattered.

This politics, however, would inevitably take a stance on the side of the dispossessed rather than the privileged. It certainly does not support the view that society is or should be governed by eternal laws. It clearly does not support the view that wealth or income are indicators of moral worth but on the contrary regards poverties of all kinds as the greatest moral challenge to every society, demanding every effort to find solutions. Wealth and success may often be the reward for talent or hard work (although the connection is not always as strong as the wealthy and successful claim) but talent and application are in any case gifts, not moral qualities or virtues. This politics does not suggest therefore that poverty or economic difficulty is somehow a natural consequence of lack of moral fibre — it simply is what it is and the challenge is to discover how to remedy it. The causes of poverty may indeed sometimes include a measure of personal culpability or error, but whether they do or not the moral response from our point of view should be based on the principles of satisfied mind, foremost among them in this instance compassion.

It might even be a relief for the "left" to abandon its obsession with economics as the field of moral debate and a source of moral value and regard it rather as the rickety science of production and distribution it really is. Let Marx rest in peace. There is no need for a vast generalization (even if it were true) about why working people do not often get very rich, especially if it masquerades as a theory about fundamental human values. As for violent revolutions, they involve outpourings of anger which may be understandable but rarely produce the positive outcomes they set out to achieve. Like any indulgence of anger, they in no way contribute to satisfied mind for anyone. Those who advocate turmoil and violence as the price of moral progress in society are either foolish or malicious. Or both.

However, very often the alternative programme of reform we are offered is empirical, seeking to change society with constant attempts to engineer and "micro-manage" people's lives. Torrents of legislation attempt to mould every aspect of society, following whatever is the latest theory about the cause of one ill or another. But the latest theories more often than not turn out to be wrong or over-simplified, or people adapt their behaviour in unforeseen ways so that the new laws do not work.

Worst of all, there is no sound value basis for all this empirically based activity, other than a vague sense that something is "not fair". Progressive politics needs sound values and currently has none. It focuses on the external and the empirical as if that were the heart of living. It misses the idea that what we do and how we live needs heart and direction, in our terms that living happily depends on values which are a matter of the inner life and its development. In its attempt to be inclusive, progressive politics consigns all values to a cultural relativism which as we have seen ultimately means abandoning values altogether. As a consequence the so-called "moral high ground" can easily be seized by anyone who offers a seemingly moral stance of their own.[86] That may be why so many less well off people accept the ideas of the right. They revere the values which are invoked even when the policies of the right cut against their interests.

For anyone who accepts that values should be based on satisfied mind and that practical politics should focus on the relief of poverties there is a genuine clash of values with those who believe that material wealth is the most important thing in life and society. On our view, people and their well-being should hold that central role. The politics of satisfied mind, politics as if people mattered, would have at its heart values built on this rational, shareable basis, making the happiness of every individual the highest common good.

Capitalism and politics

Capitalism so suffuses our culture at present that politics adopts most of its aims and strives for them without question. Few politicians, whatever their allegiances, are willing or can afford to ignore the demands of business in case investment, jobs and material prosperity slip away, for those are the benchmarks by which people now tend to judge leaders.

This makes for an uneasy, half-corrupted public life in which values are forever secondary to material success. Whatever suits the interests of business and the economy is sold to the people as anything from common sense to clever policy, but always as the right thing to do. If our public values do not stretch beyond capitalism we can expect that politics will be no more than the carrying on of business by other means.

As we have seen, to pursue material success is far from wrong, indeed material sufficiency is one of the key conditions of the happy life. But politics as the expression of the collective life of a society which recognized satisfied mind would not infer from the limited aim of sufficiency an automatic duty to grow an economy regardless of consequences, still less to grow the economy while leaving many without the means to achieve a minimum level of material comfort. If we let capitalism set our public values any opportunity to shape the society we live in so as to spread dignity and satisfied mind will be subjugated to the economic interests of whatever group happens to be strongest. Even the structures of government, perhaps even unknown to themselves, will be controlled by private economic power.

Placing happiness (in the sense we have used) at the centre of individual and public life does not incidentally lead us to advocate some formal measurement of happiness in order to gauge political success. It is fashionable at the moment to devise or discuss measures of "Gross National Happiness" (GNH) as an alternative or complement to Gross National Product (GNP). But we rejected in the first part of this book (in our brief look at utilitarianism) the idea that happiness is a quantity, from which it follows that any such measure must be misleading. In any case, not only is the individual development of the inner life something government cannot directly influence, but a society in which individuals had such a goal would grow progressively happier without government doing anything at all. So GNH, if it meant or measured anything, would certainly not measure government performance. A better strategy would be to focus on measures of absolute poverty in all its aspects and consider how government was improving them.

Values are about what we want most and we have argued throughout this book that the subjective quality of our lives lies at the centre, the heart of each individual life and therefore the heart of our collective life. Politics are about striving for our collective aims and therefore for the common good, the good we all have in common. Capitalism is one of the tools at our disposal, a mighty tool which has transformed the lives of millions and made them materially better. We should not abandon this tool but neither should we allow it to dominate us, to dazzle us into thinking that it represents all there is. We need constantly to find new ways to balance capitalism and values, in our individual lives and in our collective life. We need to frame our discussions of public goals, for example, in ways which give due weight to both, not just to economic arguments. That is the only way to create a society which aligns public goals with the common good.

Changing the world

None of the great religions, even at the heights of their spiritual appeal or temporal power, succeeded in changing the world so much that violence — killing for political ends, for example, or the will to dominate others — came to be seen as weakness and error, still less that poverty and need came to be seen as unacceptable reproaches to success and comfort. More commonly, religion sided with the rich, powerful and violent in order to enforce its own writ over dissenters.

That is not to deny that many religions in many places and times have done good work, swum against or even for a time turned back the tide of human misery. But the great religious movements which at their best have inspired people to look beyond the mundane and justified ethical living with promises of eternity have all failed to transform permanently or fundamentally the way we see each other — and that is, in the end, what ethical living requires.

We should be realistic, then, about what any set of ideas can do. The real world is and is likely to remain about business as usual, which means a world driven by greed, indifference to suffering, violence as the means to power, deceit as the means to persuade and all the rest. These negative motives are strong and deeply rooted. We probably aren't going to usher in the age of Aquarius.

Nevertheless, not to do what what we can to reduce obvious poverties, for example, is a failure of our humanity and a compromise of our inner lives, a failure of compassion and imagination. Some but very few of us can make a great difference acting alone, but collectively we have more chance to change our world. Politics inspired by values means an attempt, possibly unrewarded, to right one injustice after another, knowing that injustices are like weeds and will spring up somewhere else. The road leads to no shining city. But to leave the world slightly better than we found it is a great achievement.[87]

As with the personal transformation which can accompany the adoption of satisfied mind as a personal central goal, the point of taking this ideal into the collective sphere is not that a perfect outcome is guaranteed. We may live our private lives developing our inner skills and growing in resilience and contentment and it would be no reproach that we never perfected such skills: we would have lived as well and as fully as our time and nature allowed. Similarly, the political ideals which flow from the same source may never be fully realized in a "perfect society" but that is not their point. Values give us a direction in which to travel, ways of recognizing the way forward and ways to spot the traps and blind alleys. Ideals may help us steer a personal and political course even if their complete fulfilment is unlikely. Maybe that's why we call them ideals!

Political action is itself a part of the nourishment of the inner life by acknowledging the needs of our neighbours, even if it only extends to ordinary civic duties. Once we accept on the one hand that others are linked to us by their fundamental aspirations and the central good we have in common, and on the other that the care of others is part of the practice which will bring us to our own central goal by developing our inner skills, we cannot ignore injustices, poverties and suffering. If the world were full of "people of good will", each ruled by the values of satisfied mind, the task would be hard enough, a constant battle to choose (without sufficient information!) which policies and practical arrangements might lead us forward towards our goal. But at least it might be a co-operative effort, with disagreements honestly discussed and viewpoints respected, rather than a partisan shouting match.

So we have an approach to politics which is far from passive. On the contrary it is firm of purpose while yet not aggressive. In suggesting that external sufficiency rather than maximization on one hand or equality on the other is our key external target, it points to the necessity of political action to address accidental insufficiencies as well as man-made injustices. But it also suggests that there is more to life than economic progress, or materialism, or even politics.

The actions of a leader like M.S. Ghandi offer an example where a political approach strictly guided by values was for a time immensely successful. But his greatest success came when he mobilized people for a single cause and it is far more difficult (as it tragically proved) to inspire the same kind of commitment through the everyday trials of building and living together in a society. Only a deep and widespread acceptance of a shared approach to life and a commitment to shared values, rather than a single cause however worthy, could hope to sustain cohesion over the long haul.

Has that ever been done without using hatred of others as the unifying factor? Rare examples are scattered through history. Perhaps Nelson Mandela came closest in recent times. But could it be done, could society be based on the values we have discussed? That is the challenge, to work for such a world. Getting the institutional details and structures right and appropriate for particular times and places still presents formidable practical problems and should become the stuff of everyday political discussion. But the motivation and guidance can only come from rational, shared values at the heart of the enterprise. That in turn can only come about by individuals looking deeply at their own lives and becoming convinced that human values offer a better way to live.

Endnotes

1   (p. 3) "Foundation" is very obviously a metaphor but I think it is the right one. It does not preclude the idea that the foundation may have many different elements and it is possible that no such foundation can be found or constructed although (spoiler alert!) we will suggest it can. We will not discuss G.E. Moore's idea (Moore, "Principia Ethica", 1903) that ethical concepts have no foundation because they are not reducible to anything else, not least because nobody seems to defend that idea anymore. It is important though that a foundation is not required to be what Bernard Williams called an "Archimedean point" – a point from which the whole world can be moved, in this case an argument so powerful that even people with no interest in values have to concede that they must accept it and change their lives. Apart from anything else (see Williams, "Ethics and the Limits of Philosophy", 1985) it will always remain possible in the face of even the most powerful argument for someone to say: "I don't care about being reasonable, or about values or about anything else."

2   (p. 5) A remark attributed to the late Bill Shankly, formerly manager of Liverpool Football Club.

3   (p. 6) See my "The Lost Art of Being Happy – Spirituality for Sceptics" (2007). The term "satisfied mind" is not used in that book, but the concept of happiness explored there is the same and is developed in detail. My motive with that book was to make connections between the practice of inner skills to enhance life and happiness, on one hand, and religious spiritual practice. The connections with ethical and political practice took a little longer.

4   (p. 7) See "After Virtue" by Alasdair Macintyre (1981). My debt to Macintyre is enormous and will be clear to anyone who knows this work. "After Virtue" is of course based on deep insight and scholarship and is highly influential, even if not nearly as influential as it deserves to be.

5   (p. 9) W.B. Yeats, from "The second coming", a poem used liberally throughout – spot the quote!

6   (p. 16) We return to this later, because it is important to avoid the very prevalent mistake of reductionism, the idea that if we can explain something, particularly with a "scientific" explanation, we can explain that something away. But it is surely clear from the outset that the question of how to live is a different sort of question from the questions science asks and answers.

7   (p. 20) We have to be careful though not to do injustice to earlier times. It is a mistake generally to look at the history of thought (and of philosophy in

particular) and assume that earlier centuries were tackling the same problems as we face and just getting the answers wrong. Very often, for example, people were looking for a formula in reaction to a dominant doctrine of their day which they could see was wrong. For example, in political theory many of the versions of natural rights ("rights of man", etc.) which flourished in the seventeenth and eighteenth centuries (and eventually underpinned the US constitution) were a reaction to the pre-vailing idea of the divine right of kings. If by the nineteenth century they could be described as "nonsense upon stilts" (Bentham) that was partly at least because the debate had moved on. Macintyre (*op. cit.*) is very good on this.

8   (p. 20) Plato, "Euthyphro".

9   (p. 20) No theology intended, Plato may be presumed to have been a polytheist.

10   (p. 22) Kant, "Groundwork of the metaphysic of morals". Translated as "The Moral Law" by H.J. Paton (1948). Whole libraries of writings are justly devoted to exegesis and discussion of Kant, so to dismiss his arguments in so few words is undoubtedly disrespectful, a point which applies to other writers mentioned in this book. I apologize to a great thinker. My miti-gating plea is that this is a book about values, not about the history of thought about values. Also, those libraries cover the history far better than I could.

11   (p. 23) Rights have a long and conflicted tradition, in (relatively) modern times stretching from Hobbes and Locke up to the current idea of Human Rights and libertarianism.

12   (p. 25) Universal Declaration of Human Rights (1948), European Convention on Human Rights (1953). But the universalism of the UN version is disputed and some regard it as reflecting a predominantly Western and Christian worldview.

13   (p. 26) Bentham, "Anarchical Fallacies" (1843).

14   (p. 27) See for example C.L. Stevenson "Ethics and Language" (1944). Also and importantly Nietzsche, for example "The Happy Science", but in many other places. Nietzsche did a great service by insisting on the emptiness of the myth of law but insofar as he had a place for values at all left them as no more than an expression of individual will. Our enterprise is to explore how values could have a foundation transcending individual will and thus be shared.

15   (p. 33) The apology to Kant above is due with equal or even greater force to Marx. This briefest of references in any case is more concerned with Marxism as it has been applied in practice rather than with Marx's own writings. Right or wrong, no other secular thinker since classical times has had such influence.

16   (p. 35) Most commonly associated with the Scottish philosopher David Hume.

17   (p. 36) This distinction between fact and value is analytical and should not be taken to imply that the two never mix. There are some concepts which so mix fact and value that it is hard to tell where the boundary lies – for example "cruel" or "cowardly". Williams (*op. cit.*) calls these "thick" or "action-guiding" concepts. Certain facts have to be true for them to apply,

certainly, but their application also involves a value judgement. Nevertheless, this does not seem to invalidate the idea that <u>purely</u> factual premises cannot give us a reason for action.

18   (p. 37) Mary Midgley is particularly helpful on reductionism and many other points — see note 21.

19   (p. 37) This is broadly the thrust of Sam Harris in "The Moral Landscape" (2010). There is much to admire in that book but not this key point.

20   (p. 37) Bishop Butler, quoted by G.E. Moore, *op. cit.*

21   (p. 37) Mary Midgley, "Science and Poetry" (2000) but quoted from "The Essential Mary Midgley" (2005). There are very few books on philosophy (or anything else) in which lucid writing and intellectual power are combined with as much grace and wisdom as in this collection. It also contains her penetrating and salutary metaphor of philosophy as plumbing — sorting out the conceptual pipework which no one ever designed and no one takes any notice of until it goes wrong but on which everyone depends. Very liberating!

22   (p. 41) Associated with Jeremy Bentham and John Stuart Mill.

23   (p. 43) Sam Harris, *op. cit.*

24   (p. 47) Aristotle, "Nichomachean Ethics". Mine is the Penguin edition translated by J.A.K. Thompson which cost me five shillings in 1967. Good value.

25   (p. 47) See again Macintyre, *op. cit.*

26   (p. 49) Thus we retain from emotivism the idea that values have something to do with preference or choice, but of a very particular kind. We will see later that there are also constraints on what it makes sense to put in this central position.

27   (p. 49) Because proper tea is theft? No? O.K.

28   (p. 50) This, I believe, protects us from arguments like the "experience machine" argument of Robert Nozick ("Anarchy, State and Utopia", 1974) In a nutshell, the argument is that if the only aim is happiness and a machine could deliver it through inducing appropriate brain states while keeping you in a coma, why not just plug in rather than live real life? Very few would agree to be plugged in. There are many reasons why not, but the obvious one here is that we would still have many other aims unsatisfied because happiness, although central, is not the only aim.

29   (p. 50) "To imagine a language is to imagine a way of life." Wittgenstein, "Philosophical Investigations" (1953).

30   (p. 51) Kant, *op. cit.*

31   (p. 59) Aristotle, *op. cit.*

32   (p. 60) Except of course that there is no compulsion to be reasonable or even to care about values, so even a compelling case would not provide Williams' "Archimedean point". See note 1. Williams, *op. cit.*

33   (p. 62) See for example Susan Nieman, "Moral Clarity" (2008).

34   (p. 64) The phrase itself comes from a song by Hayes and Rhodes, covered by many iconic singers from Ella Fitzgerald to Bob Dylan and Johnny Cash. My favourite is the Jeff Buckley version.

35   (p. 65) The key theme of my 2007 book. I use this phrase rather than, say, "mind" as explained there because there are too many confusions surrounding "mind".

36 (p. 71) "For the sake of others" is the key phrase here. Martyrdom sought for personal spiritual gain doesn't count and in fact is regarded as problematic by many faiths.

37 (p. 76) See for example Timothy Gallwey, "The Inner Game of Tennis" (1974).

38 (p. 77) David Hume, "Treatise of Human Nature", Bk 2.

39 (p. 79) See for example the very clear exposition in Thich Nhat Hahn, "The Heart of the Buddha's Teaching" (1999). For more detail Nanamoli and Bodhi (Trs.), "The Middle Length Discourses of the Buddha" (1995).

40 (p. 81) Anyone new to the idea might start with Thich Nhat Hanh, "The Miracle of Mindfulness" (1991), or for clinical applications Jon Kabat-Zinn, "Full Catastrophe Living" (1991).

41 (p. 83) Called sets or circles in my earlier work, but I now like families better. This chapter is essentially a summary of the earlier work, based on a pamphlet called "The Inner Life" I wrote for Richard Docwra's "Life squared" website.

42 (p. 83) Kabat-Zinn, *op. cit.*

43 (p. 84) See for example Philip Kapleau, "The Three Pillars of Zen" (1965).

44 (p. 86) See Mihaly Csikszentmihalyi, "Flow: The Psychology of Optimal Experience" (1990).

45 (p. 86) Plato, "Apology".

46 (p. 88) See for example Thich Nhat Hahn, "The Heart of the Buddha's Teaching", cited above.

47 (p. 88) Gospel of St Mark 12:31.

48 (p. 92) Daniel Kahneman, "Thinking Fast and Slow" (2011). Brilliant and original book.

49 (p. 93) See for example Blackburn, "Being Good" (2001). A short but masterly survey in which deceptively sharp analysis is mixed with anecdotes and cartoons.

50 (p. 94) 1 Timothy 6:10.

51 (p. 112) Kant, *op. cit.*

52 (p. 113) See for example Karen Armstrong, "The Great Transformation" (2006). My favourite story is of Rabbi Hillel being impertinently asked by a heathen to teach him the whole of the Torah while standing on one foot. Hillel said: "What is hateful to you, do not do to your neighbour. That is the whole Torah — the rest is commentary."

53 (p. 117) Descartes, of course, "Discourse on the Method", which has caused no end of trouble.

54 (p. 117) The trolley car cases are a series of philosophical (ethical) dilemmas first introduced by Philippa Foot in 1967 which challenge our sense that we know how to decide moral problems. The first one, for example, concerns a trolley out of control hurtling towards a group of people on the track ahead. If it reaches them, it will certainly kill them and there is no way to warn them. You have the possibility of diverting the trolley onto a siding and saving the group, but in so doing you will certainly cause the death of a single person on the siding. What should you do? Most people say it is better to save the many than the one, but then the next problem challenges that rule, and so on. These cases and others are used to great effect in

Michael Sandel's "Justice" lectures and writing. (Sandel, "Justice: What's the Right Thing to do?", 2009.)

55 (p. 120) This is apparently very far from Kant (*op. cit.*). But there are still elements of the solution we have constructed which owe him much.

56 (p. 124) There is for example an argument that law should be designed exclusively to protect people, particularly those who have no other protection, from deliberate or reckless harm by others. Ethical considerations would therefore not generally be in point as far as the law is concerned, only external harms. But this view is probably oversimple, for the law at various times has criminalized behaviour which harms no one or self-inflicted harms.

57 (p. 125) One of the most difficult issues is that the debate stretches our concepts outside their comfort zone. Take for example the notion of a person (or even a baby). Somewhere between conception and birth a fetus, always a potential person, becomes a person. A key religious objection to abortion rests on the idea that personhood begins at conception, hence abortion is always the killing of a person. A different view is that personhood evolves over the term of pregnancy, so that (say) a newly fertilized egg is not a person while a newborn baby is. We do not need to be able to specify an exact point of change to recognize that although the change is gradual the start and end points are very different. (The law of course can and does simply define a point of change by fiat.) The issue about whether and when a fetus is a person is in itself a question neither of fact nor value but about what we think personhood involves. But personhood isn't a concept anyone devised to think about or apply in this context, so we are extending and exploring its application while we argue, conscious of the implications of the result, which is why resolution is so difficult.

58 (p. 128) See for example Blackburn, *op. cit.*

59 (p. 131) James Lovelock, "The Vanishing Face of Gaia: A Final Warning" (2009).

60 (p. 140) In one of the most celebrated (if now disputed) views of capitalism, Max Weber suggested (in "The Protestant Ethic and the Spirit of Capitalism", 1905) that driving forces in the development of capitalism were Protestant forms of Christianity, particularly Calvinism. Whereas earlier Catholicism had assured people of salvation if they did as the church told them, in Protestantism there was no such assurance and in Calvinism there was even predestination—you were already saved or not but you did not know which. Following a vocation or calling was a duty, leisure was sinful, spending was frowned on, success might be an indication of divine favour. Thus Protestant values—hard work and a frugal lifestyle—supported the growth of capitalism. But this was a historical interpretation: Weber accepted that capitalism had divorced from Protestantism by his time, so that capitalism had become "an iron cage". It is certainly hard today to argue that religious or any other values infuse capitalism, which thus needs some counterweight to prevent economic forces from dominating or even crushing human society and culture.

61 (p. 142) But there are many different interpretations (for example those of Weber, Durkheim and Habermas, while Marx himself recognized several different forms) of a phenomenon which may indeed be not one but several

different social pathologies with different causes. Division of labour is surely a major part of the problem, especially since the condition seems to originate at or around the time of the industrial revolution.

[62] (p. 155) A view stressed for example by Schumpeter, "Capitalism, Socialism and Democracy" (1943).

[63] (p. 159) Homage to E.F. Schumacher ("Small is Beautiful: A Study of Economics as if People Mattered", 1973) is intentional.

[64] (p. 162) See Roger Scruton, "Green Philosophy" (2012).

[65] (p. 171) See for example Rawls, "A Theory of Justice" (1971), the most influential work on political philosophy in (at least) the last fifty years, which revived the subject.

[66] (p. 172) Sandel (*op. cit.*) approvingly cites Barack Obama as arguing in contrast to earlier liberal opinion that ethical (in his case specifically religious) values should not be excluded from politics or the public arena but should be engaged in society. With this we agree, in fact to leave private values out of politics seems almost a guarantee of alienated politics. The difficulty is that religious values are not subject to rational discussion. Secular shared values would avoid this problem because they would take some of the sting out of unresolvable religious disagreements, as we argued earlier. The liberal call for essentially value-free politics in the name of relativism and toleration was always a political mistake, leaving the field to an increasingly passionate but closed-minded right. But it was also a philosophical mistake. Ethical relativism could not imply any <u>absolute</u> requirements, not even toleration, as Williams (*op. cit.*) pointed out.

[67] (p. 173) With a concept of values based on satisfied mind we have no need in particular of a theory about a social contract, whether thought to arise from some mythical preceding state of nature or used as a theoretical construct to underpin political theories, as in the most powerful example by Rawls (*op. cit.*). Power or authority arises in many different ways and may be embodied in many different structures. There are many questions about whether given structures are fit for purpose and about how such power is regulated, controlled or removed. But they are usually practical or institutional, not ethical, questions. The ethical questions are always how power behaves and to what ends. Institutional structures may help, impede or be neutral in respect of the general pursuit of satisfied mind or the external conditions we discuss later and may be judged accordingly but the question of whether a society is just or ethical cannot be answered by looking at institutions or structures alone. See for example Sen, "The Idea of Justice" (2009).

[68] (p. 174) But see note 7.

[69] (p. 177) They are thus examples of Williams' "thick" concepts. Williams (*op. cit.*) and see note 17.

[70] (p. 177) See for example Sen, *op. cit.*

[71] (p. 179) See for example Blackburn, *op. cit.* He quotes in this context Gibbon on Augustus "...the senate and people would submit to slavery, provided they were respectfully assured that they still enjoyed their ancient freedom".

72   (p. 183) But it is open to advocates of minimum government to show how sufficiency can really be spread widely without government action. Indeed, that is one way to frame an important political debate and challenge.

73   (p. 183) See Wilkinson (no relation!) and Pickett, "The Spirit Level" (2009).

74   (p. 187) Peter Singer's arguments (in for example "The Life You Can Save", 2009, as in earlier works) point in the same direction and are bolstered by the idea of sufficiency rather than growth as the economic aim of the affluent. The effectiveness of aid is a complex issue, at least as complex as any other large scale political or economic objective and probably more complex than most as Singer makes abundantly clear. But the complexity is not an excuse to turn away and do nothing, it is a challenge to seek out better ways to help.

75   (p. 191) Thomas Piketty, "Capital in the Twenty-First Century" (2013). Piketty suggests that the lessening in inequality in the middle part of the twentieth century was an abberation due to factors which destroyed capital and that the long term trend is reasserting itself, namely the tendency for the rate of return on capital to exceed the overall growth rate so that the rich get richer. At an earlier point in an admirable book he warns against simplistic economic explanations but in the end his explanation is very simple. The effect he mentions is surely very powerful but cannot be the whole story of economic history or the sole predictor of the economic future.

76   (p. 191) The implications are tied up with how economies which have relied on growth can handle a transition to low or zero growth without collapsing. See for example Tim Jackson, "Prosperity without Growth" (2009).

77   (p. 192) Powerful arguments against this general tendency can be found in John Hills, "Good Times, Bad Times" (2015).

78   (p. 195) What proportion is reasonable? Something significant but not overwhelming, like 20%. Lower might have too little effect and make the "scholarship" children vulnerable, higher might insulate the school too much from the need to satisfy the private market.

79   (p. 195) James Lovelock, *op. cit.*

80   (p. 198) Something I learned from many years of studying aikido.

81   (p. 200) Orson Wells' film "Citizen Kane" (1941).

82   (p. 201) Francis Fukayama has recently coined the phrase "vetocracy" to characterize the way legal action is sometimes used in the US, for example, to thwart or delay actions which have democratic support and to that extent legitimacy but are against the will or interests of a powerful lobby.

83   (p. 201) Cf. Anatole France: "In its majestic equality, the law forbids rich and poor alike to sleep under bridges, beg in the streets, and steal loaves of bread" ("The Red Lily", 1894).

84   (p. 201) Lord Acton: "Power tends to corrupt and absolute power corrupts absolutely." From a letter included in "Historical Essays and Studies", ed. Figgis and Laurence (1907). Less well known but equally powerful are sentences which closely follow: "Great men are almost always bad men..." and "There is no worse heresy than that the office sanctifies the holder of it."

85   (p. 201) In which respect Hayek, "The Road to Serfdom" (1944) was partly right but incomplete.

86 (p. 209) See Susan Nieman, *op. cit.* But the point is well made in a different way by George Lakoff, "Don't Think of an Elephant!" (2004).

87 (p. 212) Amartya Sen, one of the world's leading public thinkers with a mind-boggling breadth of intellectual interests, notes that most modern political philosophy is concerned with the specification of ideal institutions in pursuit of the perfectly just society—which he calls "transcendental institutionalism" (*op. cit.*). Such a focus is not necessarily helpful even in deciding between outcomes or states which are not perfectly just and is no good at all if we want to consider for example global or transnational justice, because suitable global institutions are never likely to exist. (For example, if justice needs law and law needs sovereignty global justice would need a global sovereign government to enforce global laws, which is unlikely.) By contrast he believes we do not need to specify an ideal or perfectly just state of affairs in order to make comparative judgements about justice. In particular we can act to eliminate obvious injustice without being able to specify perfect justice. Making the world a bit less unjust is both an understandable and a worthwhile aim.